Let's
Study
Greek

CLARENCE B. HALE

MOODY PRESS
CHICAGO

PREFACE

Let's Study Greek draws its grammatical discussions in revised form
from the author's syllabi First Year New Testament Greek as prepared in
1948 and revised in 1950, and Syllabus Greek Lessons, Greek 101-102, 1955.
The reading exercises were first used as separate lessons distributed from
day to day as the course progressed in 1954-1955. A revision of these
sheets resulted in the 1955 Syllabus. This again has been done over for
the present book.

Although some benefit is certainly to be derived from an oral use of
an ancient language like Greek or Latin and from exercises in writing translations of English sentences into Greek, the chief reason for studying Greek
is to learn to make out what written Greek means. Most of the students who
work with this book will be aiming at getting an ability to read the Greek
New Testament. They will need for this purpose a command of vocabulary,
inflectional forms, and syntax. To help master the vocabulary here presented, each word in Lessons 1-44 has been used at least five times in the
lesson where it first appears and at least ten times in the book as a whole.
The urge to attempt this method of teaching first year Greek came chiefly
from a happy experience with Using Latin I and II, published by Scott,
Foresman and Company.

The subject matter of the reading exercises, though taken from the Old
Testament, has been expressed almost entirely in New Testament vocabulary.

The appendix is intended for reference and therefore has some inflectional forms too rare to be included in the lessons. Charts have been prepared to help the student see relationships that would not otherwise be
readily grasped.

In matters of spelling and accent a serious attempt has been made to
follow Nestle, Novum Testamentum Graece, Editio vicesima prima, 1952, and
for words in the LXX but not in the New Testament, Rahlfs, Septuaginta Id
Est Vetus Testamentum Graece Iuxta LXX Interpretes, Editio tertia, 1949.

For inflectional forms used in the New Testament and for principal
parts of verbs, repeated reference has been made to the following books:
Walter Bauer, Griechisch Deutsches Wörterbuch zu den Schriften des Neuen
Testamentes und der übrigen urchristlichen Literatur, Dritte Auflage, 1937
(since most of the work on this grammar was done before the appearance of
the excellent and convenient translation by Arndt and Gingrich), Moulton
and Geden, A Concordance to the Greek Testament, Third edition reprinted
in 1953, Blass-Debrunner, Grammatik des neutestamentlichen Griechisch,
Siebente Auflage, 1943.

Acknowledgement is gratefully made to the Administration of Wheaton
College for permission to prepare this syllabus; to A. Berkeley Mickelsen,
Robert C. Stone, Merrill C. Tenney for encouragement and advice concerning
the project as a whole; to Robert D. Carlson and Gerald F. Hawthorne for
valuable detailed suggestions; to Elizabeth Terry and Gladys L. Wright for
technical advice and skill in the multilithing process; and to Ruth B.
Lewis for invaluable help in editing and for superb accuracy in typing the
exacting material of this book.

March 1957

In this second edition a number of typographical errors have been
corrected and a few changes have been made, such as removing most of the
discussion of accents from Lesson 12 to the appendix. I am indebted to
R. D. Carlson and G. F. Hawthorne for helpful devices for presenting accents
and contractions. Their alert eyes have contributed much to increasing the
accuracy of this little book.

C. B. Hale
June 1959

Wheaton College

CONTENTS

LESSON   PAGE

PREFACE   1

1   INTRODUCTION   1
        Importance of Greek language and alphabet. Alphabet. Vowels and con-
        sonants. Diphthongs. Breathings. Accents.

2   GREETINGS   3
        Sentences. Nouns. Number. Gender. Verbs. Subjects. Direct Objects.
        Appositives. Forms and Functions. Case: Nominative subject, Accusa-
        tive direct object, Vocative of direct address. Article.

3   THE MENU IS FRUIT   7
        Present tense. Active voice. Indicative and imperative moods. Number.
        Person. Conjugation. Syllables. Recessive accent.

4   A REAL DINNER THIS TIME   11
        Method of indicating gender. Genitive of possession. Ablative of sepa-
        ration or source. Distinction between genitive and ablative. Locative
        of place. Prepositions. Singular forms of the second declension. Per-
        sistent accent.

5   DOCTOR LAZARUS   15
        Dative of indirect object. Dative of direct object. Plural forms of
        second declension and the definite article. Adjectives. Agreement of
        adjectives. Adjectives of the second declension. Future tense. Pres-
        ent infinitive active. Causal clauses.

6   REVIEW   19
        Vocabulary list of Lessons 2-5. Technical terms used in 1-5. Inflec-
        tions in 1-5. Review story---"Urgent Business Interferes with Dinner."

7   TABLE TALK   22
        First declension nouns. First and second declension adjectives. Method
        of indicating declensional pattern of an adjective. Complete paradigm
        of the definite article. Instrumental of association. Instrumental of
        manner. Ascriptive attributive position of adjectives.

8   FOR OLD TIMES' SAKE   26
        Genitive used as a direct object. Imperfect indicative active tense.
        Definite temporal clauses. Predicate nominative. Locative of time.

9   BACK TO SLAVERY FOR LAZARUS   31
        Aorist tense---indicative, imperative, infinitive active. Distinction
        between present and aorist imperatives. N movable. Futures whose stems
        end in certain consonants. Principal parts of Greek verbs.

10 RESCUED: ONE LAMB, NO LAZARUS   36
        More paradigms of the first declension and of first and second declen-
        sion adjectives. Summary of first declension endings. Position of ad-
        jectives. Modifying genitives used as adjectives. Adjectives used as
        substantives.

11 AN OLD SINNER SCARED TO DIE   39
        Second aorist indicative active tense. Variations with α for ο or ε.

12 REVIEW (ON ACCENTS)   43
        Résumé of accents and breathings. Recessive accent. Persistent accent.
        Vocabulary since Lesson 6.

13 OFF TO A NEW LAND   46
        Personal pronouns. Definite article with a proper noun.

14 HALF SISTER: HALF-TRUTH   49
        The demonstrative οὗτος.

15 A CHOICE AND A PROMISE   51
        Masculine nouns of the first declension. The demonstrative
        The intensive αὐτός.

16 A GLIMPSE AT LOT'S FUTURE   54
        Future, present, and aorist of liquid and nasal verbs.

17 ABRAHAM TO THE RESCUE   58
        First and second perfect active. Summary of types of reduplication.

18 REVIEW   62
        Vocabulary in 13-17. Tables of verb, noun, and adjective endings.

iii

19 ABRAM BELIEVES GOD 64
        First and second pluperfect active.

20 WHAT DO YOU KNOW ABOUT ABRAM? 66
        Interrogative pronoun and adjective. Indefinite pronoun and adjective.
        Proclitics. Enclitics.

21 JOSEPH'S FUTURE IN EGYPT 70
        Middle voice---meaning and present and future forms. Middle of liquid
        and nasal future.

22 I NEED TO LEARN EGYPTIAN 74
        Personal pronouns. Conjugation of εἰμί. Accusative of double direct
        object.

23 RELUCTANTLY JACOB LETS BENJAMIN GO TO EGYPT 78
        Present middle imperative.

24 REVIEW 80
        Table of some related groups of verb endings. Vocabulary in 19-23.

25 BENJAMIN FRAMED 82
        More middle forms---imperfect, aorist. Secondary middle endings.

26 "I AM YOUR BROTHER." 84
        Reflexive pronouns.

27 "UNTO YOU IS BORN . . ." 87
        Aorist middle imperatives and infinitives.

28 MOSES, A MAN WITH A PAST 90
        Passive voice---meaning and some forms. Perfect and pluperfect middle
        and passive of omega verbs. Perfect middle and passive system of verbs
        whose stems end in a mute or liquid. Augment in pluperfect. Summary of
        consonant changes. Periphrastic third plural in the perfect and plu-
        perfect indicative middle and passive. Ablative of agent.

29 A PROPHETIC MEMORIAL 96
        First and second aorist passive. First and second future passive. Ao-
        rist and future passives in verbs whose stems end with a mute. Reference
        list for aorist and future passives.

30 REVIEW 100
        Vocabulary in 25-29. Reference list of the principal parts of the verbs
        previously presented.

31 PHARAOH'S FIASCO 102
        Third declension nouns and adjectives. Accusative of extent of time.
        Genitive of time. Genitive of material or content.

32 EAT A MAN! 106
        Function of the participle. Present and future active participle.

33 CALEB AND JOSHUA 109
        More third declension nouns. Aorist active participle. Significance of
        tense in participles---kind of action, relative time. Collective noun
        in singular as subject of a plural verb. Neuter noun in plural as sub-
        ject of a singular verb.

34 STIRRING WORDS FROM AN OLD SOLDIER 113
        MI aorist. Third declension nouns. Perfect active participle. Résumé
        of adjectival and substantival emphases of participles. Adverbial em-
        phasis of participles.

35 A NEW GENERATION THAT KNEW NOT THE LORD 118
        Middle participles. Comparison of the indicative and participle in the
        middle. Supplementary participle.

36 REVIEW 122
        Vocabulary in 31-35.

37 TERROR AT NIGHT 124
        Third declension nouns. Aorist and future passive participles. Geni-
        tive absolute.

38 A VOICE IN THE NIGHT 127
        Third declension noun. Indirect discourse. Translations of Greek
        tenses in indirect discourse after tenses translated as English pasts.

39 ISRAEL ASKS FOR A KING 131
        Third declension noun. Relative pronouns. Definite relative clauses.
        Reciprocal pronoun.

40 SAMUEL FINDS THE HIDDEN KING 134
      Third declension nouns in -ει and -ι.

41 WHEN THE VOICE OF THE PEOPLE WAS NOT THE VOICE OF GOD 136
      Present participle of εἰμί. Paradigms of γυνή and κρείσσων. Compara-
      tive ablative. Subjunctive mood---Deliberative question, Hortatory, and
      paradigms.

42 REVIEW 139
      Vocabulary in 37-41.

43 SAUL'S SUCCESSOR CHOSEN 141
      Present subjunctive of εἰμί. Negatives used with the subjunctive. Sub-
      junctive in strong denials, in prohibitions, and in purpose clauses.

44 A VOLUNTEER ANSWERS A CHALLENGE 143
      Conditional sentences. Result clauses with ὥστε. οὐ and μή introducing
      questions. Paradigms of εἷς and μέγας.

45 ONE LITTLE STONE 147
      Contract verbs---nature and accent. Contracts in -εω.

46 WORDS OF ENCOURAGEMENT: JOHN 14:21-26 151
      Contracts in -αω.

47 I JOHN 1:1-4 153
      Forms of ὅστις. Contracts in -οω.

48 I JOHN 1:5-10 155
      Paradigm of οὐδείς. Result clause with ἵνα. MI verbs.

49 I JOHN 2:1-11 157
      Paradigms of οἶδα. Indefinite relative clauses.

50 I JOHN 2:12-21 159

51 I JOHN 2:22-3:8 160
      Substantive clauses with ἵνα. Present progressive.

52 I JOHN 3:9-24 162

53 I JOHN 4:1-21 163

54 I JOHN 5:1-21 164
      Paradigm of βαρύς.

APPENDIX
      Nouns 165
      Pronouns 166
      Adjectives (Participles) 167
      Verbs 169
      Syntax 176

VOCABULARIES
      English-Greek 178
      Greek-English 180

INDEX 185

VERB CHART . . . . Inside Back Cover

1. IMPORTANCE OF THE GREEK LANGUAGE. You are beginning the study of one of the most important languages in the world. Its importance lies not in the number of people who now use it, for the kind of Greek presented in these lessons is no longer spoken, written, or read as an instrument of modern communication. Its importance lies rather in the literature which it has preserved from Homer on, of which the most widely known part is the New Testament. Its importance lies also in the contributions which it has made and is making to the vocabulary of the English language. A large and increasing proportion of the entries in our unabridged dictionaries are words derived from Latin and Greek, in many instances terms coined to label scientific discoveries. As you make progress in mastering this language, you will also increase your understanding both of the English language and of the Greek New Testament.

2. IMPORTANCE OF LEARNING THE GREEK ALPHABET. The first step in the study of Greek is to learn the alphabet. Learning the names, the order, and the sounds of the Greek letters will do several things for you. The barrier of strangeness between you and Greek will begin to crumble. When you see Greek letters or their names, you will experience the pleasure of recognition. When you wish to look up a word in a Greek-English lexicon, your knowledge of the order of the letters in the alphabet will enable you to find the word and to learn its meaning. When your teacher pronounces a Greek word slowly, you will have some idea of how it looks when written down. Although you will not be expected to speak this language or to understand anyone else who is speaking it, still it is often necessary in class to talk about Greek words and phrases. A knowledge of the sounds of the letters is needed for these discussions.

3. THE GREEK ALPHABET.

Forms		Names	Sounds	Forms		Names	Sounds
A	α	alpha	palm	M	μ	mu	moon
B	β	beta	big	N	ν	nu	no
Γ	γ	gamma	go (but before γ, κ, or χ as angle, anchor, ink)	Ξ	ξ	xi	breaks
				O	ο	omicron	on
				Π	π	pi	pull
				P	ρ	rho	run
Δ	δ	delta	do	Σ	σ,ς	sigma	see
E	ε	epsilon	end	T	τ	tau	to
Z	ζ	zeta	leads	Y	υ	upsilon	sur in French or über in German
H	η	eta	chaos				
Θ	θ	theta	wealth	Φ	φ	phi	philosophy
I	ι	iota	sin or machine	X	χ	chi	chaos
K	κ	kappa	king	Ψ	ψ	psi	cups
Λ	λ	lambda	lamb	Ω	ω	omega	ocean

4. CLASSIFICATION OF LETTERS.

   a. Vowels. The vowels are α, ε, η, ι, ο, υ, ω. Notice their lengths:

Always short	Either long or short		Always long
ε	long	ᾱ, ῑ, ῡ	η
ο	short	ᾰ, ῐ, ῠ	ω

   b. Consonants. The letters which are not vowels are consonants.

5. DIPHTHONGS.

   a. Proper diphthongs are combinations of two vowels pronounced in rapid succession. They are pronounced like the underlined letters in the English words below.

αι	aisle	ηυ	a (in late) plus oo (in soon): a-oo	
αυ	sauerkraut			
		οι	toil	
ει	eight or height			
		ου	through	
ευ	e (in let) plus oo (in soon): e-oo			
		υι	week	

b. <u>Improper diphthongs</u> consist of α, η, or ω and a small iota written underneath: ᾳ, ῃ, ῳ. This small letter is called <u>iota-subscript</u>. The improper diphthongs are pronounced exactly like long ᾱ, η, and ω respectively.

c. <u>Length of diphthongs and syllables</u>. All diphthongs are long, and all syllables containing diphthongs are long with certain exceptions (#425).

6. BREATHINGS. Every Greek word beginning with a vowel must have either a rough or a smooth breathing with the initial vowel or diphthong. The rough breathing is pronounced like the aspirated h in English and is written like an introductory single quotation mark (‘); the smooth breathing is pronounced with no change in the sound of the vowel or diphthong involved and is written like an apostrophe (’). ὅτι (hoti), ὢ (oh), ἑδρον (heooron), οἶνους (oinous), εἰ γὰρ λέγει (ei gar legei). Notice (1) that both breathings and accents are placed on the second vowel of diphthongs, (2) that a circumflex accent is placed above its accompanying breathing, and (3) that other accents follow their accompanying breathings.

7. ACCENTS. Three accents are used in spelling Greek words: acute (‘), circumflex (~), and grave (`). Only the last three syllables are ever accented.

8. EXERCISES.

a. Learn the letters of the alphabet so well that you can repeat their names in correct order in thirty seconds.

b. Practice writing the small letters.

c. Be able to recognize the capitals.

d. Pronounce the following Greek words. Notice their similarity to familiar English words. What do you notice about the positions of breathing marks? You need not memorize these words or their meanings, but familiarity with the sounds of the Greek letters will be very helpful.

1) φωνή: sound (cf. <u>phone</u>)
2) ἀπόστολος: apostle
3) ἄγγελος: angel, messenger
4) καρδίᾱ: heart (cf. <u>cardiac</u>)
5) φόβος: fear (cf. <u>phobia</u>)
6) Μᾶρκος: Mark
7) Νικόδημος: Nicodemus
8) Πέτρος: Peter
9) Ῥώμη: Rome
10) ὕδωρ: water (cf. <u>hydro</u>-)
11) ἐπιστολή: epistle, letter
12) μαργαρίτης: pearl (cf. English <u>Margaret</u> and Spanish <u>Margarita</u>)
13) Γαλατίᾱ: Galatia
14) Φίλιππος: Philip
15) ἔξοδος: departure (cf. <u>Exodus</u>)

e. Look up the meanings of the following words in the Greek-English vocabulary at the end of this book.

1) λαμβάνω
2) θάνατος
3) ζωή

4) ἔρχομαι
5) τίθημι
6) δίδωμι

LESSON 2

9. GREETINGS.

Πέτρος βλέπει ἄνθρωπον, καὶ ὁ ἄνθρωπος βλέπει Πέτρον.

"χαῖρε, Μᾶρκε," λέγει Πέτρος.

"χαῖρε, Πέτρε," λέγει ὁ ἄνθρωπος Μᾶρκος.

ὁ ἄνθρωπος Μᾶρκος ἔχει ἀδελφὸν Νικόδημον. Πέτρος βλέπει καὶ τὸν

5   ἀδελφὸν Νικόδημον, καὶ ὁ ἀδελφὸς βλέπει Πέτρον.

"χαῖρε, Νικόδημε," λέγει Πέτρος.

"χαῖρε, Πέτρε," λέγει Νικόδημος.

Πέτρος καὶ ἔχει ἀδελφὸν Φίλιππον. Φίλιππος καὶ βλέπει τὸν ἄνθρω-

πον Μᾶρκον καὶ τὸν ἀδελφὸν Νικόδημον.

10   "χαῖρε, Μᾶρκε," λέγει Φίλιππος.

"χαῖρε, Φίλιππε," λέγει Μᾶρκος.

"χαῖρε, Νικόδημε," λέγει Φίλιππος.

"χαῖρε, Φίλιππε," λέγει Νικόδημος.

10. VOCABULARY.

ἀδελφόν: brother (direct object of verb)

ἀδελφός: brother (subject of verb)

ἄνθρωπον: man (direct object of verb)

ἄνθρωπος: man (subject of verb)

βλέπει: sees, looks at

ἔχει: has

καί: and, also, too

λέγει: says

3

Μᾶρκε: Mark (used in direct address)

Μᾶρκον: Mark (direct object of verb)

Μᾶρκος: Mark (subject of verb)

Νικόδημε: Nicodemus (used in direct address)

Νικόδημον: Nicodemus (direct object of verb)

Νικόδημος: Nicodemus (subject of verb)

ὁ: the (used with masculine singular subject)

Πέτρε: Peter (used in direct address)

Πέτρον: Peter (direct object of verb)

Πέτρος: Peter (subject of verb)

τόν: the (used with masculine singular direct object)

Φίλιππε: Philip (used in direct address)

Φίλιππον: Philip (direct object of verb)

Φίλιππος: Philip (subject of verb)

χαῖρε: greetings, hail, welcome, good morning, farewell,
        rejoice

11. SENTENCES. A sentence is a group of words expressing a complete thought.

Πέτρος βλέπει τὸν ἄνθρωπον.
Peter sees the man.

ὁ ἄνθρωπος ἔχει ἀδελφόν.
The man has a brother.

It may ask a question, express an exclamation, give a command, or make
a statement. All the sentences in this lesson are statements or
greetings (exclamations or commands).

12. NOUNS. A noun is the name of something.

Πέτρος ἔχει ἀδελφόν.
Peter has a brother.

There are six Greek nouns in this lesson.

13. NUMBER. A noun representing one thing is singular in number. A noun
representing more than one thing is plural in number.

Brother: singular   Brothers: plural

All the nouns used in this lesson are singular.

14. GENDER. The Greek language has three grammatical genders: masculine,
feminine, and neuter. Often there is no correspondence between the
grammatical classification and the sex of the object represented, and
no satisfactory explanation can be given for this lack of correspondence.

ὁ ἄνθρωπος: the man

Here gender and sex are both masculine. All the Greek nouns used in
this lesson are masculine. Feminine and neuter nouns will appear in
later lessons.

4

15. VERBS. A verb is a word or group of words used with or without controlling nouns to make a statement, to ask a question, or to give a command. All the verbs in this lesson are used to make statements or express greetings.

ὁ ἄνθρωπος βλέπει Πέτρον.　　　　"χαῖρε, Μᾶρκε," λέγει Πέτρος.
The man sees Peter.　　　　　　　　"Good morning, Mark," says Peter.

16. SUBJECTS. A noun with whose number the verb has to agree is the subject of that verb. Not all verbs have nouns as subjects.

βλέπει. He sees. (She sees. It sees.)

The subject of βλέπει is here indicated somewhat vaguely by the verb ending -ει.

"χαῖρε, Μᾶρκε."
"Good morning /You rejoice!/, Mark."

The subject of χαῖρε is shown by the ending to be one person directly addressed. The addition of Μᾶρκε tells us who this person is. Μᾶρκε, however, is not the subject, but rather a form used in direct address.

Πέτρος βλέπει τὸν ἄνθρωπον.
Peter sees the man.

In this third example the noun Πέτρος is the subject, and βλέπει agrees with it.

17. DIRECT OBJECTS. A direct object is a word or several words representing what receives the action of the verb immediately.

Πέτρος βλέπει τὸν ἄνθρωπον.
Peter sees the man.

18. APPOSITIVES. An appositive is a word added to explain another word. It is generally in the same case as the word which it explains.

ὁ ἄνθρωπος ἔχει ἀδελφόν, Πέτρον.
The man has a brother, Peter.

19. GRAMMATICAL FUNCTIONS AND INFLECTIONAL FORMS. The functions of subject and direct object of a verb are fulfilled nearly always in English by the same form of a word. So we distinguish the subject from the direct object by the order of the words in the sentence.

Peter sees the man.　　　　　　The man sees Peter.
(Subject) (Direct Object)　　　(Subject)　　(Direct Object)

Only a few pronouns have different forms for these two functions, as "I" and "me," and "he" and "him."

　I　see　him.　　　　　　He　sees　me.
(Subject) (Direct Object)　　(Subject)　(Direct Object)

In Greek, however, masculine and feminine nouns have forms by which the subject may be distinguished from the direct object. So for the Greeks it was possible to arrange the words of a sentence in almost any order they wished. The English order was used in #9 only because this is the first reading exercise. Other patterns will be used in subsequent lessons.

Πέτρος βλέπει Φίλιππον.　　　Φίλιππος βλέπει Πέτρον.
Peter　sees　Philip.　　　　　Philip　sees　Peter.
(Subject)　(Direct Object)　　(Subject)　　(Direct Object)

Φίλιππος and Φίλιππον as well as Πέτρος and Πέτρον are inflectional

<u>forms</u>. Their endings, -ος and -ον, are interchangeable as the grammatical pattern requires.

20. CASE: NOMINATIVE SUBJECT. The nouns in #19 which serve as subjects of verbs are in the <u>nominative</u> <u>case</u>.

21. CASE: ACCUSATIVE DIRECT OBJECT. The nouns in #19 which serve as direct objects of verbs are in the <u>accusative</u> <u>case</u>.

22. CASE: VOCATIVE OF DIRECT ADDRESS. When a masculine noun such as those in #9 is used to address someone directly, it frequently has the ending -ε in the singular. This is the <u>vocative</u> <u>of</u> <u>direct</u> <u>address</u>.

"χαῖρε, <u>Μᾶρκε</u>," λέγει Πέτρος.
"Good morning, <u>Mark</u>," says Peter.

23. THE DEFINITE ARTICLE. In English the definite article is the limiting word "the" and is always spelled the same way. In Greek the form changes to correspond with the gender, number, and case of the noun with which the article is used.

ὁ ἀδελφὸς βλέπει τὸν ἄνθρωπον.
<u>The</u> brother sees <u>the</u> man.

24. THE INDEFINITE ARTICLE. In English the indefinite article is a limiting word having two forms, "a" and "an." In Greek there is no single equivalent. Often, but not always, a Greek noun without a definite article may be translated by an English noun preceded by an indefinite article.

Πέτρος βλέπει ἀδελφόν.
Peter sees <u>a</u> <u>brother</u>.

But Πέτρος is obviously not translated <u>a</u> <u>Peter</u>.

25. EXERCISES.

a. Read #9 aloud following your teacher's example.

b. Translate #9 into English.

c. Write in Greek, not putting the subject first in the sentence.

    1) Peter sees a man.
    2) Philip has the brother.
    3) The man sees the brother and Peter.
    4) The brother sees Philip.
    5) "Good morning, Mark," says Nicodemus.

d. Translate orally, using the pattern indicated for each group of sentences.

    1) Peter sees a brother. ⎫
        " " " man. ⎬ Subject--verb--direct object
        " " Nicodemus. ⎭
    2) " " Philip. ⎫
        " " the brother. ⎬ Verb--subject--direct object
        " " " man. ⎭
    3) " " Mark. ⎫
        " has the man. ⎬ Verb--direct object--subject
    4) Mark says, "Man !" ⎫
        " " , "Brother !" ⎬ Direct object--subject--verb
        " has a brother. ⎭
    5) " " man. ⎫
        " " Philip. ⎬ Direct object--verb--subject
        " " Nicodemus. ⎭

e. Fill in the blanks as you read aloud.

1) Φίλιππος ἔχει ἀδελφ___.

2) Φίλιππ__, βλέπει Πέτρον Μᾶρκος.

3) ἀδελφὸν ἔχ__ Πέτρος.

4) τ__ ἄνθρωπον καὶ τὸν ἀδελφ__ βλέπει Νικόδημος.

f. Notice carefully the following English words related to Greek words in the vocabulary of this lesson.

1) anthropology: "science of man."
2) Peter: a proper name meaning "stone."
3) Philadelphia: a proper name meaning "love of brothers."
4) Philip: a proper name meaning "lover of horses."
5) Philippians: people who lived at Philippi, a city founded by Philip of Macedon.

LESSON 3

26. THE MENU IS FRUIT.

"Μᾶρκε, ἔχεις ἄρτον;" λέγει Πέτρος.

"οὐκ ἔχω ἄρτον, Πέτρε." λέγει Μᾶρκος.

"Πέτρε καὶ Φίλιππε, ἔχετε ἄρτον;" λέγει Νικόδημος.

"οὐκ ἔχομεν ἄρτον· ἔχομεν καρπόν." λέγουσι Πέτρος καὶ Φίλιππος.

5   "Μᾶρκος καὶ Νικόδημος οὐκ ἔχουσι ἄρτον καὶ καρπόν, Φίλιππε," λέγει Πέτρος. "φέρε τὸν καρπόν."

"ἐσθίομεν καρπόν· ἐσθίετε καρπόν, Μᾶρκε καὶ Νικόδημε," λέγουσι Πέτρος καὶ Φίλιππος.

"φέρε τὸν καρπόν, Πέτρε," λέγει Φίλιππος, "Μᾶρκος καὶ Νικό-
10   δημος ἐσθιέτωσαν καρπόν."

"φερέτω Πέτρος τὸν καρπόν," λέγει Μᾶρκος.

καρπὸν ἐσθίουσι.

27. VOCABULARY.

ἄρτον: bread, loaf of bread (accusative singular of ἄρτος)

7

ἐσθίετε: eat! (second plural present imperative active), or you are
           eating, you do eat, you eat (second plural present indica-
           tive active)

ἐσθιέτωσαν: let them eat! (third plural present imperative active.
             This is a command, not a permission.)

ἐσθίομεν: we are eating, we do eat, we eat (first plural present in-
            dicative active)

ἔχεις: you are having, you do have, you have (second singular present
         indicative active)

ἔχετε: you are having, you do have, you have (second plural present
         indicative active)

ἔχομεν: we are having, we do have, we have (first plural present in-
          dicative active)

ἔχουσι: they are having, they do have, they have (third plural present
          indicative active)

ἔχω: I am having, I do have, I have (first singular present indica-
       tive active)

καρπόν: fruit (accusative singular of καρπός)

λέγουσι: they say, they ask (third plural present indicative active)

λέγει: he says, he asks (third singular present indicative active)

οὐκ: not

φέρε: bring! carry! (second singular present imperative active)

φερέτω: let him bring! let him carry! (third singular present im-
          perative active)

Greek question mark (;),   Greek semicolon (˙)

28. TENSE: PRESENT. All the verbs in this lesson represent an action as
     going on at the moment of speaking or writing. In Greek the emphasis
     on the progressive nature of the action is greater than on the present
     time.

     λέγουσι.   ἐσθίετε καρπόν
     They are saying.   Eat fruit! (as you are doing)
                                       Go on eating fruit!

     These verbs are in the present tense.

29. VOICE: ACTIVE. All the verbs in this lesson represent an action as
     performed by the subject.

     ἔχεις ἄρτον;   Φίλιππος ἔχει ἀδελφόν.   φέρε καρπόν.
     Do you have bread?   Philip has a brother.   Bring fruit.

     These verbs are in the active voice.

30. MOOD: INDICATIVE. Some of the verbs in this lesson make a statement
     or ask a question.

     οὐκ ἔχω ἄρτον.   ἔχετε ἄρτον;
     I do not have bread.   Do you have bread?

     These verbs are in the indicative mood.

31. MOOD: IMPERATIVE. Other verbs in this lesson express a command.

8

φέρε τὸν καρπόν.   ὁ ἄνθρωπος φερέτω τὸν καρπόν.
Bring the fruit.   **Let** the man **bring** the fruit.

These verbs are in the **imperative mood**.

32. NUMBER. Verbs like nouns may be singular or plural. With verbs the number indicates whether the subject of the verb is singular or plural.

Singular: ἔχω.   Plural: ἔχομεν.
         I <u>have</u>.   We <u>have</u>.

33. PERSON. If the subject of a verb is the person or the group of persons <u>speaking</u>, the verb is in the <u>first person</u>. If the subject of a verb is the person or the group of persons <u>spoken to</u>, the verb is in the <u>second person</u>. If the subject of a verb is the person or the thing or the group <u>spoken of</u>, the verb is in the <u>third person</u>.

	Indicative	Imperative
1st Sing.:	ἔχω.	(There are no 1st person
	I <u>have</u>.	imperative forms.)
1st Pl.:	ἔχομεν.	
	We <u>have</u>.	
2nd Sing.:	ἔχεις.	ἔχε.
	You <u>have</u>.	Have !
2nd Pl.:	ἔχετε.	ἔχετε.
	You <u>have</u>.	Have !
3rd Sing.:	ἔχει.	ἐχέτω.
	He (she, <u>it</u>) has.	<u>Let</u> him (her, <u>it</u>) <u>have</u> !
3rd Pl.:	ἔχουσι.	ἐχέτωσαν.
	<u>They</u> have.	<u>Let</u> them <u>have</u> !

34. CONJUGATION. All this information about the verb can be briefly summed up by the following tabular arrangement called the <u>conjugation</u> of the present indicative active and present imperative <u>active</u> of ἔχω. A conjugation is the inflection or paradigm of a verb. Because ἔχω has an omega as its last letter, it is called an <u>omega verb</u>.

Present Active

	Indicative		Imperative	
	Sing.	Plural	Sing.	Plural
1st per.	ἔχω	ἔχομεν	(No forms exist)	
2nd per.	ἔχεις	ἔχετε	ἔχε	ἔχετε
3rd per.	ἔχει	ἔχουσι	ἐχέτω	ἐχέτωσαν

35. SYLLABLES: NUMBER IN EACH WORD. To describe the location of an accent we must understand something about syllables. A Greek word has as many syllables as the sum of its diphthongs and separately pronounced vowels.

ἄνθρωπος has three separately pronounced vowels and therefore three syllables. ἔχουσι has one diphthong and two separately pronounced vowels and therefore three syllables.

36. SYLLABLES: NAMES OF THE LAST THREE. The last syllable of a Greek word is called the ultima (ἔχου/σι); the next to the last, the <u>penult</u> (ἔ/χου/σι); the second from the last, the <u>antepenult</u> (ἔ/χουσι).

37. SYLLABLES: LENGTH. If the vowel or the diphthong in a syllable is long, the syllable is long. Otherwise, the syllable is short.

38. ACCENT: RECESSIVE. The accent of the verbs presented in this lesson backs up as far from the ultima as it can. If the ultima is short, an

'acute accent stands on the antepenult where the verb has as many as three syllables.

βλέπετε, ἔχομεν, ἔχουσι, λεγέτωσαν.

Even if the ultima is short, the accent stands on the penult, of course, if the verb has only two syllables.

ἔχε, φέρε, βλέπε.

If the ultima is long, an acute accent stands on the penult.

βλέπω, φέρεις, ἔχει, βλεπέτω.

39. EXERCISES.

a. Read #26 aloud imitating your teacher.

b. Translate #26 into English.

c. Write in Greek:

    1) I see bread.
    2) I bring bread.
    3) I eat bread.
    4) Nicodemus says, "I see fruit, I bring fruit, I eat fruit."
    5) Mark says, "We have a man; we bring the man, we do not eat the man."
    6) Is Peter saying, "Welcome"?
    7) Nicodemus and Mark are asking, "Do Philip and Peter have a man?"
    8) Philip and Peter say, "We do not have a man, Nicodemus and Mark."

d. Translate orally:

    1) I eat fruit.
    2) You eat fruit, Peter.
    3) Philip eats fruit.
    4) We eat fruit.
    5) You eat fruit, Mark and Nicodemus.
    6) Peter and Philip eat fruit.
    7) Eat fruit, Nicodemus!
    8) Let Nicodemus eat fruit!
    9) Eat fruit, Mark and Nicodemus!
   10) Let Peter and Philip eat fruit!
   11) - 20)   (Substitute "bring" for "eat" in 1) - 10).)

e. Accent the following verb forms in accordance with principles of recessive accent.

    1) ἐχουσι
    2) βλεπετωσαν
    3) λεγετε
    4) φερομεν
    5) ἐσθιε
    6) ἐσθιετω
    7) ἐχεις
    8) λεγω

40. A REAL DINNER THIS TIME.

"ἔχομεν δεῖπνον ἐν τῷ κήπῳ, Φίλιππε καὶ Πέτρε;" λέγει τὸ τέκνον
Νικοδήμου. Νικόδημος γὰρ τέκνον ἔχει.

Πέτρον καὶ Νικόδημον καὶ τὸ τέκνον καὶ Μᾶρκον ἐκ τοῦ οἴκου
Φίλιππος πέμπει.

"δοῦλε," Φίλιππος λέγει, "φέρε τὸν ἄρτον Πέτρου καὶ τὸν οἶνον
Μάρκου ἐκ τοῦ οἴκου."

"ἐσθίετε τὸ ἀρνίον, Φίλιππε;" λέγει ὁ δοῦλος Φιλίππου.

"φέρε τὸ ἀρνίον εἰς τὸν κῆπον. ἐσθίομεν γὰρ ἀρνίον, δοῦλε," λέγει
Φίλιππος.

ἐκ τοῦ οἴκου Φιλίππου φέρει ὁ δοῦλος τὸν ἄρτον καὶ τὸν οἶνον καὶ
τὸ ἀρνίον.

"Πέτρε, ἔχεις ὀψάριον;" λέγει τὸ τέκνον.

"οὐκ ἔχω ὀψάριον, τέκνον," λέγει Πέτρος.

"ὀψάριον ἔχει Φίλιππος;" λέγει τὸ τέκνον.

"οὐκ ἔχει Φίλιππος ὀψάριον," λέγει Πέτρος.

"πίνομεν τὸν οἶνον Μάρκου ἐκ τοῦ ποτηρίου," τὸ τέκνον λέγει.
"οὐ πίνομεν τὸν ἄρτον. ἐσθίομεν γὰρ τὸν ἄρτον."

"δοῦλε, φέρεις δεῖπνον καλόν," λέγει Νικόδημος. "Φίλιππε, ἔχεις
δοῦλον καλόν."

Φίλιππος πέμπει τὸν καλὸν δοῦλον ἀπὸ τοῦ κήπου, καὶ ὁ δοῦλος
φέρει καρπὸν καλὸν εἰς τὸν κῆπον Φιλίππου.

τὸν καλὸν καρπὸν Φίλιππος βλέπει καὶ λέγει, "Νικόδημε καὶ Μᾶρκε
καὶ ἀδελφὲ Πέτρε καὶ τέκνον καὶ δοῦλε, ἐσθίετε τὸν καλὸν καρπὸν τοῦ
δούλου."

"ἔχομεν δεῖπνον καλὸν ἐν τῷ κήπῳ Φιλίππου," τὸ τέκνον Νικοδήμου
λέγει.

41. VOCABULARY.

ἀπό: from, away from

ἀπὸ τοῦ κήπου: away from the garden

ἀρνίον, τό: lamb, little lamb

γάρ: for (generally put as the second word in its clause)

δεῖπνον, τό: dinner, supper

δοῦλος, ὁ: slave, bondslave

εἰς: **into**

εἰς τὸν κῆπον: into the garden

ἐκ: from, out of, from within

ἐκ τοῦ οἴκου: out of the house

ἐκ τοῦ ποτηρίου: out of the cup

ἐν: in, within, among

ἐν τῷ κήπῳ: in the garden

καλόν: beautiful, good, excellent, fair, noble

κῆπος, ὁ: garden

οἶκος, ὁ: house

οἶνος, ὁ: wine

οὐ: not (used before a word beginning with a consonant)

οὐκ: not (used before a word beginning with a vowel having a smooth breathing)

ὀψάριον, τό: fish

πέμπω: I send

πίνω: I drink

ποτήριον, τό: cup

τέκνον, τό: child

τό: the

42. METHOD OF INDICATING GENDER IN VOCABULARIES. In the vocabulary just given and in all following vocabularies the gender of nouns is shown by the gender of the definite article which is added.

"ἄρτος, ὁ: bread" is a masculine noun.
"δεῖπνον, τό: dinner, supper" is a neuter noun.

43. CASE: GENITIVE OF POSSESSION. In the following expressions the under-lined words indicate possessors.

τὸ τέκνον Νικοδήμου
the child of Nicodemus

τὸν καλὸν καρπὸν τοῦ δούλου
the slave's good fruit

τὸν οἶνον Μάρκου
Mark's wine

ὁ δοῦλος Φιλίππου
Philip's slave

τὸν ἄρτον Πέτρου
Peter's bread

These Greek words, ending in -ου and shown by the context to indicate possession, are called genitives of possession.

44. CASE: ABLATIVE OF SEPARATION OR SOURCE. In #40 the nouns in the phrases ἐκ τοῦ οἴκου and ἀπὸ τοῦ κήπου name things from which there occurs separation by the action of the verb. The words ἀπό, away from, and ἐκ, out of, state the ideas of separation.

ὁ δοῦλος φέρει τὸ ἀρνίον ἐκ τοῦ οἴκου.
The slave brings the lamb out of the house.

12

In this sentence it is clear that the house is the source from which the slave brings the lamb.

Because in #40 the nouns οἴκου and κήπου end in -ου and because at the same time the immediate contexts have words expressing the idea of separation or source, these nouns are called <u>ablatives of separation or source</u>.

45. CASE: DISTINCTION BETWEEN GENITIVE AND ABLATIVE. It can be observed that Νικοδήμου, Πέτρου, Μάρκου, Φιλίππου, and δούλου (called genitives in #43), and οἴκου and κήπου (called ablatives in #44), all have the same inflectional ending. It is clear, then, that the two cases are not distinguished by their inflectional forms but by their contexts.

46. CASE: LOCATIVE OF PLACE. In #40 the noun in the phrase ἐν τῷ κήπῳ, <u>in the garden</u>, names the place in which the dinner is served. Because κήπῳ ends in -ῳ and because at the same time the immediate context has a word expressing the idea of location, this noun is called a <u>locative of place</u>.

47. PREPOSITIONS. In #40 ἀπό, <u>away from</u>, εἰς, <u>into</u>, ἐκ, <u>out of</u>, ἐν, <u>in</u>, have been used with nouns. These words are called prepositions. Their function is to help show the relation which the accompanying noun has to its context. The inflectional ending of the noun limits the noun to some extent, but the preposition adds a stricter limitation.

48. RÉSUMÉ OF INFLECTIONAL FORMS USED THUS FAR. For masculine nouns the following inflectional endings have been used.

Nominative   -ος
Genitive ⎫
Ablative ⎭   -ου
Locative   -ῳ
Accusative   -ον
Vocative   -ε

The endings for neuter nouns are the same as those for masculine nouns except in the nominative and vocative.

Nominative   -ον
Genitive ⎫
Ablative ⎭   -ου
Locative   -ῳ
Accusative   -ον
Vocative   -ον

49. SINGULAR FORMS OF THE SECOND DECLENSION. Both the masculine and the neuter nouns used so far belong to the <u>Second Declension</u>. A <u>declension</u> is an inflection or a paradigm of a noun, an adjective, or a pronoun. Adjectives and pronouns will be studied later. Only singular forms have been used.

		Masculine		Neuter
N.		ἀδελφός		τέκνον
G. Ab.		ἀδελφοῦ		τέκνου
L.		ἀδελφῷ		τέκνῳ
Ac.		ἀδελφόν		τέκνον
V.		ἀδελφέ		τέκνον

N.	ὁ	δοῦλος	τό	ποτήριον
G. Ab.	τοῦ	δούλου	τοῦ	ποτηρίου
L.	τῷ	δούλῳ	τῷ	ποτηρίῳ
Ac.	τόν	δοῦλον	τό	ποτήριον
V.	--	δοῦλε	--	ποτήριον

50. ACCENT: PERSISTENT. Unlike the accent of verbs, which recedes as far from the ultima as the length of the ultima permits (see #38), the accent of nouns tends to stay where it is in the nominative form. For this reason the accent of nouns is called <u>persistent</u>. Notice the position of the accent in the preceding paradigms.

καρπός is accented like ἀδελφός.

ἀρνίον, Πέτρος, and ἄρτος are accented like τέχνον.

δεῖπνον, κῆπος, οἶνος, and οἶκος are accented like δοῦλος.

ἄνθρωπος, ὀψάριον, and Φίλιππος are accented like ποτήριον.

In all of these examples in #49 except ποτηρίου and ποτηρίῳ the accent remains on the same syllable throughout the paradigm. In these two exceptions the long ultima draws the accent from the antepenult to the penult. An acute accent on the ultima, as occurs in some forms of καρπός and ἀδελφός, is changed to a grave accent when another word follows without intervening punctuation. Enclitics (#170) are exceptions to this principle.

For the present these paradigms may be consulted in placing accents on nouns.

51. EXERCISES.

a. Read #40 aloud to increase your fluency in pronouncing Greek. This control of the language will make the Gospels much more vivid when you come to study them.

b. Translate #40 into English.

c. Write in Greek:

   1) I do not drink wine.
   2) You (sing.) do not drink good wine.
   3) He does not drink good wine in the garden.
   4) We eat fruit.
   5) You (pl.) eat dinner.
   6) Eat (pl.) the lamb in the house.
   7) They bring the good bread.
   8) Bring (sing.) the fish away from the slave.
   9) From (out of) the house I see the garden.
   10) Out of the cup we drink in the garden.

d. Translate orally:

   1) We see Peter.
   2) We do not eat Peter.
   3) You (pl.) have a little lamb.
   4) You (pl.) say, "Drink, little lamb."
   5) The little lamb drinks.
   6) The little lamb does not drink wine.
   7) Send (sing.) the fish into the garden.
   8) Send (pl.) the child into the garden.
   9) Carry (sing.) the cup into the house.
   10) Carry (pl.) the cup out of the house away from Philip.

e. Translate the English words in parentheses so as to fit the sentence in which each stands, e. g.,
   ὁ δοῦλος (Philip's) ἐσθίει δεῖπνον.
   ὁ δοῦλος <u>Φιλίππου</u> ἐσθίει δεῖπνον.

   1) τὸ ἀρνίον (Peter's) βλέπει τὸ τέχνον.

14

2) πίνετε ἐν τῷ κήπῳ (the child's).

3) ἔχομεν τὸν ἄρτον (the man's).

4) πέμπε τὸν δοῦλον ἀπὸ (the fruit).

5) βλέπουσι τὸν ἄνθρωπον ἐν (the house).

6) πίνεις ἐκ (the cup).

7) τὸ γὰρ ποτήριον πέμπομεν εἰς (the garden).

LESSON 5

52. DOCTOR LAZARUS.

πυρετοὺς ἔχουσι τὰ τέκνα Μάρκου καὶ Νικοδήμου καὶ Πέτρος καὶ Φίλιππος. ἄρτον καὶ ἀρνίον οὐκ ἐσθίουσι. τοῖς τέκνοις καὶ τοῖς ἀνθρώποις ἄρτους καὶ ὀψάρια οἱ δοῦλοι φέρουσι. οὐκ ἐσθίουσι καὶ οὐκ ἰσχύουσι ἐσθίειν καὶ πίνειν ὅτι πυρετοὺς κακοὺς ἔχουσι.

5 θεραπεύειν πυρετοὺς ἰσχύει ὁ δοῦλος Λάζαρος. τοὺς κακοὺς πυρετοὺς
τῶν ἀνθρώπων καὶ τῶν τέκνων θεραπεύειν ἰσχύσει. θεραπεύσει τοὺς κακοὺς
πυρετούς.

Φιλίππῳ Λάζαρος λέγει, "θεραπεύσω τὰ τέκνα καὶ τοὺς ἀνθρώπους."

Φιλίππῳ δουλεύει Λάζαρος. Λάζαρον ἀπολύσει Φίλιππος ὅτι τοὺς κα-
10 κοὺς πυρετοὺς θεραπεύειν ἰσχύσει ὁ δοῦλος. ὅτι Φίλιππος τὸν καλὸν
δοῦλον Λάζαρον ἀπολύσει, οὐ δουλεύσει Λάζαρος Φιλίππῳ.

λέγει Φίλιππος τῷ καλῷ δούλῳ Λαζάρῳ, "Λάζαρε, ἀπολύσω τὸν καλὸν
δοῦλον. οὐ δουλεύσεις Φιλίππῳ."

53. VOCABULARY.

ἀπολύω: I release, set free, let go

ἀπολύσω: I shall release, etc.

δουλεύω: I serve as a slave, am a slave to (with dat. dir. obj.)

δουλεύσω: I shall serve as a slave, etc. (with dat. dir. obj.)

θεραπεύω: I treat, cure, heal

θεραπεύσω: I shall treat, etc.

θεραπεύειν: to treat, etc.

ἰσχύω: I am able, strong, powerful

ἰσχύσω: I shall be able, etc.

κακός: bad, evil, wicked

καλός: beautiful, good, excellent, fair, noble

Λάζαρος, -ου, ὁ: Lazarus

ὅτι: because, that

πυρετός, -οῦ, ὁ: fever

54. METHOD OF INDICATING THE DECLENSIONAL PATTERN OF NOUNS IN VOCABULARIES. The vocabulary entry "πυρετός, -οῦ, ὁ: fever" by the part "-οῦ" indicates that the second inflectional form is πυρετοῦ. With this start we can go on to use the pattern of declension used for ἀδελφός, δοῦλος, and ἄνθρωπος.

55. CASE: DATIVE OF INDIRECT OBJECT. In #52 the word Φιλίππῳ has the same endings as τῷ κήπῳ, which in #46 is called a locative of place. You will remember that the ending -ῳ plus the use of the preposition ἐν (ἐν τῷ κήπῳ, in the garden) determined the construction. But in #52 we have Φιλίππῳ Λάζαρος λέγει, Lazarus says to Philip. By grammatical tradition this is called a dative of <u>indirect object</u>. What Lazarus says is the direct object of the verb λέγει. Philip receives the action of this less immediately than the words that are spoken.

56. CASE: DATIVE OF DIRECT OBJECT. In #52 Φιλίππῳ is used in another construction.

Φιλίππῳ δουλεύει Λάζαρος.
Lazarus is a slave <u>to Philip</u>.

Since Φιλίππῳ receives the action of the verb immediately, it is the direct object of δουλεύει although not in the accusative, but in the dative case.

57. PLURAL FORMS OF SECOND DECLENSION NOUNS AND OF THE DEFINITE ARTICLE. Until this lesson only singular nouns and articles have been used. In this lesson the plural endings of the second declension have all been used, and the masculine and neuter forms of the definite article. Two complete paradigms follow.

A Masculine Noun   A Neuter Noun

Singular   Singular

N.	ὁ	ἄνθρωπος	τὸ	τέκνον	(the child)
G. Ab.	τοῦ	ἀνθρώπου	τοῦ	τέκνου	(of the child)
D. L.	τῷ	ἀνθρώπῳ	τῷ	τέκνῳ	(to or for the child)
Ac.	τὸν	ἄνθρωπον	τὸ	τέκνον	(the child)
V.		ἄνθρωπε		τέκνον	(O child)

Plural   Plural

N.	οἱ	ἄνθρωποι	τὰ	τέκνα	(the children)
G. Ab.	τῶν	ἀνθρώπων	τῶν	τέκνων	(of the children)
D. L.	τοῖς	ἀνθρώποις	τοῖς	τέκνοις	(to or for the children)
Ac.	τοὺς	ἀνθρώπους	τὰ	τέκνα	(the children)
V.		ἄνθρωποι		τέκνα	(O children)

16

58. ADJECTIVES. An adjective is a word which describes or qualifies the
meaning of a noun or pronoun. The definite article is an adjective.

καλὸς δοῦλος   ὁ δοῦλος   ὁ καλὸς δοῦλος
a <u>good</u> slave   <u>the</u> slave   <u>the</u> <u>good</u> slave

59. AGREEMENT OF ADJECTIVES. Adjectives agree with the nouns or pronouns
which they modify by having the same gender, number, and case.

καλῷ δούλῳ   τὰ τέκνα   τοὺς κακοὺς πυρετούς
for a <u>good</u> slave   <u>the</u> children   <u>the</u> <u>bad</u> fevers

60. ADJECTIVES OF THE SECOND DECLENSION. The adjectives used thus far belong to the second declension in their masculine and neuter forms.
Consequently, they employ the same endings as the nouns which they modify.

τ<u>οὺς</u> κακ<u>οὺς</u> πυρετ<u>ούς</u>

τ<u>ὰ</u> καλ<u>ὰ</u> τέκν<u>α</u>

τ<u>ῶν</u> καλ<u>ῶν</u> ἀνθρώπ<u>ων</u>

δούλ<u>οις</u> κακ<u>οῖς</u>

ο<u>ἱ</u> καλ<u>οὶ</u> κῆπ<u>οι</u>

The agreement of nouns and adjectives will not always involve the rhym-
ing of endings. In later lessons nouns and adjectives of different declensions and of different endings will be used together.

61. TENSE: FUTURE. The verb forms used before this lesson have all belonged
to the present tense. In this lesson the following verb forms are not
in the present tense.

ἀπολύσει   θεραπεύσει
ἀπολύσω   θεραπεύσω
δουλεύσει   ἰσχύσει
δουλεύσεις

These are future forms and are to be recognized by the sigma just before
the personal endings.

ἀπολύσει   θεραπεύσω

The <u>future tense</u> represents an action as going on or as about to occur
after the moment of speaking or writing.

62. FUTURE INDICATIVE ACTIVE COMPARED WITH PRESENT INDICATIVE ACTIVE.

Present   Future

ἰσχύω   ἰσχύσω
ἰσχύεις   ἰσχύσεις
ἰσχύει   ἰσχύσει

ἰσχύομεν   ἰσχύσομεν
ἰσχύετε   ἰσχύσετε
ἰσχύουσι   ἰσχύσουσι

All the other new verbs in this lesson form their future active indicative as ἰσχύω does, but the verbs given in Lessons 2, 3, and 4 do
not follow this pattern and will be explained later.

63. PRESENT INFINITIVE ACTIVE. The form θεραπεύειν is a present active
infinitive translated <u>to heal</u> or <u>heal</u>, depending upon the English verb
introducing the infinitive in the translation. It may be called a

complementary <u>infinitive</u> since it completes the idea in ἰσχύω. It is really a direct object of ἰσχύω.

ἰσχύω θεραπεύειν.
I am able <u>to heal</u>, (or) I can <u>heal</u>.

All the verbs given thus far can form their present active infinitives by adding -ειν to the present active stem.

	Indicative	Infinitive
	βλέπω	βλέπειν
	πίνω	πίνειν
	ἐσθίω	ἐσθίειν

64. CAUSAL CLAUSES. A clause introduced by ὅτι may in a suitable context indicate the reason for the statement to which the clause is subordinate.

Φίλιππος τὸν δοῦλον ἀπολύει <u>ὅτι ὁ δοῦλος τέκνα θεραπεύει</u>.
Philip releases the slave <u>because the slave heals children</u>.

65. EXERCISES.

a. Read #52 aloud trying to group together the words that are grammatically allied. This should help you to understand what you are reading.

b. Translate #52 into good English.

c. Write in Greek.

1) I shall let the slave go.
2) You will let the slave go, Peter.
3) She will let the slave go.
4) We are letting the slave go.
5) You are letting the slave go, Mark and Nicodemus.
6) They are letting the slave go.
7) Serve as a slave to Philip, Lazarus!
8) Will you be a slave to Philip, Lazarus?
9) I will not be a slave to Philip, Peter.
10) I can not be a slave to Philip, Peter.
11) Will you be able to be a slave to Philip, Nicodemus?
12) Cure Philip, Lazarus!
13) Good morning, Philip.

d. Translate the following forms and give their corresponding present forms.

1) ἀπολύσομεν

2) δουλεύσετε

3) θεραπεύσουσι

4) ἰσχύσεις

5) θεραπεύσομεν

6) δουλεύσουσι

7) ἀπολύσετε

8) θεραπεύσεις

9) δουλεύσομεν

10) ἀπολύσει

11) ἰσχύσουσι

12) θεραπεύσετε

13) ἀπολύσουσι

14) ἰσχύσομεν

15) ἰσχύσετε

16) δουλεύσει

17) ἀπολύσω

18) δουλεύσεις

66. VOCABULARY IN LESSONS 2-5. You should know all these words perfectly.

NOUNS	PREPOSITIONS	CONJUNCTIONS
ἀδελφός	ἀπό	γάρ
ἄνθρωπος	εἰς	καί
ἀρνίον	ἐκ	ὅτι
ἄρτος	ἐν	
δεῖπνον		
δοῦλος	VERBS	ADJECTIVES
καρπός		
κῆπος	ἀπολύω	κακός
Λάζαρος	βλέπω	καλός
Μᾶρκος	δουλεύω	ὁ
Νικόδημος	ἐσθίω	τό
οἶκος	ἔχω	
οἶνος	θεραπεύω	
ὀψάριον	ἰσχύω	
Πέτρος	λέγω	ADVERBS
ποτήριον	πέμπω	
πυρετός	πίνω	
τέκνον	φέρω	οὐ
Φίλιππος	χαῖρε	οὐκ

NOTE: Some of these words will be used with meanings different from those given so far. Whenever the context seems to require a new meaning, look in the Greek-English vocabulary in the back of the book.

67. TECHNICAL TERMS DEFINED OR ILLUSTRATED IN LESSONS 1-5. These terms will be used constantly as long as you study Greek. Know them well!

Ablative	Improper Diphthong
Accent	Indefinite Article
Accusative	Indicative Mood
Active Voice	Inflectional Form
Adjective	Locative
Agreement	Nominative
Alphabet	Nouns
Antepenult	Number
Appositive	Penult
Breathing	Persistent Accent
Case	Person
Causal Clause	Preposition
Conjugation	Present Infinitive Active
Consonant	Present Tense
Dative	Proper Diphthong
Declension	Recessive Accent
Definite Article	Sentence
Direct Object	Subject
Future Tense	Syllable
Gender	Ultima
Genitive	Verb
Grammatical Function	Vocative
Imperative Mood	Vowel

68. INFLECTIONS IN LESSONS 2-5.

SECOND DECLENSION

ὁ	ἄνθρωπος	τὸ	τέκνον
τοῦ	ἀνθρώπου	τοῦ	τέκνου
τῷ	ἀνθρώπῳ	τῷ	τέκνῳ
τόν	ἄνθρωπον	τό	τέκνον
	ἄνθρωπε		τέκνον

οἱ   ἄνθρωποι   τά   τέκνα
τῶν   ἀνθρώπων   τῶν   τέκνων
τοῖς ἀνθρώποις   τοῖς τέκνοις
τούς ἀνθρώπους   τά   τέκνα
      ἄνθρωποι   τέκνα

PRESENT INDICATIVE ACTIVE

ἰσχύω   ἰσχύομεν
ἰσχύεις   ἰσχύετε
ἰσχύει   ἰσχύουσι

PRESENT INFINITIVE ACTIVE

ἰσχύειν

PRESENT IMPERATIVE ACTIVE

ἴσχυε   ἰσχύετε
ἰσχυέτω   ἰσχυέτωσαν

FUTURE INDICATIVE ACTIVE

ἰσχύσω   ἰσχύσομεν
ἰσχύσεις   ἰσχύσετε
ἰσχύσει   ἰσχύσουσι

69. OBJECTIVE TESTS.

a. Select the Greek item at the right which illustrates the technical
    term at the left.

1) Accented   a) κακός
    Antepenult   b) πέμπειν
                      c) ὀψάριον
                      d) δοῦλος
                      e) ἄρτος   1.( )

2) Improper   a) ῳ
    Diphthong   b) οι
                      c) ει
                      d) η
                      e) ιο   2.( )

3) Preposition   a) γάρ
                      b) εἰς
                      c) οὐκ
                      d) ὅτι
                      e) τόν   3.( )

4) Smooth Breathing a) ὅτι
    and Circumflex   b) ἄρτος
    Accent   c) ἀρνίον
                      d) οὖ
                      e) οἶκος   4.( )

5) Agreement of   a) οἶνος κακός
    Noun and   b) οἴνου κακός
    Adjective   c) οἴνῳ κακοί
                      d) οἶνον κακῷ
                      e) οἴνων κακόν   5.( )

6) Grammatical Gen- a) ὁ ἀδελφός
    der Differing   b) τοῦ ἀνθρώπου
    from Natural   c) τῷ τέκνῳ
    Gender   d) Λάζαρον
                      e) τά ποτήρια   6.( )

7) Imperative Mood	a) b) c) d) e)	λέγει φέρε πίνειν δουλεύουσι βλέπεις	7.( )
8) Genitive Case (Choose among the underlined words.)	a) b) c) d) e)	ἀπὸ τοῦ οἴκου ἐκ τοῦ κήπου τὸ ἀρνίον τοῦ τέκνου εἰς τὸ ποτήριον οὐ βλέπει, Φίλιππε	8.( )
9) Recessive Accent	a) b) c) d) e)	Νικόδημε Λάζαρον Φίλιππος θεραπεύω ποτήριον	9.( )
10) Long Syllable	a) b) c) d) e)	ἐν ὁ γάρ οὐ ἐκ	10.( )

b. Make each of the following a meaningful expression by filling each blank with an appropriate inflectional ending.

1) θεραπεύ____ τὰ τέκνα Λάζαρος.

2) θεράπευ____ τὰ τέκνα, Λάζαρε.

3) θεραπεύσ____ τὰ τέκνα, Λάζαρε;

4) ἰσχύσει θεραπεύ____ τὰ τέκνα;

5) δουλεύομεν Πέτρ____.

6) βλέπε, Μᾶρκ____, τοὺς καρπούς.

7) φέρετε τὸν δεῖπν____ εἰς τ____ κῆπον.

8) τὰ ποτήρι____ τοῦ οἴν____ οὐκ ἔχουσι οἱ δοῦλοι.

9) τὰ ἀρνία βλεπέτωσαν οἱ ἀδελφ____.

10) ἐκ τ____ οἴκ____ καὶ ἀπὸ τ____ κήπ____ φέρομεν τὰ δεῖπν____.

70. URGENT BUSINESS INTERFERES WITH DINNER. (This little story uses just about all you have learned so far. If you have mastered all the lessons before this review, you should be able to translate this exercise at sight with a little study.)

Πέτρος καὶ Φίλιππος: "ἐν τῷ οἴκῳ δεῖπνον καλὸν ἐσθίομεν. ἐν τῷ κήπῳ ἀνθρώπους βλέπομεν. Νικόδημον καὶ Μᾶρκον βλέπομεν. λέγομεν τοῖς ἀδελφοῖς, 'χαίρετε (plural of χαῖρε), ἄνθρωποι καλοί. χαῖρε, Νικόδημε. χαῖρε, Μᾶρκε.' φέρομεν τοὺς καλοὺς ἀδελφοὺς εἰς τὸν οἶκον καὶ λέγομεν,

5 'ἰσχύσετε ἐν τῷ οἴκῳ δεῖπνον ἐσθίειν;"

Νικόδημος καὶ Μᾶρκος: "οὐκ ἰσχύσομεν ἐσθίειν, Πέτρε καὶ Φίλιππε, ὅτι κακοὺς δούλους ἀπὸ τοῦ κήπου πέμπομεν. οἱ γὰρ δοῦλοι τοῖς καλοῖς τέκνοις ποτήρια οἴνου φέρουσι. οὐ φέρει οἶνον τοῖς τέκνοις ὁ καλὸς

21

δοῦλος Λάζαρος. θεραπεύει πυρετοὺς ὁ καλὸς Λάζαρος. τὸν καλὸν δοῦλον
10 Φίλιππος ἀπολυέτω. τὰ τέκνα καὶ οἱ δοῦλοι καλῶν ἀνθρώπων ὀψάριον καλὸν ἐσθίουσι καὶ οὐ πίνουσι κακὸν οἶνον. οἶνον κακὸν κακοὶ δοῦλοι
πινέτωσαν. οἴνῳ γὰρ καὶ οὐκ ἀνθρώποις δοῦλοι κακοὶ δουλεύουσι. ὁ γὰρ
κακὸς οἶνος τοὺς κακοὺς δούλους οὐκ ἀπολύσει."

Πέτρος καὶ Φίλιππος: "ἀπὸ τοῦ οἴκου καὶ ἀπὸ τοῦ κήπου καὶ ἀπὸ
15 τῶν τέκνων τοὺς κακοὺς δούλους πέμπετε. λέγετε τοῖς καλοῖς τέκνοις,
'ἐσθίετε ἄρτον καὶ ἀρνίον καὶ καρπὸν καὶ ὀψάριον.'"

Νικόδημος καὶ Μᾶρκος: "χαίρετε, Πέτρε καὶ Φίλιππε."

Πέτρος καὶ Φίλιππος: "χαίρετε, Νικόδημε καὶ Μᾶρκε."

LESSON 7

71. TABLE TALK.

σὺν τοῖς ἰδίοις ἀδελφοῖς, Πέτρῳ καὶ Φιλίππῳ, ἐσθίει ἀρνίον καὶ
ὀψάριον Μαρία. περὶ τοῦ ἐλευθέρου Λαζάρου λέγουσι.

Πέτρος: "οὐκέτι δουλεύσει Φιλίππῳ ὁ ἐλεύθερος Λάζαρος."

Μαρία: "πάντοτε τοὺς πυρετοὺς τῶν τέκνων θεραπεύει;"

5 Φίλιππος: "ναί. δικαίαν γὰρ καρδίαν ἔχει Λάζαρος."

Πέτρος: "καὶ νῦν δωρεὰς ἔχει ὁ μακάριος Λάζαρος."

Φίλιππος: "χρείαν δωρεῶν ἔχει ὅτι οὐκέτι ἐν τῷ οἴκῳ Πέτρου καὶ
Φιλίππου σὺν τοῖς δούλοις ἐσθίει."

Μαρία: "Νικόδημος καὶ Μᾶρκος Λαζάρῳ δωρεὰς πέμπουσι;"

10 Πέτρος: "ναί, ἀλλὰ πέμπουσι τοὺς ἰδίους κακοὺς δούλους ἀπὸ τῶν
ἰδίων μακαρίων τέκνων."

Μαρία: "δικαίας καρδίας ἔχουσι πάντοτε."

Φίλιππος: "παρρησίαν νῦν ἔχει ὁ μακάριος Λάζαρος. παρρησίᾳ
λέγειν ἰσχύει."

22

15   Μαρία: "παρρησίαν καὶ ἔχομεν, ἀλλὰ οὐκ ἔχουσι δοῦλοι."

       Πέτρος: "ἀλλὰ ἔχουσι αἱ καρδίαι καλῶν δούλων δικαίαν ἐπιθυμίαν

παρρησίας."

       Φίλιππος: "ναί, ἀλλὰ ἐπιθυμίαν οἴνου ἔχουσι αἱ καρδίαι κακῶν

δούλων."

20   Μαρία: "τὸν μακάριον καὶ ἐλεύθερον Λάζαρον, ἀδελφοί, εἰς τὸν

ἴδιον οἶκον φέρετε."

       Πέτρος καὶ Φίλιππος: "ἔχομεν καὶ ἐπιθυμίαν ἐν ταῖς ἰδίαις καρ-

δίαις καὶ χρείαν λέγειν σὺν Λαζάρῳ. ἰσχύσεις βλέπειν Λάζαρον. ἰσχύ-

σομεν φέρειν τὸν ἐλεύθερον Λάζαρον καὶ λέγειν παρρησίᾳ περὶ τῶν δωρεῶν.

72. VOCABULARY.

ἀλλά: but

δίκαιος, -ᾱ, -ον: righteous, just

δωρεά, -ᾶς, ἡ: gift

ἐλεύθερος, -ᾱ, -ον: free

ἐπιθυμίᾱ, -ᾱς, ἡ: longing, desire

ἴδιος, -ᾱ, -ον: one's (my, our, your, his, her, its, their) own,
                  belonging to one's self

καρδίᾱ, -ᾱς, ἡ: heart

μακάριος, -ᾱ, -ον: happy, blessed

Μαρίᾱ, -ᾱς, ἡ: Mary

ναί: yes

νῦν: now

οὐκέτι: no longer, no more

πάντοτε: always, at all times, at any time

παρρησίᾱ, -ᾱς, ἡ: freedom (of speech), confidence, boldness, openness

παρρησίᾳ (instrumental of παρρησία used as an adverb):   freely, frankly,
          plainly

περί: (with gen. in figurative sense)   around, about, concerning

σύν: (with instr.)   with

χρείᾱ, -ᾱς, ἡ: need, necessity

73. PARADIGMS OF THE FIRST DECLENSION. Until this lesson all the nouns
have belonged to the second declension and have been either masculine
or neuter in gender. In this lesson the nouns δωρεά, ἐπιθυμίᾱ, καρδίᾱ,
Μαρίᾱ, παρρησίᾱ, and χρείᾱ belong to the first declension and are feminine in gender. It will be noticed that all of these nouns end in -ᾱ
preceded by ε or ι. When as in these examples the stem of a first declension noun ends in ε, ι, or ρ followed by α in the nominative singu-

23

lar, the following pattern prevails.

	Singular	Plural	Endings	
N. V.	καρδίᾱ	καρδίαι	-ᾱ	-αι
G. Ab.	καρδίᾱς	καρδιῶν	-ᾱς	-ων
D. L. I.	καρδίᾳ	καρδίαις	-ᾳ	-αις
Ac.	καρδίᾱν	καρδίᾱς	-ᾱν	-ᾱς

	Singular	Plural
N. V.	δωρεά	δωρεαί
G. Ab.	δωρεᾶς	δωρεῶν
D. L. I.	δωρεᾷ	δωρεαῖς
Ac.	δωρεάν	δωρεάς

74. PARADIGM OF THE FEMININE **OF** FIRST AND SECOND DECLENSION ADJECTIVES.
The feminine forms of the adjectives introduced as new vocabulary in
this lesson (δίκαιος, ἐλεύθερος, ἴδιος, and μακάριος) have the same
endings as the feminine nouns discussed in #73.

	Singular	Plural
N. V.	δικαίᾱ	δίκαιαι
G. Ab.	δικαίᾱς	δικαίων
D. L. I.	δικαίᾳ	δικαίαις
Ac.	δικαίᾱν	δικαίᾱς

The accent of the genitive and ablative plural is not a circumflex on
the ultima as in #73.

75. COMPLETE PARADIGM OF A FIRST AND SECOND DECLENSION ADJECTIVE. The
following paradigm gives the pattern for adjectives of this declension
whose stems end in ε, ι, or ρ.

Singular

	Masculine	Feminine	Neuter
N.	δίκαιος	δικαίᾱ	δίκαιον
G. Ab.	δικαίου	δικαίᾱς	δικαίου
D. L. I.	δικαίῳ	δικαίᾳ	δικαίῳ
Ac.	δίκαιον	δικαίᾱν	δίκαιον
V.	δίκαιε	δικαίᾱ	δίκαιον

Plural

	Masculine	Feminine	Neuter
N. V.	δίκαιοι	δίκαιαι	δίκαια
G. Ab.	δικαίων	δικαίων	δικαίων
D. L. I.	δικαίοις	δικαίαις	δικαίοις
Ac.	δικαίους	δικαίᾱς	δίκαια

There is no distinct vocative form except in the masculine singular.

76. METHOD OF INDICATING IN THE VOCABULARY THE DECLENSIONAL PATTERN OF AN
ADJECTIVE. The vocabulary entry "δίκαιος, -ᾱ, -ον" is an abbreviated
way of giving the nominative singular forms as written out in full in
#75. This style of entry will be used from now on.

77. COMPLETE PARADIGM OF THE DEFINITE ARTICLE. Since some of the feminine
forms of the definite article have been used in #71, it will be helpful to see all the forms at once.

NOTE: Although ὁ, ἡ, τό usually means "the," rather often a definite
article may have the force of a possessive adjective.

Πέτρος βλέπει τὸν ἀδελφόν.
Peter sees his brother.

	Singular		
	Masculine	Feminine	Neuter
N.	ὁ	ἡ	τό
G. Ab.	τοῦ	τῆς	τοῦ
D. L. I.	τῷ	τῇ	τῷ
Ac.	τόν	τήν	τό
V.	None	None	None

	Plural		
N.	οἱ	αἱ	τά
G. Ab.	τῶν	τῶν	τῶν
D. L. I.	τοῖς	ταῖς	τοῖς
Ac.	τούς	τάς	τά
V.	None	None	None

78. CASE: INSTRUMENTAL OF ASSOCIATION. At the beginning of #71 occurs the phrase σὺν τοῖς ἰδίοις ἀδελφοῖς, with her own brothers. Although the underlined Greek words have the same endings as the forms labeled "Dative" and "Locative" in paradigms, this expression will be called an instrumental of association. The meaning of σύν, with, explains "association." The term "instrumental" is rather arbitrary.

79. CASE: INSTRUMENTAL OF MANNER. In the sentence παρρησίᾳ λέγειν ἰσχύει Λάζαρος, Lazarus can speak freely, the underlined Greek word expresses the way in which Lazarus can speak. Again, somewhat arbitrarily παρρησίᾳ will be called an instrumental of manner.

80. POSITION OF ADJECTIVES: ASCRIPTIVE ATTRIBUTIVE. In the expression σὺν τοῖς ἰδίοις ἀδελφοῖς, with her own brothers, the position of ἰδίοις between the noun and its definite article is described as ascriptive attributive.

81. EXERCISES.

a. Read #71 aloud.

b. Translate #71 into English.

c. Match the adjectives in List II with the nouns in List I so that the two words will agree.

List I	List II
1) χρείαις	α) τά
2) τέκνῳ	β) δικαίας
3) παρρησίαν	γ) ἰδίαν
4) πυρετούς	δ) μακαρίων
5) Μαρίᾳ	ε) ἴδιος
6) ποτηρίων	ζ) ἐλευθέρα
7) καρδιῶν	η) δικαίῳ
8) ὀψάρια	θ) καλῶν
9) ἐπιθυμίας	ι) ἰδίᾳ
10) οἶκος	κ) κακούς
	λ) δικαίαις
	μ) μακάριε
	ν) ἴδιοι
	ξ) ἐλεύθεραι

d. Translate orally the underlined words:

1) His own gifts are here.
2) The price of the gifts was high.
3) We serve a free man.
4) You came with happy Mary.

25

5) Let's talk about our own needs.
6) Noble brother, listen!
7) Do you see the happy children?
8) He cannot heal his own fever.
9) These brothers are free.
10) What desires do you have in your own just hearts?

e. Conjugate in the present indicative and imperative active.

1) ναί, πάντοτε λέγω παρρησίᾳ.

2) νῦν οὐκέτι λέγω περὶ χρειῶν.

3) ἀλλὰ νῦν λέγω περὶ παρρησίας.

f. Conjugate in the future indicative active.

1) οὐκέτι θεραπεύσω πάντοτε πυρετούς.

2) ναί, ἀπολύσω τοὺς δούλους Μαρίας.

3) νῦν δουλεύσω Μαρίᾳ.

g. Translate the Greek sentences in e. and f. into English.

h. Notice carefully the following English words related to new Greek words in this lesson.

1) Theodore: a proper name meaning gift of God.
2) idiom: a way of speaking peculiar to a group of people, their own way of speaking.
3) cardiac: related to the heart.
4) Mariolatry: veneration of Mary, the mother of Jesus.
5) perimeter: the distance around a geometric figure.

LESSON 8

82. FOR OLD TIMES' SAKE.

ἐν χρόνῳ μικρῷ πέμπει ἀπὸ τοῦ οἴκου Φιλίππου εἰς τὸν οἶκον
Λαζάρου ἄγγελον Πέτρος. λέγειν Λαζάρῳ ἐλπίζει.

"χαῖρε, Λάζαρε," λέγει ὁ ἄγγελος.

"χαῖρε, ἄγγελε," λέγει Λάζαρος.

5 "μνημονεύουσι Μαρία καὶ Πέτρος καὶ Φίλιππος," λέγει ὁ ἄγγελος,
"τὸν χρόνον ὅτε ἦς μικρὸς δοῦλος. τότε ἦτε ὁμοῦ πάντοτε, Μαρία καὶ
Πέτρος καὶ Φίλιππος καὶ Λάζαρος. ἐλπίζουσι πάλιν βλέπειν Λάζαρον ἐν

τῷ οἴκῳ Φιλίππου καὶ πάλιν ἐσθίειν σὺν Λαζάρῳ καὶ λέγειν περὶ τῶν

χρόνων ὅτε ἦσαν τέκνα ἐλεύθερα καὶ ὅτε ἦς μικρὸς δοῦλος."

10   "λέγε Μαρίᾳ καὶ Πέτρῳ καὶ Φιλίππῳ," λέγει Λάζαρος, "'μνημονεύω

ὅτε ἤμην μικρὸς δοῦλος, ὅτε ἠσθίομεν ὁμοῦ, ὅτε ἰσχύετε λέγειν παρρη-

σίᾳ, ἀλλὰ ὅτε οὐκ ἴσχυον λέγειν παρρησίᾳ. μνημονεύετε ὅτι εἴχομεν

δεῖπνον ἐν τῷ κήπῳ; τότε ἄρτον καὶ ὀψάριον ἤσθιον, ἀλλὰ οὐκ ἔπινον

οἶνον. μακάριοι ἦμεν.'"

15   τότε πάλιν εἰς τὸν οἶκον Φιλίππου τὸν ἄγγελον Λάζαρος πέμπει.

    τότε Λάζαρος μνημονεύει τοῦ χρόνου ὅτε ἦν μικρὸς δοῦλος καὶ ὅτε

ἦν τέκνον ἐν τῷ οἴκῳ Φιλίππου.

    "ἀρνίον μικρὸν εἶχε Μαρία," λέγει Λάζαρος. "ἦμεν τέκνα ὁμοῦ.

ἤμην μακάριον τέκνον ἐν τοῖς χρόνοις ὅτε τὸ ἀρνίον Μαρίας ἤσθιε σὺν

20   Πέτρῳ καὶ Φιλίππῳ καὶ Λαζάρῳ. ἐλπίζω ὅτι μνημονεύει πάλιν Μαρία τοῦ

ἀρνίου, καὶ ἐλπίζω λέγειν παρρησίᾳ σὺν Μαρίᾳ καὶ τοῖς ἀδελφοῖς Μαρίας

περὶ τῶν μακαρίων χρόνων."

83.   VOCABULARY.

ἄγγελος, -ου, ὁ: angel, messenger

ἐλπίζω (future will be given later): I hope

ἦμεν: we were

ἤμην: I was

ἦν: he (she, it) was

ἦς: you (sing.) were

ἦσαν: they were

ἦτε: you (pl.) were

μικρός, -ά, -όν: small, little

μνημονεύω: I remember (followed by accusative or more frequently by
                      genitive direct object)

ὁμοῦ: together

ὅτε: when

πάλιν: again, back

τότε: then, at that time

χρόνος, -ου, ὁ: time

84.   CASE: GENITIVE USED AS A DIRECT OBJECT. In #82 genitives are twice
used as direct objects of the verb μνημονεύω. This construction will
be found with several other verbs.

85. TENSE: IMPERFECT. In this lesson a new tense has been used. Such forms as εἶχε, ἔπινον, ἦν, ἦσαν, ἤσθιον, ἰσχύετε, and ἴσχυον belong to the **imperfect indicative active**. This new tense belongs to the present system of the Greek verb but has different endings. The imperfect represents an action or a state as continuing or as being repeated in past time. It may be translated in several ways.

ἤσθιον: I was eating.
I used to eat.
I continued to eat.
I kept on eating.
I ate and ate and ate.
I ate repeatedly.

86. PARADIGMS OF THE IMPERFECT INDICATIVE ACTIVE.

a. πίνω   ἔπινον   ἐπίνομεν
ἔπινες   ἐπίνετε
ἔπινε   ἔπινον

The ε at the beginning is called an **augment**, that is, an increase in the length of the word as compared with the present. Since this **ε** adds a syllable to the word, it is called **syllabic** augment.

After ἐπιν- the next letter is always either **ο** or **ε**. These letters are referred to as the **variable** or **thematic vowel**.

The personal endings follow the variable vowel.

b. ἐσθίω   ἤσθιον   ἠσθίομεν
ἤσθιες   ἠσθίετε
ἤσθιε   ἤσθιον

The η does not add a syllable to the word, but it does add length to the first syllable. For this reason, the lengthening of the ε in ἐσθίω to η in ἤσθιον is called **temporal augment**, that is, an increase in the time necessary to pronounce the first syllable.

c. ἀπολύω   ἀπέλυον   ἀπελύομεν
ἀπέλυες   ἀπελύετε
ἀπέλυε   ἀπέλυον

Notice that the augment is placed between the prepositional prefix ἀπό and the verb λύω and that the **ο** in ἀπ**ό** is elided (omitted) before the augment.

d. ἔχω   εἶχον   εἴχομεν
εἶχες   εἴχετε
εἶχε   εἶχον

In ἔχω the ε is lengthened to ει in εἶχον. This is another form of temporal augment. Whether η or ει is used as an augment of ε must be learned by observation.

e. ἰσχύω   ἴσχυον   ἰσχύομεν
ἴσχυες   ἰσχύετε
ἴσχυε   ἴσχυον

Here a short ι in ἰσχύω is made a long ι in ἴσχυον.

f. εἰμί: I am   ἤμην   I was
ἦς   you were
ἦν   he (she, it) was

ἦμεν and ἤμεθα   we were
ἦτε   you were
ἦσαν   they were

28

This verb is being introduced in the imperfect because of certain difficulties in the present and future. For now it will be best to memorize these forms since they are commonly used. The points in which this verb differs from the other paradigms just given will be better understood after -μι verbs have been studied. ἤμην and ἤμεθα are middle forms in common use in the New Testament. ἤμεθα and ἦμεν have the same meaning.

87. A REFERENCE LIST OF THE VERBS GIVEN SO FAR.

Present	Imperfect
ἀπολύω	ἀπέλυον
βλέπω	ἔβλεπον
δουλεύω	ἐδούλευον
εἰμί: I am	ἤμην
ἐλπίζω	ἤλπιζον
ἐσθίω	ἤσθιον
ἔχω	εἶχον
θεραπεύω	ἐθεράπευον
ἰσχύω	ἴσχυον
λέγω	ἔλεγον
μνημονεύω	ἐμνημόνευον
πέμπω	ἔπεμπον
πίνω	ἔπινον
φέρω	ἔφερον

88. DEFINITE TEMPORAL CLAUSES. A definite time may be described by a clause introduced by ὅτε, <u>when</u>, and using a verb in the indicative.

ὅτε ἔβλεπε Μαρίαν, μακάριος ἦν Λάζαρος.
<u>When he used to see</u> Mary, Lazarus was happy.

89. CASE: NOMINATIVE IN THE PREDICATE. In previous lessons the nominative case has been used to indicate the subject of a verb. In this lesson the nominative has been used after forms of εἰμί: I am.

Μαρία καὶ Λάζαρος ἦσαν τέκνα.
Mary and Lazarus were <u>children</u>.

μικρὸς Λάζαρος ἦν δοῦλος.
Little Lazarus was <u>a slave</u>.

This usage is called the <u>predicate nominative</u>.

90. CASE: LOCATIVE OF TIME. In #46 the locative of place has been explained as showing where an action belongs in spatial relationships. This case may show also where an action belongs in temporal relationships.

ἐν χρόνῳ μικρῷ πέμπει ἄγγελον.
<u>In a little while</u> he sends a messenger.

91. EXERCISES.

a. Read #82 through silently, trying to understand as much as possible while your eye first follows the lines without jumping back. Then reread if necessary.

b. Translate #82 into good English.

c. In translating the sentences below notice that a Greek verb in the future tense should be indicated in the corresponding English by <u>should</u> and <u>would</u> (not <u>shall</u> and <u>will</u>) when this Greek future is in a clause subordinate to an imperfect verb, e. g.

ὁ ἄγγελος ἔλεγε ὅτι δουλεύσουσι οἱ ἀδελφοί.
The messenger was saying that the brothers <u>would</u> serve.

29

1) Λάζαρον ἀπέλυε Φίλιππος ὅτε τέκνα ἐθεράπευε Λάζαρος.

2) ὅτε δουλεύσομεν τοῖς ἀνθρώποις ἐν τῷ κήπῳ, ἰσχύσομεν ἐσθίειν τοὺς καρποὺς τοῦ κήπου.

3) ἐλέγομεν ὅτι οὐκ ἠσθίομεν τοὺς καρποὺς καὶ οὐκ ἐπίνομεν τὸν οἶνον Πέτρου.

4) ἠλπίζετε ὅτι οἶνον οὐκ ἰσχύσουσι πίνειν οἱ δοῦλοι;

5) ναί, ὅτε ἔπινον οἱ κακοὶ ἄνθρωποι, ἠλπίζομεν ὅτι οὐκέτι δουλεύσουσι οἴνῳ.

6) Μᾶρκε, ἔφερες ὀψάριον Νικοδήμῳ;

7) ναί, ἔφερον ὀψάριον καὶ ἄρτον τῷ ἀδελφῷ καὶ ἔπεμπον τοὺς καρποὺς ἐκ τοῦ κήπου.

8) ἔπεμπες ποτήρια οἴνου τοῖς τέκνοις;

9) οὐκ ἔπεμπον, οὐ γὰρ ἴσχυον πίνειν οἶνον.

10) Μᾶρκε καὶ Νικόδημε, ὅτε ἦτε μικρὰ τέκνα, ἰσχύετε μνημονεύειν πάντοτε τὰς ἰδίας χρείας;

11) ὅτε ἦς ἐν τῷ οἴκῳ, ἔβλεπες τὰ ἀρνία;

12) ἤλπιζε ὁ ἄγγελος ὅτι ἦτε μακάριοι.

13) ναί, ἤμην μακάριος τότε καὶ ἦμεν μακάριοι πάντοτε.

14) ἤμην σὺν Μαρίᾳ, τότε γὰρ ὁμοῦ ἦμεν πάντοτε.

15) ἦν ἐλευθέρα, ἀλλὰ δοῦλος ἤμην.

16) ἦτε οἱ ἀδελφοὶ Μαρίας.

d. Change the verbs in the following sentences into the imperfect tense.

1) ἐλπίζουσι βλέπειν τοὺς ἀγγέλους.

2) μνημονεύετε τὸν χρόνον ὅτε ἀπολύσομεν τὸν καλὸν δοῦλον.

3) ἔλπιζε πέμπειν τὰς ἰδίας δωρεάς.

4) λέγει παρρησίᾳ περὶ τῶν ἐπιθυμιῶν Πέτρου.

5) λέγουσι Μαρία καὶ τὸ τέκνον περὶ τῆς παρρησίας Λαζάρου.

e. By combining the personal endings in List II with the stems in List I form at least fifteen finite verbs. Add correct accents, and translate.

List I

ἤλπιζ___
ἐμνημονευ___
ἐφερ___
εἶχ___
ἤσθι___
ἀπελυ___
ἰσχυ___

List II

-ε
-ες
-ετε
-ομεν
-ον

f. Notice carefully the following English words related to new Greek words in this lesson.

1) <u>angel</u>: a heavenly <u>messenger</u>.

30

2) <u>mnemonic</u>: related to <u>memory</u>.
3) <u>chronology</u>: the study of the measurement of <u>time</u>.
4) <u>micro</u>scope: an instrument by means of which <u>one</u> is able to
            see very <u>small</u> objects.
5) <u>palin</u>genesis: a being <u>born again</u>.
6) <u>synchronous</u>: occurring at the same <u>time</u>.

LESSON 9

92. BACK TO SLAVERY FOR LAZARUS.

ὅτε ἤσθιον δεῖπνον ἐν τῷ οἴκῳ Λάζαρος καὶ Μαρία καὶ οἱ ἀδελφοὶ
Μαρίας, ἀπὸ τοῦ κήπου ἀπέλυσε τὸ ἀρνίον Μαρίας κακὸς γεωργός. ἐν τῇ
σκοτίᾳ τὸν γεωργὸν οἱ δοῦλοι Φιλίππου καὶ Πέτρου οὐκ ἔβλεψαν, ἀλλὰ
ἤκουσαν τοῦ ἀρνίου, καὶ ἔλεγον τῷ ἀνθρώπῳ.

5   ἐν τῷ οἴκῳ ἔλεγον οἱ δοῦλοι Φιλίππῳ καὶ Πέτρῳ, "ἠκούσαμεν ἄνθρωπον ἐν τῷ κήπῳ.

"'ἀπέλυσας τὸ ἀρνίον;' ἐν τῇ σκοτίᾳ ἐλέγομεν.

"'ναί, ἀπέλυσα,' ἠκούσαμεν. 'ἀλλὰ οὐκ ἐβλέψατε ὅτε ἀπέλυσα τὸ
ἀρνίον. νῦν ἐλπίζω φέρειν τὸ ἀρνίον εἰς τὸν ἴδιον οἶκον. χαίρετε,

10   δοῦλοι.'"

ὅτε τοὺς δούλους ἤκουσε Μαρία, οὐκέτι μακαρία ἦν. τότε οὐκέτι
μακάριος ἦν Λάζαρος ὅτι οὐκέτι μακαρία ἦν Μαρία.

"σήμερον ἐν τῷ κήπῳ ἔβλεψα ἄνθρωπον μικρόν. ἔβλεπεν τὸ ἀρνίον,"
ἐμνημόνευσε δοῦλος. "οὐκ ἦν δοῦλος, ἀλλὰ ἦν ἐλεύθερος."

15   τότε Λάζαρος κακοῦ μικροῦ γεωργοῦ ἐμνημόνευσε.

"ἐλπίζω σήμερον βλέψαι καὶ φέρειν πάλιν τὸ ἀρνίον Μαρίᾳ," ἔλεγε
Λάζαρος. "χαῖρε, Μαρία. χαίρετε, ἀδελφοί. χαίρετε, δοῦλοι."

οὐκ ἴσχυε Λάζαρος βλέψαι ἐν τῇ σκοτίᾳ, ἀλλὰ ἐμνημόνευσε τὸν οἶκον
τοῦ κακοῦ γεωργοῦ. ἤλπιζεν ἰσχύειν βλέψαι τὸ ἀρνίον ἐν τῷ οἴκῳ τοῦ

20   γεωργοῦ.

μετὰ μικρὸν χρόνον ἔβλεψε Λάζαρος τὸ ἀρνίον ἐν τῷ οἴκῳ τοῦ γεωργοῦ.

31

ἀλλὰ ἤκουσεν ὁ γεωργὸς σὺν τοῖς ἰδίοις δούλοις. ἔπεμψεν ἐκ τοῦ οἴκου καὶ περὶ τὸν οἶκον τοὺς ἰδίους δούλους.

"βλέψατε· φέρετε Λάζαρον εἰς τὸν οἶκον, δοῦλοι," ἔλεγεν ὁ
25 γεωργός. μετὰ μικρὸν χρόνον εἰς τὸν οἶκον Λάζαρον φέρειν ἴσχυσαν.

"βλέψον τοὺς δούλους, Λάζαρε," ἔλεγε ὁ γεωργός. "οὐ γὰρ ἰσχύσεις φέρειν τὸ ἀρνίον πάλιν Μαρίᾳ. οὐ λέγω, 'ἀπολυσάτωσαν Φίλιππος καὶ Πέτρος Λάζαρον.' ἀλλὰ λέγω, 'δουλευσάτω Λάζαρος τῷ γεωργῷ. δοῦλοι, μνημονεύσατε, ἔχετε πάντοτε Λάζαρον.'"

30 ὅτε ὁ κακὸς γεωργὸς παρρησίᾳ ἔλεγεν, οὐκέτι ἐλεύθερος ἦν Λάζαρος, ἀλλὰ ἤλπιζεν ὅτι μνημονεύει Μαρία τοῦ ἀρνίου καὶ Λαζάρου.

93. VOCABULARY.

ἀκούω, ἀκούσω, ἤκουσα: I hear, listen (followed by acc. or gen.
                                                direct object)

γεωργός, -οῦ, ὁ: farmer

μετά: (with gen.) with; (with acc.) after

μή: not (used with imperatives)

περί: (with acc. in local sense) around, about

σήμερον: today

σκοτία, -ᾱς, ἡ: darkness

94. TENSE: AORIST. This lesson introduces the aorist tense, which indicates the simple occurrence of an action. In the indicative the occurrence is usually understood to be in past time, but even in the indicative the chief emphasis is on the point-like quality of the action
rather than on its past time. In the subjunctive, optative, and imperative moods there is no indication of past time. It is important,
therefore, from our first acquaintance with this tense to form the
habit of thinking in terms of simple occurrence rather than of past
time. Several translations of the aorist are possible.

ἤκουσα: I heard (on one occasion).
         I did hear.
         I began to hear.

95. PARADIGMS OF THE FIRST OR SIGMATIC AORIST INDICATIVE ACTIVE.

a. ἀκούω   ἤκουσα   ἠκούσαμεν
                ἤκουσας   ἠκούσατε
                ἤκουσε   ἤκουσαν

    This group of forms has temporal augment like some verbs in the
    imperfect indicative. To the augmented stem ἠκου- is added the
    tense suffix -σα- (except in the third person singular where -σε
    is used). The sigma in the suffix accounts for the designation
    "sigmatic." To the suffix are added the personal endings:
    -, -ς, -, -μεν, -τε, -ν.

b. βλέπω   ἔβλεψα   ἐβλέψαμεν
                 ἔβλεψας   ἐβλέψατε
                 ἔβλεψε   ἔβλεψαν

Here the syllabic augment is used. To the stem ἐβλεπ- is added -σα- or -σε- with the result that ἔβλεπσα is written with -πσ- combined as -ψ-. πέμπω follows this pattern.

c. ἀπολύω   ἀπέλυσα   ἀπελύσαμεν
                ἀπέλυσας   ἀπελύσατε
                ἀπέλυσε   ἀπέλυσαν

Here as in the imperfect indicative the augment is inserted between the prepositional prefix and the verb stem: ἀπο-ε-λυσα. Then the vowel -ο- in ἀπο- is elided. The tense suffix -σα- and the personal endings are the same as in the two previous paradigms.

96. PARADIGMS OF THE FIRST OR SIGMATIC AORIST IMPERATIVE ACTIVE.

a. ἀκούω   ἄκουσον   ἀκούσατε
             ἀκουσάτω   ἀκουσάτωσαν

It is quite important to notice that the aorist imperative has no augment. Only the indicative mood has augment. The ending -σον requires attention in memorizing since it does not have the suffix -σα-. The accent is recessive in the imperative as it is in the indicative.

b. βλέπω   βλέψον   βλέψατε
            βλεψάτω   βλεψάτωσαν

c. ἀπολύω   ἀπόλυσον   ἀπολύσατε
                ἀπολυσάτω   ἀπολυσάτωσαν

97. DISTINCTION BETWEEN PRESENT AND AORIST IMPERATIVES. Just as the present indicative indicates continued or repeated action, the present imperative commands an action that is intended to be kept in progress or to be repeated. The aorist, on the other hand, whether indicative or imperative, emphasizes point action. The aorist may put the spotlight on the beginning of the action, on the effect of the action, or on the action as a whole, but not on its progress or its repetition.

βλεψάτω.
Let him begin to look.

βλεπέτω.
Let him keep on looking.
Let him look repeatedly.

μὴ βλεπέτω.
Let him not keep on looking.
Let him stop looking.

No example of μή with the aorist imperative will be given since prohibitions of this kind were as a rule expressed by μή with the aorist subjunctive. The subjunctive will be studied later. (#324)

98. FIRST OR SIGMATIC AORIST INFINITIVE ACTIVE.

a. ἀκούω: ἀκοῦσαι

b. βλέπω: βλέψαι

c. ἀπολύω: ἀπολῦσαι

The ending of the aorist infinitive active is -σαι. The accent falls on the penult, an acute on a short syllable and a circumflex on a long syllable. The principle of recessive accent does not apply to infinitives.

99. N MOVABLE. In the statement ὁ Φίλιππος ἀπέλυσεν τὸ ἀρνίον the verb is a third singular aorist indicative active of ἀπολύω. But it has at its end a letter not shown in the paradigm. This letter is called ν movable. The ν movable is sometimes used at the end of (1) third singular verb forms ending in -ε, and (2) all words ending in -σι, -ξι or -ψι.

$$λύσουσιν$$
$$ἔβλεπεν$$

100. FUTURES OF VERBS WHOSE STEMS END IN CERTAIN CONSONANTS.

a. Verbs in π, β, or φ. Just as βλέπω forms its aorist ἔβλεψα by combining π and σ into ψ, this verb forms its future also by using this same combination.

Present	Future
βλέπω	βλέψω
πέμπω	πέμψω

Similarly β or φ may join with σ to form ψ.

b. Verbs in π, β, or φ. When σ is added to a verb stem ending in κ, γ, or χ, the result is ξ. The future of ἔχω is ἕξω. The rough breathing is an irregularity that should be carefully noted, but it will not be explained here.

c. Verbs in τ, δ, or θ. The letters τ, δ, and θ are dropped when σ is added. (This is not illustrated in the future tense until #210. There we learn that the future of πείθω is πείσω.)

101. PRINCIPAL PARTS OF GREEK VERBS. The following forms of ἀπολύω are its principal parts. Each is an indicative in the first person singular. The tense and voice are given in parentheses.

a. ἀπολύω   (present active)
b. ἀπολύσω   (future active)
c. ἀπέλυσα   (aorist active)
d. ἀπολέλυκα   (perfect active)
e. ἀπολέλυμαι   (perfect middle and passive)
f. ἀπελύθην   (aorist passive)

Of these six the first three have been introduced for ἀπολύω and several other verbs. Eventually you will be able to develop any form (with few exceptions) of a Greek verb if you know its principal parts.

For several lessons the principal parts of all verbs will be given in the vocabularies as far as they have been introduced.

102. EXERCISES.

a. Translate #92.

b. Become thoroughly familiar with the principal parts of the following verbs as listed in this summary. Some of the blank spaces in this list will be filled by information appearing in later lessons.

Present	Future	Aorist
ἀκούω	ἀκούσω	ἤκουσα
ἀπολύω	ἀπολύσω	ἀπέλυσα
βλέπω	βλέψω	ἔβλεψα
δουλεύω	δουλεύσω	ἐδούλευσα
ἐλπίζω	---	ἤλπισα
ἐσθίω	---	---
ἔχω	ἕξω	---
θεραπεύω	θεραπεύσω	ἐθεράπευσα

34

Present	Future	Aorist
ἰσχύω	ἰσχύσω	ἴσχυσα
λέγω	---	---
μνημονεύω	---	ἐμνημόνευσα
πέμπω	πέμψω	ἔπεμψα
πίνω	---	---
φέρω	---	---

c. Find in List II a correct translation for each Greek form in List I.

I	II
1) πεμψάτωσαν	α) Keep on listening.
2) ἐμνημόνευεν	β) To carry and carry.
3) ἴσχυσε	γ) They will hope.
4) θεραπευέτω	δ) She used to be able.
5) ἔλπισον	ε) You took one look.
6) ἐδουλεύετε	ζ) You used to be slaves.
7) ἐβλέψατε	η) Begin to hope.
8) ἄκουε	θ) Go on hoping.
9) φέρειν	ι) She was remembering.
10) μὴ ἐχέτωσαν	κ) He remembers.
	λ) Let them start to send.
	μ) They are about to send.
	ν) He became able.
	ξ) She will be able.
	ο) Let us heal.
	π) Let it heal repeatedly.
	ρ) Let them stop holding.

d. Complete each of the following sentences with the proper form of ὁ γεωργός or ἡ σκοτία as the context seems to require.

1) πέμπετε _____ μετὰ τῶν ἀδελφῶν.

2) ἐν _____ ἦσαν οἱ καλοὶ ἄγγελοι;

3) ἐκ _____ ἐβλέψαμεν τὰς δωρεὰς περὶ _____ .

4) πυρετοὺς _____ μὴ θεραπευέτω μετὰ μικρὸν χρόνον.

5) σὺν _____ ἐν _____ ἦμεν πάντοτε μακάριαι.

6) μὴ πίνε οἶνον, _____ .

7) μετὰ _____ σήμερον ἔπεμψας δοῦλον περὶ τὸν οἶκον.

8) περὶ τὸν κῆπον ἐν _____ ἦτε;

9) σήμερον ἔβλεψε καλὰ ἀρνία περὶ Μαρίαν _____ .

e. Notice carefully the following English words related to new Greek words in this lesson.

1) acoustic: related to hearing.
2) George: a man's name meaning farmer.
3) perimeter: the distance around a geometric figure.
4) metaphysics: the next treatise after physics in Aristotle's
                works.

103. RESCUED: ONE LAMB, NO LAZARUS.

Ἰάκωβος, ὁ γεωργὸς ὁ κακός, μακάριος ἦν ὅτι Λάζαρον τὸν ἐλευ-
θερὸν καὶ τὸ Μαρίας ἀρνίον εἶχεν.

Ἰάκωβος: "χρείαν δείπνου καλοῦ, δοῦλοι, ἔξω. ἐπιθυμίαν τοῦ
μικροῦ ἀρνίου νῦν ἔχω. ἐν ἀληθείᾳ ἔξω καλὸν δεῖπνον, Λάζαρε."

5   Λάζαρος: "κακὲ Ἰάκωβε, πῶς ἰσχύεις ἐλπίζειν ἐσθίειν τὸ Μαρίας
ἀρνίον τὸ μικρόν; ἔχεις γὰρ πλοῦτον ἐν ἀληθείᾳ. ἕξεις οὐ χρείαν τοῦ
Μαρίας ἀρνίου."

Ἰάκωβος: "πῶς ἰσχύεις λέγειν τὴν ἀλήθειαν παρρησίᾳ; δοῦλος
λέγειν παρρησίᾳ οὐκ ἰσχύει, καὶ δοῦλος κακὸς λέγειν τὴν ἀλήθειαν οὐκ
10   ἰσχύει. δοῦλε Λάζαρε, μὴ λέγε περὶ τοῦ πλούτου Ἰακώβου."

Λάζαρος: "κακέ, μετὰ μικρὸν χρόνον ἀπολύσουσι Λάζαρον καὶ τὸ
Μαρίας ἀρνίον οἱ ἄνθρωποι τῆς κώμης. βλέψεις μετὰ μικρὸν χρόνον,
Ἰάκωβε κακέ."

Ἰάκωβος: "μὴ λέγε, κακέ."

15   Λάζαρος: "ἐν ἀληθείᾳ σήμερον Φίλιππος καὶ Πέτρος, ἐλεύθεροι,
τοὺς ἰδίους δούλους μετὰ τῶν ἐλευθέρων τῆς κώμης πέμψουσιν εἰς τὸν
τοῦ κακοῦ γεωργοῦ οἶκον."

Ἰάκωβος: "πῶς ἰσχύεις λέγειν περὶ τῆς ἀληθείας; ἡ γὰρ ἀλήθεια
Λάζαρον, τὸν κακὸν δοῦλον, οὐκ ἀπολύσει."

20   Λάζαρος: "πῶς ἰσχύσεις ἔχειν ἐλεύθερον;"

Ἰάκωβος: "ἔξω τὸν δοῦλον τὸν ἴδιον ἐν σπηλαίῳ σὺν τῷ ἰδίῳ πλού-
τῳ. οὐ βλέψεις τὸν πλοῦτον ἐν τῇ τοῦ σπηλαίου σκοτίᾳ. πῶς βλέψεις
τὸν πλοῦτον τοῦ σπηλαίου ἐν τῇ σκοτίᾳ; οἱ τῆς κώμης ἐλεύθεροι οὐ
βλέψουσι Λάζαρον καὶ οὐ πέμψουσι τὸν πλοῦτον Ἰακώβου εἰς τὴν κώμην."

25   μετὰ μικρὸν χρόνον ἔπεμψαν Φίλιππος καὶ Πέτρος τοὺς δούλους τοὺς
ἰδίους σὺν τοῖς τῆς κώμης ἀνθρώποις εἰς τὸν Ἰακώβου οἶκον. ἀλλὰ οὐκ
ἐν τῷ οἴκῳ ἦν Λάζαρος. ἴσχυσαν τὸ ἀρνίον πάλιν Μαρίᾳ φέρειν, ἀλλὰ οὐ
Λάζαρον τὸν ἐλεύθερον βλέψαι.

104. VOCABULARY.

ἀλήθειᾰ, -ᾱς, ἡ: truth, truthfulness

ἔχω, ἕξω, (aor. later): I have, hold

'Ιάκωβος, -ου, ὁ: James

κακός, -ή, -όν: bad, evil, wicked

καλός, -ή, -όν: fair, beautiful, good, excellent, noble

κώμη, -ης, ἡ: village, town

πλοῦτος, -ου, ὁ: wealth, riches

πῶς: how?

σπήλαιον, -ου, τό: cave

105. MORE PARADIGMS OF THE FIRST DECLENSION. In #73 the forms of καρδία
and δωρεά were presented. These paradigms set the pattern for all
first declension nouns ending in -εᾱ, -ιᾱ, or -ρᾱ.

In this lesson three other patterns are being used: nouns ending in
-η, in -ᾰ, and in -εᾰ, -ιᾰ, or -ρᾰ.

a. A noun in -η.   b. A noun in -ᾰ. (#180)

κώμη	κῶμαι		γλῶσσᾰ	γλῶσσαι
κώμης	κωμῶν		γλώσσης	γλωσσῶν
κώμῃ	κώμαις		γλώσσῃ	γλώσσαις
κώμην	κώμᾱς		γλῶσσᾰν	γλώσσᾱς

Notice that the plural endings are the same as those shown in #73.

c. A noun in -εᾰ, -ιᾰ, or -ρᾰ.

ἀλήθειᾰ	ἀλήθειαι
ἀληθείᾱς	ἀληθειῶν
ἀληθείᾳ	ἀληθείαις
ἀλήθειᾰν	ἀληθείᾱς

106. SUMMARY OF FIRST DECLENSION ENDINGS STUDIED THUS FAR. Since the
plural of these first declension nouns are all the same, our special
attention must be directed to the differences in the singular.

Singular				Plural
after ε, ι, ρ		not after ε, ι, ρ		
-ᾱ	-ᾰ	-η	-ᾰ	-αι
-ας	-ᾱς	-ης	-ης	-ων
-ᾳ	-ᾳ	-ῃ	-ῃ	-αις
-ᾱν	-ᾰν	-ην	-ᾰν	-ᾱς

107. MORE PARADIGMS OF FIRST AND SECOND DECLENSION ADJECTIVES. In #75
δίκαιος was presented as an example of a first and second declension
adjective whose feminine nominative singular ends in -εᾱ, -ιᾱ or -ρᾱ.
Another kind of first and second declension has a feminine nominative
singular which ends in -η. These two patterns include nearly all the
adjectives of the first and second declensions.

Singular			Plural		
καλός	καλή	καλόν	καλοί	καλαί	καλά
καλοῦ	καλῆς	καλοῦ	καλῶν	καλῶν	καλῶν
καλῷ	καλῇ	καλῷ	καλοῖς	καλαῖς	καλοῖς
καλόν	καλήν	καλόν	καλούς	καλᾱς	καλά
καλέ	καλή	καλόν			

37

108. POSITION OF ADJECTIVES.

a. **Ascriptive attributive.** (See #80). The adjective stands between the modified noun and its definite article.

ὁ κακὸς γεωργός.
the <u>wicked</u> farmer.

b. **Restrictive attributive.** The adjective stands after the modified noun and a repeated definite article.

ὁ γεωργὸς ὁ κακός.
the farmer the <u>wicked</u> ⟨one⟩.

This position is somewhat more emphatic than the ascriptive attributive and may be translated in the present example "the farmer, ⟨I mean⟩ the wicked ⟨one⟩," as if implying that there are other farmers who are not wicked.

c. **Predicate.** The adjective stands in neither of the positions described in a. and b. but modifies a noun which has a definite article.

ὁ γεωργὸς κακός   (or)   κακὸς ὁ γεωργός.
The farmer ⟨is⟩ <u>wicked</u>.

ὁ γεωργὸς ἦν κακός.
The farmer was <u>wicked</u>.

Notice (1) the absence of the verb in the first two examples---a common occurrence in Greek, and (2) the fact that these predicate adjectives are also predicate nominatives. (See #89).

d. **Ambiguous.** When a noun is not modified by a definite article, it is frequently impossible to assign any position to an accompanying adjective.

γεωργὸς κακός may mean
"a farmer ⟨is⟩ <u>wicked</u>"   (or)   "a farmer, <u>I mean a wicked</u> one."

109. MODIFYING GENITIVES USED AS ADJECTIVES. A genitive of a noun may sometimes serve as the equivalent of an adjective.

τὸ Μαρίας ἀρνίον.
<u>Mary's</u> lamb.

εἰς τὸν τοῦ γεωργοῦ οἶκον.
into <u>the farmer's</u> house.

Μαρίας and τοῦ γεωργοῦ are used as adjectives in ascriptive attributive position.

110. ADJECTIVES USED AS SUBSTANTIVES. In #103 we have several instances of adjectives used without any expressed nouns for them to modify. Take as an example ... τοὺς ἰδίους δούλους μετὰ τῶν ἐλευθέρων πέμψουσιν..., "... they will send their own slaves with the <u>free</u> ⟨men⟩..." The context helps us to understand with ἐλευθέρων the noun ἀνθρώπων, but the adjective itself here serves as a substantive. Suppose we had αἱ ἐλεύθεραι. This we should translate "the free women" unless the context pointed to some other feminine plural Greek noun to be understood. Likewise τὰ ἐλεύθερα would usually mean "the free things."

111. EXERCISES.

a. Translate #103.

b. Write in Greek:

38

1) wicked hearts.
2) the wicked hearts.
3) the hearts, I mean the wicked ones.
4) the cups (were) small.
5) out of the small cups.
6) into the cups, I mean the small ones.
7) for the brothers, the free ones.
8) within the beautiful house.
9) (o) happy farmer.
10) around her own wealth.
11) See the village, I mean the happy one.

c. Give the forms of καλός, μακάριος, and δίκαιος that will agree with each of the following:

1) τῆς ἀληθείας
2) κώμῃ
3) γεωργοῖς
4) τὰς χρείας
5) ἀγγέλους
6) καρδίᾱ

7) δωρεάν
8) σπηλαίων
9) Ἰάκωβε
10) σκοτίᾳ
11) κώμην
12) κώμη

d. Associate the following English words with new Greek words used in this lesson.

1) Alethea: a woman's name meaning "truth."
2) cacophony: an unpleasant (bad) sound.
3) plutocrat: one who has power because of his wealth.
4) spelaean: related to caves.

LESSON 11

112. AN OLD SINNER SCARED TO DIE.

Λάζαρον εἰς τὸ σπήλαιον Ἰάκωβος ἤγαγεν καὶ ἦλθεν εἰς τὸν ἴδιον οἶκον πάλιν.

"ἐνέγκατε νῦν ὀψάριον καὶ ἄρτον, δοῦλοι. χρείᾱν γὰρ ἔσχον φαγεῖν," εἶπεν Ἰάκωβος.

5   τότε ἤνεγκαν ὀψάριον καὶ ἄρτον Ἰακώβῳ.

"εἴπατε ὅτι τὸ Μαρίᾱς ἀρνίον ἠγάγετε πάλιν εἰς τὸν κῆπον Φιλίππου;" εἶπεν Ἰάκωβος.

"οὐκ ἠγάγομεν, Ἰάκωβε, ἀλλὰ οἱ ἐλεύθεροι τῆς κώμης καὶ οἱ
Φιλίππου δοῦλοι τὸ ἀρνίον ἐκ τοῦ οἴκου ἤγαγον," εἶπαν οἱ δοῦλοι.

10   "οὐκέτι τὸ ἀρνίον ἔχω, ἀλλὰ ἔξω πάντοτε Λάζαρον," εἶπεν ὁ κακὸς
γεωργός. "νῦν σὺν Ἰακώβῳ φαγέτωσαν καὶ πιέτωσαν οἱ δοῦλοι."

    "λαβέτω τὸ ποτήριον οἴνου καλοῦ ὁ μακάριος γεωργός," εἶπαν οἱ
δοῦλοι.

    ἔπιε καὶ ἔπιον. ἔπινε καὶ ἔπινον. ὅτε ἔπινε, πυρετὸς Ἰάκωβον
15 ἔλαβεν. κακὸς ἦν ὁ πυρετός.

    μετὰ μικρὸν χρόνον ὁ κακὸς ἀπέθνησκεν. τότε ἐμνημόνευσεν ὅτι ἦν
κακὸς ἄνθρωπος καὶ ὅτι οὐκ ἦν ἕτοιμος ἀποθανεῖν. οὐκέτι ἦν μακάριος.

    "ἐλθὲ νῦν εἰς τὸ σπήλαιον," εἶπε δούλῳ. "Λάζαρον ἄγαγε. ἐλπίζω
ὅτι θεραπεύσει τὸν κακὸν γεωργόν."

20   ἦλθεν εἰς τὸν οἶκον μετὰ μικρὸν χρόνον Λάζαρος.

    "κακὸν πυρετὸν ἔχω, ναί, κακὸν πυρετόν. χρείαν Λαζάρου ἔχω.
θεράπευσον τὸν γεωργὸν τὸν κακὸν καὶ ἰσχύσεις ἐλθεῖν πάλιν εἰς τὸν
ἴδιον οἶκον," εἶπε Ἰάκωβος.

    "ὅτι πυρετοὺς θεραπεῦσαι ἰσχύω ἤκουσας; ἤκουσας τὴν ἀλήθειαν,"
25 εἶπε Λάζαρος.

    "πῶς ἰσχύσω ἀποθανεῖν; κακὸς ἀποθανεῖν οὐκ ἐλπίζει. νῦν, Λάζαρε,
θεράπευσον τὸν γεωργὸν τὸν κακόν. οὐκέτι ἀκούσεις, 'σήμερον κακὸς
ἦν Ἰάκωβος,'" εἶπε ὁ γεωργός.

    "ἐλπίζω ὅτι λέγεις τὴν ἀλήθειαν," εἶπε Λάζαρος.

30   ἐθεράπευσε τὸν πυρετόν, καὶ ὁ γεωργὸς Λάζαρον ἀπέλυσε καὶ ἔπεμψε
δωρεὰς καλὰς ἐκ τοῦ ἰδίου πλούτου εἰς τὸν οἶκον Λαζάρου.

113. VOCABULARY.

ἄγω, ἄξω, ἤγαγον: I lead, bring, go

ἀποθνήσκω, (fut. later), ἀπέθανον: I die

ἐσθίω, (fut. later), ἔφαγον: I eat

ἕτοιμος, -η, -ον: prepared, ready

ἔχω, ἕξω, ἔσχον: I hold, have

ἦλθον, (pres. and fut. later): I went, came

λαμβάνω, (fut. later), ἔλαβον: I take, receive, seize

λέγω, (fut. later), εἶπον: I say, speak, declare

πίνω, (fut. later), ἔπιον: I drink

φέρω, οἴσω, ἤνεγκα: I carry, bring, endure

114. TENSE: SECOND AORIST INDICATIVE ACTIVE. Such forms as ἦλθεν, εἶπεν, φαγεῖν, and ἠγάγομεν used in this lesson, are in the second aorist. In meaning this aorist is just like the aorist using -σα, which is generally called the _first aorist_. Few verbs have both first and second aorist forms. In formation, however, the second aorist differs from the first aorist and is quite similar to the imperfect. Both second aorist and imperfect have (1) augment, (2) the thematic vowel ο/ε, and (3) the endings -ν, -σ, -, -μεν, -τε, -ν, known as the secondary active endings. The imperfect can usually be distinguished from the second aorist by its stem. Compare the following examples of the two tenses.

Present	Imperfect	Second Aorist
ἄγω	ἦγον	ἤγαγον
ἀποθνήσκω	ἀπέθνησκον	ἀπέθανον
ἐσθίω	ἤσθιον	ἔφαγον
ἔχω	εἶχον	ἔσχον
λαμβάνω	ἐλάμβανον	ἔλαβον
λέγω	ἔλεγον	εἶπον
πίνω	ἔπινον	ἔπιον

The differences in stem are due to several causes.

a. Different roots are used in ἤσθιον and ἔφαγον, and in ἔλεγον and εἶπον. Compare in English I _was going_ with I _went_.

b. _Suffixes used in the present system, to which the imperfect belongs_, account for the following differences.

Imperfect	Suffix	Second Aorist
ἀπέθνησκον	-σκ-	ἀπέθανον

(-θνη- is a changed form of -θαν-)

ἐλάμβανον	-αν-	ἔλαβον

(a -μ- also crept into the present system stem.)

ἔπινον	-ν-	ἔπιον

c. The second aorist of ἄγω reduplicates (doubles) its root, that is, ἀγ- becomes ἀγαγ-.

d. εἶχον is developed from ἔ-σεχ-ον by the loss of the intervocallic σ and the contraction of ε+ε to ει, and ἔσχον uses the stem -σχ-.

115. PARADIGMS OF THE SECOND AORIST ACTIVE.

a. Indicative.

ἤγαγον	ἦλθον	ἔσχον	ἔλαβον
ἤγαγες	ἦλθες	ἔσχες	ἔλαβες
ἤγαγε	ἦλθε	ἔσχε	ἔλαβε
ἠγάγομεν	ἤλθομεν	ἔσχομεν	ἐλάβομεν
ἠγάγετε	ἤλθετε	ἔσχετε	ἐλάβετε
ἤγαγον	ἦλθον	ἔσχον	ἔλαβον

b. Imperative.

ἄγαγε	ἐλθέ (Note Accent)	σχές	λάβε
ἀγαγέτω	ἐλθέτω	σχέτω	λαβέτω
ἀγάγετε	ἔλθετε	σχέτε	λάβετε
ἀγαγέτωσαν	ἐλθέτωσαν	σχέτωσαν	λαβέτωσαν

c. Infinitive: Notice the accents.

ἀγαγεῖν	ἐλθεῖν	σχεῖν	λαβεῖν

41

116. VARIATIONS WITH A FOR O OR E. The endings of the first aorist and the perfect tenses had an influence on the second aorist which resulted in the appearance of α for o or ε in scattered instances. This substitution was not consistently made, but be ready to meet such forms as would give us a paradigm like the following one if they were collected.

a. Indicative

εἶπα   εἴπαμεν
εἶπας   εἴπατε
εἶπε   εἶπαν

b. Imperative

εἶπον and εἰπέ   εἴπατε
εἰπάτω   εἰπάτωσαν

c. Infinitive

εἰπεῖν

Notice that the substitution of α does not occur in the underlined forms.

117. EXERCISES.

a. Read #112 silently in Greek, trying to get the meaning as you go along.

b. Read the speeches in #112 aloud, trying to group the words that naturally go together and to emphasize the places that call for emphasis.

c. Locate the following verb forms by giving whenever possible (1) tense, (2) mood, (3) voice, (4) person, (5) number, and (6) first principal part.

1) ἔπεμψεν   10) εἰπέ
2) ἔχει   11) ἠνέγκατε
3) θεραπεῦσαι   12) σχεῖν
4) ἦν   13) οἴσετε
5) ἰσχύσουσιν   14) εἶπαν
6) σχές   15) λαμβανέτωσαν
7) λάβετε   16) ἐλθεῖν
8) ἀγαγεῖν   17) ἔσχες
9) εἴχετε

d. Translate orally.

1) I was eating the fish.
2) I did eat the fish.
3) You were not drinking your own wine, Peter.
4) You did not drink your own wine, Peter.
5) She was ready to go into the house.
6) She did go into the house.
7) We brought the lamb (just once).
8) We brought the lamb (every evening).
9) Let them keep on speaking.
10) Let them speak (just once).
11) She was ready to keep on speaking.
12) We were ready to speak (just once).
13) The gift came from the man, the /one/ ready to die.

e. Associate ἔφαγον with "sarcophagus" (flesh-eating): a limestone coffin used by the Greeks for the rapid disintegration of a corpse.

42

118. VOCABULARY IN LESSONS 7-11.

Review thoroughly.

NOUNS	VERBS	ADJECTIVES
ἄγγελος	ἄγω	δίκαιος
ἀλήθειᾰ	ἀκούω	ἐλεύθερος
γεωργός	ἀποθνῃσκω	ἕτοιμος
δωρεά	εἶπον	ἴδιος
ἐπιθυμίᾱ	ἐλπίζω	κακός
Ἰάκωβος	ἔξω	καλός
καρδίᾱ	ἔφαγον	μακάριος
κώμη	ἔχω	μικρός
Μαρίᾱ	ἦλθον	
παρρησίᾱ	ἤμην	ADVERBS
πλοῦτος	ἤνεγκα	ναί
σκοτίᾱ	λαμβάνω	νῦν
σπήλαιον	μνημονεύω	ὁμοῦ
χρείᾱ	οἴσω	οὐκέτι
χρόνος		πάλιν
	PREPOSITIONS	πάντοτε
CONJUNCTIONS		παρρησίᾳ
	μετά	πῶς
ἀλλά	περί	σήμερον
ὅτε	σύν	τότε

119. Complete the following sentences with adjectives that are suitable in form and meaning:

δίκαιοι	ἰδίᾱς	καλῶν
ἐλευθερᾶν	ἴδιον	μακάριοι
ἐλεύθερος	κακὸν	μικρῷ
ἕτοιμα	καλᾱς	μικρῶν

1. ὁ _____ γεωργὸς τὸν _____ πλοῦτον ἐν τῷ _____

σπηλαίῳ ἕξει.

2. τῶν ἀρνίων τῶν _____ μνημονεύσομεν;

3. ἕτοιμοι περὶ τὴν _____ κώμην ἐνεγκεῖν τὰς δωρεᾶς τὰς

_____ ἦσαν οἱ _____ ἄγγελοι.

4. πίνετε, _____ ἀδελφοί.

120. Arrange the following Greek words, or as many of them as you need, so as to put the adjective (1) in ascriptive attributive position, (2) in restrictive attributive position, and (3) in predicate position: καρδίᾱ, ἥν, ἡ, μακαρίᾱ, ἡ.

121. DISTINCTION OF TENSES.

a. After reviewing the distinct meanings of the imperfect (#85) and aorist (#94) tenses, translate the underlined verbs.

1. While <u>we were</u> <u>looking</u> at the lambs,   _____

Mary <u>heard</u> the messenger.   _____

2. Philip <u>began</u> <u>to eat</u>, but the   _____

slave <u>kept</u> <u>on</u> <u>speaking</u>.   _____

3. He <u>did</u> not <u>die</u> <u>repeatedly</u>! _____

4. Lazarus, where <u>were</u> <u>you</u> <u>carrying</u> _____

   the lamb?

b. After reviewing the distinct implications of the present and aorist imperatives (#97), translate the underlined verbs.

1. <u>Carry</u> the cups to Mark every day, _____

   my slaves.

2. Lazarus, <u>start</u> <u>treating</u> the little _____

   child.

3. <u>Stop</u> <u>looking</u> <u>at</u> me, Mary. _____

4. <u>Get</u> <u>possession</u> <u>of</u> (a form of ἔχω) _____

   the wealth, noble messengers.

122. ACCENTS IN PARTS OF SPEECH OTHER THAN FINITE VERBS, ADJECTIVES, AND NOUNS: To be learned by observation.

123. EXERCISES ON ACCENTS AND BREATHINGS.

a. Résumé of material on accents and breathings.

   1) Breathings: #6.
   2) Kinds of accents: #7.
   3) Syllables and accents: #7, 35, 36, 37.
   4) Recessive accent: #38.
   5) Persistent accent: #50.

b. Table of accents permitted on the last three syllables of Greek words.

	IF THE ACCENT FALLS ON THE			
	ANTEPENULT	PENULT		ULTIMA
		Short	Long	
When a word has a <u>short</u> ultima	Acute ἄνθρωπος	Acute λόγος	Circumflex δοῦλος	Acute or Grave καλὸν ἀδελφός
When a word has a <u>long</u> ultima	(No accent) (ever does!)	Acute λόγων	Acute δούλων	Acute or Circum- flex or Grave ἀδελφοός ἀδελφῶν καλοὺς ἀδελφοός

c. The following words are the only ones thus far studied which have the rough breathing:

αἱ
ἕξω (plus other future forms
     of ἔχω)
ἕτοιμος
ἡ

ὁ
οἱ
ὁμοῦ
ὅτε
ὅτι

If you are familiar with this list, it will be easy to put smooth breathings everywhere else when a word begins with a vowel in the following exercises.

d. Applying the principle of recessive accent, put accents and breathings on the following finite verbs:

1) λαμβανετε

2) ηγαγον

3) εχουσί

4) αποθνησκει

5) εμνημονευσᾰν

6) ησᾰν

7) ισχυεις

8) απελυσᾱς

9) πεμψομεν

10) εβλεψεν

e. After being sure you know where the accent falls in the nominative singular of each of the following adjectives, put the right accents and breathings on the right syllables.

1) κακου

2) δικαιοι

3) ιδιᾳ

4) ελευθεραις

5) μικρα τεκνα

6) μακαριᾱ Μαριᾱ

f. After being sure you know where the accent falls in the nominative singular of each of the following nouns, put the right accents and breathings on the right syllables.

1) κωμην

2) αρτῳ

3) Φιλιππου

4) οινους

5) αγγελων

6) δωρεων

7) Λαζαρῳ

8) χρονους

9) αδελφοις

10) σπηλαιοις

g. Putting into action all your information on accents, arrange breathings and accents properly in the following sentences:

1) μνημονευετε των τεκνων εν τῳ σπηλαιῳ;

2) οι γεωργοι ελαβον τον πλουτον περι της κωμης.

124. OFF TO A NEW LAND.

    ὁ κύριος τῷ Αβραμ εἶπεν, "ἔλθε ἐκ τῆς γῆς σοῦ καὶ ἐκ τοῦ οἴκου σοῦ."

    τότε ἐν τῇ Μεσοποταμίᾳ ἦν ὁ Αβραμ. ἀλλὰ οἱ ἄνθρωποι ἐν τῇ Μεσοποταμίᾳ ἦσαν κακοί, οὐ δίκαιοι, οὐχ ἕτοιμοι δουλεύειν τῷ κυρίῳ.

5   ἦλθον οὖν ἐκ τῆς γῆς τῆς Μεσοποταμίας ὁ Αβραμ καὶ ἡ Σαρα καὶ ὁ Λώτ.

    ὅτε ὁ Αβραμ ἐκ τῆς ἰδίας γῆς ἦλθεν, τάχα εἶπαν ὁμοῦ ὁ Αβραμ καὶ ἡ Σαρα.

    Σαρα: "Αβραμ, ἀδελφὲ ἐμοῦ, εἶπεν ἄγγελος τοῦ κυρίου σοί;"

    Αβραμ: "οὐχί. ἐγὼ ἤκουσα τοῦ κυρίου ἡμῶν ἐν τῇ σκοτίᾳ. εἶπεν

10 ἐμοί, 'ἐγὼ ὁ κύριος ἄξω ὑμᾶς ἐκ τῆς γῆς ὑμῶν καὶ ἐκ τοῦ οἴκου ὑμῶν, καὶ βλέψετε ὑμεῖς γῆν μακαρίαν, καὶ ἕξετε τὴν γῆν, σὺ καὶ ὁ οἶκος σοῦ. σὺ γὰρ ἦς δίκαιος. ἐγὼ γὰρ ἔβλεψα σέ.'"

    Σαρα: "πάντοτε οὖν κακοὶ ἦσαν οἱ ἄνθρωποι περὶ ἡμᾶς;"

    Αβραμ: "ναί. ἡμεῖς, σὺ καὶ ἐγὼ καὶ Λώτ, ἐδουλεύομεν τῷ κυρίῳ,

15 ἀλλὰ οἱ ἄνθρωποι τῆς Μεσοποταμίας οὐκ ἐδούλευον τῷ κυρίῳ σὺν ἡμῖν. πολλάκις οὖν ἔπεμπον ἐμὲ ἐκ τῶν ἰδίων οἴκων ὅτι ἐγὼ ἐδούλευον τῷ κυρίῳ. ὑμῖν, σοὶ καὶ τῷ Λώτ, κακὰ εἶπαν οἱ κακοὶ τῆς γῆς ὅτι ὑμεῖς, σὺ καὶ Λώτ, ἐδουλεύετε τῷ κυρίῳ;"

    Σαρα: "ναί, πολλάκις ἔλεγον κακὰ ἡμῖν, ἐμοὶ καὶ τῷ Λώτ."

20   Αβραμ: "μακάριος οὖν ἤμην ἐγὼ ὅτε ἐμοὶ εἶπεν ὁ κύριος, 'ἐγὼ ἄξω ὑμᾶς ἐκ τῆς γῆς ὑμῶν, καὶ τὴν ἰδίαν γῆν τὴν μακαρίαν βλέψετε ὑμεῖς.'"

    Σαρα: "πῶς οὖν ἄξει ἡμᾶς ὁ κύριος ἡμῶν;"

    Αβραμ: "βλέψομεν ἡμεῖς. τάχα οἱ κακοὶ τῆς Μεσοποταμίας οὐ βλέψουσιν, ἀλλὰ ἡμεῖς βλέψομεν."

125. VOCABULARY.

Αβραμ (indecl.), ὁ: Abram

γῆ, γῆς, ἡ: earth, land, country, ground

ἐγώ: I

ἐμέ (acc. of ἐγώ): me

ἐμοῦ (abl., gen. of ἐγώ)

ἐμοί (dat., instr., loc. of ἐγώ)

ἡμᾶς (acc. of ἡμεῖς): us

ἡμεῖς: we

ἡμῖν (dat., instr., loc. of ἡμεῖς)

ἡμῶν (abl., gen. of ἡμεῖς)

κύριος, -ου, ὁ: Lord, lord, master

Λώτ (indecl.), ὁ: Lot

Μεσοποταμία, -ᾱς, ἡ: Mesopotamia

οὖν: consequently, therefore, then

οὐχ (form of οὐ used before a word with a rough breathing): not

οὐχί (emphatic form of οὐ): not at all, no, no indeed

πολλάκις: often, many times

Σαρα, -ας, -α, -αν, ἡ: Sarai

σέ (acc. of σύ)

σοῦ (abl., gen. of σύ)

σοί (dat., instr., loc. of σύ)

σύ: you (sing.), thou

τάχα: perhaps

ὑμᾶς (acc. of ὑμεῖς)

ὑμεῖς: you (pl.)

ὑμῖν (dat., instr., loc. of ὑμεῖς)

ὑμῶν (abl., gen. of ὑμεῖς)

126. DECLENSION OF γῆ. Since it is a contract noun from the form γέα, γῆ
has a circumflex accent throughout its declension.

γῆ
γῆς   (No plural is in use in
γῆ   the New Testament.)
γῆν

127. PERSONAL PRONOUNS.

First Person

Singular		Plural	
ἐγώ	(I)	ἡμεῖς	(we)
ἐμοῦ	(of me)	ἡμῶν	(of us)
ἐμοί	(for me)	ἡμῖν	(for us)
ἐμέ	(me)	ἡμᾶς	(us)

Second Person

σύ	(you)	ὑμεῖς	(you)
σοῦ	(of you)	ὑμῶν	(of you)
σοί	(for you)	ὑμῖν	(for you)
σέ	(you)	ὑμᾶς	(you)

128. DEFINITE ARTICLE WITH A PROPER NOUN. The definite article is sometimes used with a proper noun, but only rarely can such definite
articles be translated.

οὐ δουλεύει τῷ Φιλίππῳ.
He is not a slave to Philip.

129. EXERCISES.

a. As you read #124, bear in mind (1) that the definite article before proper nouns usually does not influence the translation, and
(2) that more personal pronouns are used in this passage than are
absolutely necessary.

b. Supply the Greek personal pronouns needed to complete the following sentences.

1) πέμπετε οὖν τάχα τὸν πλοῦτον _____ (your) εἰς τὸν οἶκον
_____ (my).

2) χαῖρε, Ἰάκωβε. λέγει οὐχ ὁ ἀδελφός _____ (your) παρρησίᾳ
σήμερον, ἀλλὰ ὁ ἄγγελος ____ (our) λέγει.

3) οἴσομεν τάχα _____ (our) ἄρτους.

4) οὐχί. οὐ δουλεύετε πολλάκις _____ (me).

5) ουχί. οὐκ ἰσχύσομεν φαγεῖν _____ (you), τὰ τέκνα _____ (my).

6) πολλάκις _____ (to us) δωρεὰς ἔπεμπον.

7) ἐμνημόνευσε _____ (us) ὁ Πέτρος, οὐχ ἡ Μαρία.

8) βλέψουσι _____ (you), Μᾶρκε.

9) εἴπομεν _____ (to you), ἀδελφοί, ὅτι ἔφερε τὴν δωρεὰν _____ (your)
Νικόδημος.

10) βλέπετε _____ (me), ἄγγελοι, _____ (I) ἰσχύω ὀψάριον φαγεῖν.

c. Write in Greek, remembering that personal pronouns used as subjects often add emphasis to the personal idea in the inflectional
endings of the verb. The underlining in the following sentences
is intended to add emphasis.

1) Are you speaking to me, Philip?
2) No. I am not speaking to you, but Mary is hoping to speak to
you.
3) Yes. I am speaking to you, not to Mary.
4) Mary, did they carry your little lamb away from the garden?
5) Yes, Mark, and they have our fish, too.

d. Add to the predicate of each of the following sentences personal
pronouns agreeing with the subject in person but differing from
it in number, e. g., ἀπολύομεν τὸν δοῦλον ἐμοῦ.

1) οὐχ ἕξω τοὺς καρποὺς _____.

2) οὐχ ἕξεις τοὺς καρποὺς _____.

3) οὐχ ἕξομεν τοὺς καρποὺς _____.

4) οὐχ ἕξετε τοὺς καρποὺς _____.

5) ἔπεμπον ἐγὼ τὸν ἄγγελον _____.

6) ἐπέμπετε τὸν ἄγγελον _____.

7) ἔπεμπες τὸν ἄγγελον _____.

8) θεραπεύσω _____.

9) θεραπεύσεις _____.

10) θεραπεύσετε _____.

e. Associate the following English words with new Greek words in this lesson.

1) Cyril: a man's name meaning "lordly."
2) egotism: excessive use of the pronoun "I."
3) geography: a description of the earth.

LESSON 14

130. HALF SISTER: HALF-TRUTH.

ἐπεὶ εἰς τὴν γῆν τὴν μακαρίᾱν ἦλθεν ὁ Αβραμ σὺν τῇ Σαρα καὶ τῷ Λῶτ ἐν ταύτῃ τῇ γῇ χρείᾱν ἄρτου ἔσχον. εἰς τὴν Αἴγυπτον οὖν ἦλθον ὁ Αβραμ καὶ ἡ Σαρα ἡ γυνή.

ἐπεὶ οὖν εἰς τὴν Αἴγυπτον ἦλθε, τῇ Σαρα εἶπεν οὗτος, "ἐπεὶ
5 βλέψουσι σὲ οἱ Αἰγύπτιοι, οὗτοι τάχα φονεύσουσιν ἐμὲ καὶ οἴσουσι σὲ εἰς τὸν οἶκον τοῦ Φαραώ, σὲ τὴν καλὴν Σαραν. ἐγὼ γὰρ τούτους τοὺς Αἰγυπτίους φονεῦσαι οὐκ ἰσχύσω, ἀλλὰ οὗτοι οἱ Αἰγύπτιοι ἐμὲ φονεῦσαι ἰσχύσουσι. εἰπὲ οὖν τότε τούτοις τοῖς Αἰγυπτίοις, 'βλέπετε τὴν ἀδελφὴν τούτου τοῦ Αβραμ.'"

10 ὅτι γὰρ ἡ Σαρα ἦν ἀδελφὴ τοῦ Αβραμ, τοῦτο ἦν ἡ ἀλήθεια, ἀλλὰ ἦν καὶ ἡ γυνὴ τοῦ Αβραμ.

ἐν τῇ Αἰγύπτῳ οὖν ἡ Σαρα ἡ γυνὴ καὶ ἡ ἀδελφὴ τοῦ Αβραμ εἶπε ταῦτα τοῖς Αἰγυπτίοις, καὶ οὗτοι τὸν Αβραμ οὐκ ἐφόνευσαν, ἀλλὰ τὴν ἀδελφὴν τούτου ἤγαγον εἰς τὸν οἶκον τοῦ Φαραώ. τότε τούτῳ, τῆς Σαρας τῷ
15 ἀδελφῷ, δωρεὰς καλὰς ἔπεμψεν ὁ Φαραώ.

μετὰ τοῦτο ἔλαβεν ὁ Φαραώ ἀπὸ τοῦ κυρίου κακά. ἐπεὶ οὖν ἤκουσε ὁ Φαραώ ὅτι αὕτη ἦν ἡ γυνὴ τοῦ Αβραμ, τούτῳ εἶπεν ὁ Φαραώ, "οὐ παρρησίᾳ ἐμοὶ εἶπες περὶ ταύτης. σὺ γὰρ εἶπες καὶ αὕτη εἶπεν, 'βλέπεις

τὴν ἀδελφὴν τοῦ Αβραμ.' λάβε οὖν ταύτην καὶ ἔλθετε ἐκ τῆς γῆς καὶ σὲ

20   οὐ φονεύσω."

   ἐπεὶ ὁ Φαραὼ ταῦτα εἶπε τούτῳ καὶ ταύτῃ, ἐκ τῆς Αἰγύπτου ἦλθον

Αβραμ καὶ Σαρα, ἡ γυνή, καὶ Λῶτ.

131. VOCABULARY.

ἀδελφή, -ῆς, ἡ: sister

Αἰγύπτιος, -ᾱ, -ον: Egyptian

Αἴγυπτος, -ου, ἡ: Egypt

γυνή (not a first declension noun, other forms to be given later),
      woman, wife

ἐπεί: after, when, since, because

οὗτος, αὕτη, τοῦτο: this

Φαραώ (indecl.), ὁ: Pharaoh

φονεύω, φονεύσω, ἐφόνευσα: I kill, murder

132. THE DEMONSTRATIVE οὗτος.

   a. Its use. Such words as ταύτῃ, τούτους, and οὗτοι are inflectional
       forms of the demonstrative οὗτος, αὕτη, τοῦτο: this, which can be
       used either as a pronoun by itself or as an adjective.

   Adjectival use.   Pronominal use.

   ἐν ταύτῃ τῇ γῇ.   τῇ Σαρα εἶπεν οὗτος.
   in this land.   This (man) said to Sarai

   Notice that the Greek demonstrative adjective is in predicate position (#108c). It either precedes or follows the combination of
   definite article and noun; it is not placed between them.

   b. Its declension.

   Masculine   Feminine   Neuter

   οὗτος   αὕτη   τοῦτο
   τούτου   ταύτης   τούτου
   τούτῳ   ταύτῃ   τούτῳ
   τοῦτον   ταύτην   τοῦτο

   οὗτοι   αὗται   ταῦτα
   τούτων   τούτων   τούτων
   τούτοις   ταύταις   τούτοις
   τούτους   ταύτας   ταῦτα

133. EXERCISES.

   a. Translate #130.

   b. Translate orally.

      1) Kill this Egyptian.   3) These caves.
      2) These sisters.   4) In this fish.

5) Concerning this land.	11) About these needs.
6) For these children.	12) In these truths.
7) Of these lambs.	13) Away from these farmers.
8) Take this cup.	14) With these sisters.
9) Out of this cup.	15) For these lords.
10) We shall not kill these Egyptians.	

c. Match the adjectives in List II with the nouns in List I.

LIST I	LIST II
1) τοῖς ἀνθρώποις	α) τούτῳ
2) τὰ ἀργία	β) ταύτην
3) τοὺς ἄρτους	γ) τοῦτο
4) τὸ δεῖπνον	δ) ταύταις
5) τῷ δούλῳ	ε) αὕτη
6) τὴν ἐπιθυμίαν	ζ) τούτους
7) ταῖς καρδίαις	η) ταῦτα
8) ἡ παρρησία	θ) ταύτης
9) τῇ σκοτίᾳ	ι) ταύτῃ
10) τῆς ἀληθείας	κ) τούτοις

d. Notice carefully the following English words related to new Greek words in this lesson.

1) Egyptology: scientific study of ancient Egypt.
2) gynarchy: rule by women.
3) gynecologist: a medical doctor who specializes in the treatment of women.
4) phonomania: an insane desire to murder.

LESSON 15

134. A CHOICE AND A PROMISE.

πάλιν εἰς τὴν γῆν τῆς ἐπαγγελίας τοῦ κυρίου ἤγαγον τὰ πρόβατα
αὐτῶν καὶ τοὺς καμήλους αὐτῶν οἱ ἄνθρωποι Αβραμ καὶ Λωτ. ἀλλὰ οὐκ ἐν
τῷ αὐτῷ τόπῳ ἴσχυον ἐσθίειν καὶ πίνειν οἱ κάμηλοι καὶ τὰ πρόβατα.
μικρὸς γὰρ ἦν ὁ τόπος.

5 εἶπεν οὖν ὁ Αβραμ τῷ Λωτ, "οὐκ ἰσχύσομεν ἔχειν τὸν πλοῦτον ἡμῶν
ἐν τῷ αὐτῷ τόπῳ. βλέπε περὶ ἡμᾶς. βλέπε ἐκείνην τὴν γῆν, τὴν γῆν
τοῦ Ἰορδάνου, καὶ ταύτην τὴν γῆν περὶ ἡμᾶς. σὺ λάβε ἐκείνην καὶ
ταύτην ἔξω ἐγώ, ἢ λάβε ταύτην καὶ ἐκείνην ἔξω."

τότε ἔβλεψεν ὁ Λωτ τὴν γῆν τοῦ Ἰορδάνου, γῆν καλήν. καὶ αὐτὸς

10 ἔλαβεν αὐτήν. εἰς οὖν ἐκείνην τὴν γῆν ἤγαγεν ὁ Λὼτ τοὺς καμήλους καὶ τὰ πρόβατα ἀπὸ τοῦ Αβραμ.

μετὰ τοῦτο τῷ Αβραμ αὐτὸς ὁ κύριος εἶπεν, "σὺ ἕξεις ταύτην τὴν γῆν, σὺ καὶ τὰ τέκνα σοῦ." αὕτη ἦν ἡ ἐπαγγελία τοῦ κυρίου τῷ Αβραμ.

135. VOCABULARY.

αὐτός, αὐτή, αὐτό: self, even, very, same, he, she, it

ἐκεῖνος, ἐκείνη, ἐκεῖνο: that

ἐπαγγελία, -ᾱς, ἡ: promise

ἤ: or, than

'Ιορδάνης, -ου, ὁ: Jordan

κάμηλος, -ου, ὁ or ἡ: camel

πρόβατον, -ου, τό: sheep

τόπος, -ου, ὁ: place, spot, locality

136. MASCULINE NOUNS OF THE FIRST DECLENSION. The nouns of the first declension studied thus far are feminine and end in -ᾱ, -ᾰ, and -η. In this lesson a first declension masculine noun ending in -ης has been used. The endings differ from the patterns already presented only in the first and second inflectional forms of the singular.

'Ιορδάνης
'Ιορδάνου
'Ιορδάνῃ
'Ιορδάνην

No plural is in use for this noun. The plural endings, however, for this type of first declension noun are the same as for the other types.

137. THE DEMONSTRATIVE ἐκεῖνος. As οὗτος is used to point out persons or things near at hand, so ἐκεῖνος is used to point out what is more remote.

ἐκεῖνος	ἐκείνη	ἐκεῖνο
ἐκείνου	ἐκείνης	ἐκείνου
ἐκείνῳ	ἐκείνῃ	ἐκείνῳ
ἐκεῖνον	ἐκείνην	ἐκεῖνο

ἐκεῖνοι	ἐκεῖναι	ἐκεῖνα
ἐκείνων	ἐκείνων	ἐκείνων
ἐκείνοις	ἐκείναις	ἐκείνοις
ἐκείνους	ἐκείνᾱς	ἐκεῖνα

No vocative is used.

138. THE INTENSIVE αὐτός: ITS DECLENSION. The declension of αὐτός is like that of ἐκεῖνος except for the accent.

αὐτός	αὐτή	αὐτό
αὐτοῦ	αὐτῆς	αὐτοῦ
αὐτῷ	αὐτῇ	αὐτῷ
αὐτόν	αὐτήν	αὐτό

αὐτοί	αὐταί	αὐτά
αὐτῶν	αὐτῶν	αὐτῶν
αὐτοῖς	αὐταῖς	αὐτοῖς
αὐτούς	αὐτᾱς	αὐτά

No vocative is used.

52

139.   THE INTENSIVE αὐτός: ITS USES. There are three uses for αὐτός.

a.   To emphasize the noun or pronoun with which it agrees.

Αβραμ αὐτὸς εἶχε δούλους.
Abram <u>himself</u> had slaves.

ὁ ἄνθρωπος <u>αὐτός</u> (or) <u>αὐτὸς</u> ὁ ἄνθρωπος.
The man <u>himself</u> (or) the <u>very</u> man.

Notice that either meaning fits either order and that αὐτός
meaning <u>self</u> cannot come between a noun and its definite article.

b.   To identify a noun or pronoun with something already mentioned.

ἐν τῷ <u>αὐτῷ</u> τόπῳ.
in the <u>same</u> place.

αὐτός meaning <u>same</u> must come between its noun and definite article.

c.   To serve as a personal pronoun.

ἡ γῆ ἦν καλή, καὶ <u>αὐτὴν</u> ἔλαβεν Λώτ.
The land was beautiful, and Lot took <u>it</u>.

140.   EXERCISES.

a.   Translate #134.

b.   Write in Greek.

1)   This promise.
2)   That promise.
3)   The same promise.
4)   The promise itself.
5)   His promise.
6)   Her promise.
7)   Its promise.
8)   These camels or those sheep.
9)   The same sheep.
10)   In that place or in this place.
11)   In the Jordan itself.
12)   Into the same Jordan.
13)   These /things7 or those /things7.
14)   The camels themselves or the sheep themselves.
15)   That promise or the same gift.

c.   Translate orally.

1)   ἡ αὐτὴ γυνὴ ἦν ἡ ἀδελφὴ αὐτή.

2)   τὰ πρόβατα ἐκεῖνα καὶ οἱ κάμηλοι οὗτοι ἦσαν τούτῳ ἢ ἐκείνῳ;

3)   ἐκ τοῦ 'Ιορδάνου αὐτοῦ.

4)   εἰς ἐκεῖνον τὸν 'Ιορδάνην.

5)   ἤμεθα ἐν τῇ αὐτῇ σκοτίᾳ.

6)   ἦτε σὺν τῷ 'Ιακώβῳ αὐτῷ;

7)   ἐκεῖνοι οἱ γεωργοὶ ἦσαν ἕτοιμοι τούτοις τοῖς καμήλοις.

8)   ἤγαγον ἐκείνους περὶ τὴν αὐτὴν κώμην.

9)   βλέπετε τούτους τοὺς ἐλευθέρους;

10) οὐχί. ἀλλὰ ἐγὼ βλέπω τοὺς δούλους ἐκείνους.

11) ὁ Ἰορδάνης ἦν ὁ τόπος;

12) οὐκ ἦν ὁ Ἰορδάνης ἀλλὰ τὰ Σόδομα.

13) ὁ Ἰορδάνης οὐκ ἦν τῷ Λὼτ ἢ τῷ Αβραμ.

d. Associate the following English words with new Greek words in this lesson.

1) <u>automobile</u>: a vehicle that moves <u>itself</u>.
2) <u>camel</u>: the English word <u>camel</u> is <u>derived</u> from Greek through Latin.
3) <u>topography</u>: map making (a drawing of a <u>place</u>).

LESSON 16

141. A GLIMPSE AT LOT'S FUTURE.

"μενῶ ἐν τοῖς Σοδόμοις," ἐρεῖ Λὼτ τάχα ὅτε ἕξει τόπον τοῖς καμήλοις αὐτοῦ καὶ τοῖς προβάτοις αὐτοῦ ἐν τῇ γῇ τοῦ Ἰορδάνου.

"ἀποστελῶ ἄγγελον εἰς τὰ Σόδομα καὶ ἐρῶ, ʼμενοῦμεν ἐν τῇ αὐτῇ γῇ
σὺν ὑμῖν.ʼ"

5   ἀποστελεῖ δὲ τάχα ὑπηρέτην ὁ Λὼτ πρὸς τοὺς ἀνθρώπους τῶν Σοδόμων
ἐπεὶ ἄξει τὰ πρόβατα καὶ τοὺς καμήλους ἀπὸ τοῦ Αβραμ εἰς τὴν γῆν τοῦ
Ἰορδάνου.

οἱ δὲ ἄνθρωποι τῶν Σοδόμων οἱ κακοὶ οὐκ ἀποκτενοῦσι Λὼτ καὶ τοὺς
ὑπηρέτας αὐτοῦ. μενοῦσι οὖν Λὼτ καὶ ἡ γυνὴ αὐτοῦ ἐν τοῖς κακοῖς τῶν
10 Σοδόμων καὶ βλέψουσι τὰ κακὰ τοῦ τόπου ἐκείνου.

ὅτε οἱ ἐχθροὶ τῶν Σοδόμων οἴσουσι τοὺς ἀνθρώπους τῶν Σοδόμων καὶ
τὸν πλοῦτον αὐτῶν ἀπὸ τῆς γῆς τοῦ Ἰορδάνου, τότε ἐροῦσι τάχα ἐκεῖνοι
τῷ Λὼτ, "οὐ μενεῖτε ἐν τούτῳ τῷ τόπῳ, σὺ καὶ ἡ γυνή σοῦ καὶ ὁ πλοῦτος
σοῦ. ὑπηρέτην δὲ οὐκ ἀποστελεῖς πρὸς Αβραμ. οὐχί. ἀλλὰ ἡμεῖς σε
15 καὶ τούτους τοὺς ἀνθρώπους οἴσομεν εἰς γῆν μακράν."

ὑπηρέτην δὲ Λὼτ ἀποστελεῖ πρὸς Αβραμ περὶ τῶν ἐχθρῶν τούτων.

καὶ Αβραμ οὐ μενεῖ ἐν τῷ ἰδίῳ τόπῳ ὅτε ἀκούσει. αὐτὸς δὲ ὁ Αβραμ οἴσει τὸν Λωτ καὶ τὸν πλοῦτον ἀπὸ τῶν ἐχθρῶν ἐν ἐκείνῃ τῇ μακρᾷ γῇ.

142. VOCABULARY.

ἀποκτείνω, ἀποκτενῶ, ἀπέκτεινα: I kill

ἀποστέλλω, ἀποστελῶ, ἀπέστειλα: I send away, send forth

δέ: but, and, now (not in temporal sense)

ἐλπίζω, ἐλπιῶ, ἤλπισα (final stem consonant dropped before -σ- of tense suffix): I hope

ἐχθρός, -οῦ, ὁ: enemy

λέγω, ἐρῶ, εἶπον: I say, speak, declare

μακρός, -ά, -όν: long, far distant

μένω, μενῶ, ἔμεινα: I stay, remain, wait for

πρός: (with loc.) near; (with acc.) to, towards, with

Σόδομα, -ων, τά: Sodom (a place name with plural form but singular meaning)

ὑπηρέτης, -ου, ὁ: assistant, servant, attendant

143. FUTURE OF LIQUID AND NASAL VERBS. In this lesson future forms of ἀποκτείνω, ἀποστέλλω, λέγω (ἐρῶ), and μένω have been used. The future stems of these verbs are called liquid (when ending in λ or ρ) and nasal (when ending in μ or ν). These futures differ from those previously observed in having no -σ- in the tense suffix and in having circumflex accents.

Indicative

μενῶ	μενοῦμεν
μενεῖς	μενεῖτε
μενεῖ	μενοῦσι

These forms seem to be descended from the following, which are <u>not</u> in use:

Indicative

μενέσω	μενέσομεν
μενέσεις	μενέσετε
μενέσει	μενέσουσι

The -σ- disappeared and the vowels on each side of the -σ- combined to produce the endings presented in the paradigms above. Although not having a liquid or nasal stem, ἐλπίζω has as its future active indicative ἐλπιῶ, ἐλπιεῖς etc.

144. PRESENT OF LIQUID AND NASAL VERBS. In most of the verbs used before this lesson the future has been built upon the present stem by adding -σο/ε- (or to state the same fact in other words) by inserting a -σ- between the present stem and the present endings, e. g.

Present	Future
ἀπολύ-ω	ἀπολύ-σ-ω

In the regular pattern of liquid and nasal verbs the verb stem, e. g., ἀποστελ- , was changed by the addition of -ίω, -ίεις, etc. to form the present. The -ῐ- was assimilated to a -λ-.

(ἀποστελῐω)   ἀποστέλλω
(ἀποστελῐεις)   ἀποστέλλεις

In μένω the nasal pattern for the present tense is not followed.

145. AORIST OF LIQUID AND NASAL VERBS. The first or sigmatic aorist was presented in #94-98 and the second aorist in #114-116. In #141 verbs with liquid and nasal stems have been used in the future. These same verbs usually have peculiarities in the aorist, where the stem differs from that of the future, and where no -σ- appears in the tense suffix.

Indicative

ἔμεινα   ἐμείναμεν
ἔμεινας   ἐμείνατε
ἔμεινε   ἔμειναν

Imperative

μεῖνον   μείνατε
μεινάτω   μεινάτωσαν

Infinitive

μεῖναι

These forms seem to be descended from the following, which are not in use:

Indicative

ἔμενσα   ἐμένσαμεν
ἔμενσας   ἐμένσατε
ἔμενσε   ἔμενσαν

Imperative

μένσον   μένσατε
μενσάτω   μενσάτωσαν

Infinitive

μένσαι

It is supposed that -μεν- became -μειν- to make up for the loss of the -σ-. The aorist stems of ἀποκτείνω and ἀποστέλλω exhibit the same relationship with their future stems:

Future   Aorist

ἀποκτενῶ   ἀπέκτεινα
(ἀποκτενέσω)   (ἀπέκτενσα)

ἀποστελῶ   ἀπέστειλα
(ἀποστελέσω)   (ἀπέστελσα)

146. EXERCISES.

a. Translate #141.

b. Change every future to an aorist in #141 unless the result does not make good sense.

c. Write in Greek.

56

1) You (sing.) are speaking to (πρός) the attendant.
2) You (sing.) will speak to (πρός) the attendant.
3) You (sing.) did speak to (πρός) the attendant.
4) We do not kill the enemy.
5) We shall not kill the enemy.
6) We did not kill the enemy.
7) They remain in a far distant land.
8) They will remain in a far distant land.
9) They did remain in a far distant land.
10) She sends forth an assistant to (πρός) a far distant village.
11) She will send forth an assistant to (πρός) a far distant village.
12) She sent (once) forth an assistant to (πρός) a far distant village.

d. Translate into English.

1) ἐλπιοῦμεν ἀποκτεῖναι τοὺς ἐχθρούς.

2) οὐκ ἐλπιεῖτε, ἐχθροί, ἀποστεῖλαι ἡμᾶς πρὸς τοὺς ὑπηρέτᾱς.

3) μὴ μεινάτωσαν πρὸς τοῖς Σοδόμοις.

4) ἄνθρωποι τῶν Σοδόμων, ἐλπιεῖτε ἀποκτεῖναι ἡμᾶς;

5) ἐχθρέ, ἐλπιεῖς μεῖναι ἐν τῷ αὐτῷ οἴκῳ σὺν ἡμῖν;

6) ὁ ὑπηρέτης ἀποστειλάτω τὸν ἐχθρὸν πρὸς μακρὰν γῆν.

7) ἀπόκτεινον ἡμᾶς, ἐχθρέ· ἐλπιοῦμεν δὲ ὅτι ὁ κύριος μενεῖ σὺν ἡμῖν.   (NOTE: The raised period is the Greek semicolon.)

8) ἐλπιεῖτε μεῖναι ἐν τούτῳ τῷ τόπῳ;

9) δοῦλε, ἀποστελεῖς ἀρνίον πρὸς τὸν ἀδελφὸν ἐμοῦ;

10) πῶς ἀπέστειλας τὸ ἀρνίον;

11) ἀπόκτεινον τὸ ἀρνίον.

12) μὴ ἀποκτεινάτω τὸ ἀρνίον.

13) μὴ ἀποκτεινάτωσαν ἀρνία.

14) ἀποστείλατε αὐτὰ ἀπὸ τῶν Σοδόμων.

15) ἔμεινας σὺ ἐν τῷ τόπῳ ἐκείνῳ· ἡμεῖς δὲ ἀπεστείλαμεν τοὺς ἀγγέλους ἀπὸ σοῦ.

16) ἐμείνατε· ἐλπίζομεν δὲ ὅτι οὐκ ἐμείνατε χρόνον μακρόν.

17) ἀπόστειλον ὑπηρέτην πρὸς ἐμέ.

18) μείνατε ἐν τῇ ἀληθείᾳ.

19) ἐμείνατε ἐν τῇ ἀληθείᾳ.

20) ἀποκτείνατε τοὺς κακοὺς ἐχθρούς, τοὺς δὲ καλοὺς ὑπηρέτᾱς ἀποστείλατε πρὸς τὸν Αβραμ.

21) Αβραμ, ἀπόστειλον ἐμὲ εἰς τὰ Σόδομα.

22) Αβραμ καὶ Λωτ μεινάτωσαν πρὸς τούτῳ τῷ τόπῳ.

23) Λωτ μεινάτω ἀλλὰ Αβραμ καὶ Σαρα ἀποστειλάτωσαν ἄγγελον.

24) ὁ ὑπηρέτης τῶν Σοδόμων μεινάτω πρὸς τοῖς Σοδόμοις.

e. Associate the following English words with new Greek words in
   the lesson:

   1) <u>apostle</u>: one whom Jesus <u>sent forth</u> to preach.
   2) <u>macron</u>: a mark over a vowel to indicate that its pronuncia-
      tion is <u>long</u>.

LESSON 17

147. ABRAM TO THE RESCUE.

ὅτε ἔμενε Λῶτ ἐν τοῖς Σοδόμοις, ἐχθροὶ ἦλθον καὶ ἔλαβον αὐτόν.
ἄγγελος δὲ πρὸς Αβραμ ἦλθε καὶ εἶπεν, "εἰλήφᾱσιν οἱ τῶν Σοδόμων ἔχ-
θροὶ τὸν Λῶτ καὶ ἄλλους καὶ ἐληλόθᾱσι πρὸς γῆν μακρᾱ́ν."

ἐπεὶ δὲ ἤκουσεν Αβραμ τοῦτο, ἔλαβε τοὺς ἰδίους ἀνθρώπους καὶ
5 ἐδίωξαν τοὺς ἐχθρούς. ἐν τῇ σκοτίᾳ Αβραμ αὐτὸς καὶ οἱ ἴδιοι ἀπέλυσαν
Λῶτ καὶ τοὺς ἄλλους. πάλιν δὲ πρὸς τὰ Σόδομα ἦλθεν Αβραμ. οὐ γὰρ
ἐδίωξαν αὐτὸν οἱ ἐχθροὶ τῶν Σοδόμων.

ἦλθε δὲ ὁ βασιλεὺς τῶν Σοδόμων πρὸς Αβραμ ὅτε οὗτος ἦλθε πάλιν
σὺν τῷ Λῶτ καὶ τοῖς ἄλλοις. ἄλλος δὲ βασιλεὺς ἤνεγκεν ἄρτους καὶ
10 οἶνον τῷ Αβραμ. οὗτος ὁ βασιλεὺς ἦν ὑπηρέτης τοῦ κυρίου. οὗτος οὖν
καλὰ τῷ Αβραμ εἶπε καὶ ἔλαβε δωρεᾶς καλᾱς ἀπὸ τοῦ Αβραμ.

τότε δὲ εἶπεν ὁ βασιλεὺς Σοδόμων πρὸς Αβραμ, "μενέτωσαν οἱ ἄνθρωποι ἐμοῦ σὺν ἐμοί, τὰ δὲ ἄλλα ἕξεις. εἴληφας γὰρ ἐκεῖνα ἀπὸ τῶν ἐχθρῶν. ἕξεις οὖν ἐκεῖνα."

15 πρὸς δὲ αὐτὸν εἶπεν Αβραμ, "εἴρηκα τῷ κυρίῳ, 'οὐχ ἕξω ἐκεῖνα.
οὐχί. ὁ βασιλεὺς τῶν Σοδόμων οὐκ ἐρεῖ, "Αβραμ ἔχει τὸν πλοῦτον ἐμοῦ."'
ἀπέλυσα τοὺς ἀνθρώπους σοῦ καὶ σοὶ αὐτοὺς ἤγαγον. λάβε αὐτοὺς καὶ
ἐκεῖνα. μεμενήκᾱσι σὺν σοὶ καὶ μενοῦσι."

148. VOCABULARY.

ἄλλος, -η, -ο: other, another; οἱ ἄλλοι: the rest, the others
βασιλεύς (nom. sing.; other forms to be given later), ὁ: king

διώκω, διώξω, ἐδίωξα: I pursue, run after, put to flight, persecute

εἴληφας (perf. ind. act. 2nd s. of λαμβάνω): you have taken

εἰλήφασιν (perf. ind. act. 3rd pl. of λαμβάνω): they have taken

εἴρηκα (perf. ind. act. 1st s. of λέγω): I have said

ἐληλύθᾱσι (perf. ind. act. 3rd pl. of the same verb as ἦλθον): they
         have gone.

149. FIRST PERFECT ACTIVE. In #147 εἴρηκα, I have said is a first perfect.
This tense indicates an action completed in the past and leaving behind its completion a more or less lasting result. Here Abram is
represented as saying, "I made this statement and it still stands."

                          Indicative

         εἴρηκα   εἰρήκαμεν
         εἴρηκας   εἰρήκατε
         εἴρηκε   εἰρήκᾱσι

                          Infinitive
                          εἰρηκέναι

The first perfect is made up of (1) reduplication (εἰ-), (2) the verb
stem, (3) the tense suffix -κα (κε inf. & 3rd sing.), (4) the primary
active endings (-μι, -ς, -σι, -μεν, -τε, -νσι). Notice that -μι and
-σι do not appear in the 1st and 3rd sing., and that -νσι is modified
to -σι with the preceding -α- lengthened to compensate for the loss
of the ν. The active infinitive ending is -ναι.

Another and more common type of reduplication appears in μεμενήκᾱσι.

                          Indicative

         μεμένηκα   μεμενήκαμεν
         μεμένηκας   μεμενήκατε
         μεμένηκε   μεμενήκᾱσι

                          Infinitive
                          μεμενηκέναι

The initial μ in the simple verb stem is repeated with ε before the
verb stem -μενη-to form the reduplication.

150. SECOND PERFECT ACTIVE. In #147 εἰλήφᾱσιν, they have taken, and
ἐληλύθᾱσι, they have gone are second perfects. The second perfect
does not differ in meaning from the first perfect, and in formation it
differs only in the spelling of the tense suffix, which here has only
-α- (-ε- in 3rd sing.).

                          Indicative

         εἴληφα   εἰλήφαμεν
         εἴληφας   εἰλήφατε
         εἴληφε   εἰλήφᾱσι

                          Infinitive
                          εἰληφέναι

Another type of reduplication appears in ἐληλύθᾱσι.

Indicative

ἐλήλυθα	ἐληλύθαμεν
ἐλήλυθας	ἐληλύθατε
ἐλήλυθε	ἐληλύθασι

Infinitive

ἐληλυθέναι

In this verb -ἐλ- is the reduplication; -ηλυθ- is the verb stem (-η- being a lengthened form of -ε-); -α- or -ε- after -θ- is the tense suffix; and -ναι- the active infinitive ending.

151. SUMMARY OF TYPES OF REDUPLICATION USED IN THIS LESSON.

a. A prefix made up of the initial consonant of the verb plus ε (μεμένηκα).

b. A prefix which earlier in the history of the language probably was the initial consonant of the verb stem plus ε (εἴληφα from σέσληφα, or εἴρηκα from FεFρηκα, wewreka).

c. A prefix made up of the first two letters of the verb stem (ἐλήλυθα from stem ἐλυθ-).

152. EXERCISES.

a. Translate #147.

b. Drill on the following list of principal parts in order to add the perfect tense to the present, future, and aorist tenses, most of which you already know from #102. Some, but not all, of the blank spaces in this list will be filled by information appearing in later lessons.

Present	Future	Aorist	Perfect
ἄγω	ἄξω	ἤγαγον	---
ἀκούω	ἀκούσω	ἤκουσα	ἀκήκοα
ἀποθνήσκω	---	ἀπέθανον	---
ἀποκτείνω	ἀποκτενῶ	ἀπέκτεινα	---
ἀπολύω	ἀπολύσω	ἀπέλυσα	---
ἀποστέλλω	ἀποστελῶ	ἀπέστειλα	ἀπέσταλκα
βλέπω	βλέψω	ἔβλεψα	---
διώκω	διώξω	ἐδίωξα	---
δουλεύω	δουλεύσω	ἐδούλευσα	δεδούλευκα
εἰμί	---	---	---
ἐλπίζω	ἐλπιῶ	ἤλπισα	ἤλπικα
ἐσθίω	---	ἔφαγον	---
---	---	ἦλθον	ἐλήλυθα
ἔχω	ἕξω	ἔσχον	ἔσχηκα
θεραπεύω	θεραπεύσω	ἐθεράπευσα	---

60

Present	Future	Aorist	Perfect
ἰσχύω	ἰσχύσω	ἴσχυσα	---
λαμβάνω	---	ἔλαβον	εἴληφα
λέγω	ἐρῶ	εἶπον	εἴρηκα
μένω	μενῶ	ἔμεινα	μεμένηκα
μνημονεύω	---	ἐμνημόνευσα	---
πέμπω	πέμψω	ἔπεμψα	πέπομφα
πίνω	---	ἔπιον	πέπωκα
φέρω	οἴσω	ἤνεγκα	---
φονεύω	φονεύσω	ἐφόνευσα	---

c. Translate into English.

1) πέπωκας οἶνον, κακὲ ἐχθρέ; *have you drunk;* — *1st. perf.*

2) μεμενήκᾱσιν ἐν τῷ οἴκῳ. *they had remained* — *1st. perf.*

3) ἀπέσταλκε τὸ τέκνον ὁ βασιλεύς; *he had sent.* — *1st. perf.*

4) ἀκηκοέναι. — *2 perf. infve.*

5) οὐκ πεπόμφαμεν. — *perf.*

6) τὸν ἄγγελον ἀπεστάλκατε; — *1st. perf.*

7) ἤλπικα σχεῖν ἄρτον. — *perf.*

8) ὁ Λὼτ τῷ Αβραμ οὐ δεδούλευκε. — *1st. perf.*

9) ἐλήλυθε εἰς τὰ Σόδομα. — *perf.*

10) ἐσχήκατε τοὺς ἄλλους ὑπηρέτᾱς. — *perf.*

11) πῶς εἴληφας τοὺς ἐχθρούς; — *perf.*

12) ὑμῖν εἰρήκαμεν; — *perf.*

d. Translate into Greek orally.

1) We have hoped.
2) The king has served as a slave of the Lord.
3) You, Peter, have sent forth the slave.
4) They have spoken.
5) I have not hoped to see you.

e. Associate the following English words with new Greek words in this lesson.

1) <u>allopath</u>: one who practices medicine based on the theory that remedies producing in a well person symptoms dif-ferent from those found in the sick person will heal the disease whose symptoms have been produced.
2) <u>basilic</u>: <u>kingly</u>.

153. NEW VOCABULARY IN LESSONS 13-17.

NOUNS

Ἀβραμ
ἀδελφή
Αἴγυπτος
βασιλεύς
γῆ
γυνή
ἐπαγγελίᾱ
ἐχθρός
Ἰορδάνης
κάμηλος
κύριος
Λώτ
Μεσοποταμίᾱ
πρόβατον
Σαρα
Σόδομα
τόπος
ὑπηρέτης
Φαραώ

PRONOUNS

αὐτός
ἐγώ
ἐκεῖνος
ἡμεῖς
οὗτος
σύ
ὑμεῖς

VERBS

ἀποκτείνω
ἀποστέλλω
διώκω
ἐλπιῶ
ἐρῶ
ἤλπισα
μένω
φονεύω

ADJECTIVES

Αἰγύπτιος
ἄλλος
μακρός

ADVERBS

οὐχ
οὐχί
πολλάκις
τάχα

CONJUNCTIONS

δέ
ἐπεί
ἤ
οὖν

PREPOSITION

πρός

154. TABLE OF VERB ENDINGS. (Full inflections are given in the appendix, #412 forward.)

Indicative								
Pres.	Fut. (usual)	Fut. (liq. & nasal)	Aor. (1st)	Aor. (liq.& nasal)	Perf. (2nd)	Perf. (1st)	Aor. (2nd)	Imperf
-ω	-σω	-ῶ	-σα	-α	-α	-κα	-ον	-ον
-εις	-σεις	-εῖς	-σας	-ας	-ας	-κας	-ες	-ες
-ει	-σει	-εῖ	-σε(ν)	-ε(ν)	-ε	-κε	-ε(ν)	-ε(ν)
-ομεν	-σομεν	-οῦμεν	-σαμεν	-αμεν	-αμεν	-καμεν	-ομεν	-ομεν
-ετε	-σετε	-εῖτε	-σατε	-ατε	-ατε	-κατε	-ετε	-ετε
-ουσι(ν)	-σουσι(ν)	-οῦσι(ν)	-σαν	-αν	-ᾱσι	-κᾱσι	-ον	-ον
Imperative								
-ε	None	None	-σον	-ον	None	None	-ε	None
-έτω			-σάτω	-άτω			-έτω	
-ετε			-σατε	-ατε			-ετε	
-έτωσαν			-σάτωσαν	-άτωσαν			-έτωσαν	
Infinitive								
-ειν	Rare -σειν	Rare -εῖν	-σαι	-αι	-έναι	-κέναι	-εῖν	None

Tenses using augment: imperfect and aorist.
Tense using reduplication: perfect. (Note aorist of ἄγω.)
Tenses showing change of stem from the present in addition to augment
and to the endings given above: liquid and nasal future and aorist,
and 2nd aorist.

155. LOCATION DRILL. Locate the following verb forms by studying their
(1) endings, (2) stems, and (3) augments. A location consists of a

correct indication of (1) tense, (2) mood, (3) voice, (4) person, (5) number, (6) first principal part.

Example: ἤγαγον   (1) 2nd aorist, (2) indicative, (3) active,
                (4) {first, (5) {singular, (6) ἄγω.
                      {third   {plural

ἤγαγ ον
     1st sing. act. or 3rd pl. act.

2nd aor. indic. ἄγω

1) ἀποστελεῖτε   8) φαγεῖν *ἐσθίω.*   15) ἕξεις *2.pers. ἔχω.*
fut.ind.act. 2.p.pl. ἀποστέλλω   *fut.inf.act.*

2) ἔσχομεν   9) βλέψει *βλέπω.*   16) ἀπολῦσαι
2.aor.ind.act.1.p.pl. ἔχω.   *fut.ind.act.*   *3.p.sing.*   *1st.aor.inf.apoλύω.*

3) ἔμειναν *μένω.*   10) ἠκούσαμεν *ἀκούω.*   17) θεράπευσον
aor.liqu.+nasal ind.act.3p.pl.   *1.aor.ind.1.pl.*   *1st.aor.imp.act.2ot.pers.sing. θεραπεύω.*

4) ἐμένομεν   11) ἐλπισάτωσαν *ἐλπίζω.*   18) εἴχετε
imp.ind.act.1.p.pl. μένω.   *Pres.imp.*   *3.p.pl.*   *2.perf.ind.act.2pers.plur. ἔχω*

5) ἀπολυέτω   12) λάβε *λαμβάνω.*   19) σχεῖν
imp.ind.act.3p.s. ἀπολύω.   *Pres.imp.imper.2.pers.s.ng.*   *2.aor.2nd.act.inf.*

6) ἤσθιεν   13) εἰπεῖν *εἶπα.*   20) ἦμεν+ἤμεθα
imp.ind.act.3p.s. ἐσθίω.   *2d.aor.inf. λέγω.*   *imp.ind.act.1st.pers.plur. ἤμην.*

7) ἐσθίειν   14) ἐροῦμεν   21) εἰρήκασι
inf.ind.act. ἐσθίω.   *fut.ind.act.1st.pers.plur. λέγω.*   *1st.perf.ind.act.3pers.plur. λέγω.*

156. TABLE OF NOUN ENDINGS. (Also see #383.)

A or First Declension

Singular

After ε, ι, or ρ   Not after ε, ι, or ρ

-ᾱ	-ᾰ	-η	-ᾰ	-ης
-ᾱς	-ᾱς	-ης	-ης	-ου
-ᾳ	-ᾳ	-ῃ	-ῃ	-ῃ
-ᾱν	-ᾱν	-ην	-ᾰν	-ην

Plural

   -αι   (The middle column above
   -ων   will be used in #180.)
   -αις
   -ᾱς

O or Second Declension

Singular		Plural	
-ος	-ον	-οι	-ᾰ
-ου	-ου	-ων	-ων
-ῳ	-ῳ	-οις	-οις
-ον	-ον	-ους	-ᾰ
-ε			

157. TABLE OF ADJECTIVE ENDINGS: COMBINATION OF A AND O DECLENSIONS. (Also see #383 and #384.)

Singular

Masc.	Fem.		Neut.
	After ε, ι, or ρ	Not after ε, ι, or ρ	
-ος	-ᾱ	-η	-ον
-ου	-ᾱς	-ης	-ου
-ῳ	-ᾳ	-ῃ	-ῳ
-ον	-ᾱν	-ην	-ον
-ε	-ᾱ	-η	-ον

	Plural	
Masc.	Fem.	Neut.
—οι	—αι	—ᾰ
—ων	—ων	—ων
—οις	—αις	—οις
—ους	—ᾱς	—ᾰ

158. LOCATION DRILL. Give the number, gender, and possible case of the following nouns and adjectives.

a. Nouns.

1) δεῖπνα *1st. pers. plu. neut. nom.*

2) ἀδελφῇ *fem. sing. gen.*

3) πλοῦτοι *plur. mas. nom.*

4) ἐπαγγελίαις *plur. fem. nom.*

5) κυρίους *plur. mas. nom. acc.*

b. Adjectives.

1) μακαρίων *plur. mas. gen.*

2) ἐλεύθερε *sing. mas. voc.*

3) μακρῷ *sing. dat. mas.*

4) μικρόν *sing. mas. acc.*

5) Αἰγύπτιαι *plur. fem. nom.*

LESSON 19

159. ABRAM BELIEVES GOD.

ἐπεὶ ὁ Λὼτ ἐμεμενήκει ἐν τοῖς Σοδόμοις τοῖς κακοῖς καὶ ἐπεὶ ὁ *first plup active* Ἀβραμ ἀπέλυσε τὸν Λὼτ ἀπὸ τῶν ἐχθρῶν Σοδόμων καὶ ἐπεὶ ἐληλύθει πρὸς *sec. Perf.* Ἀβραμ ὁ βασιλεὺς τῶν Σοδόμων καὶ ἐπεὶ ὁ ἄλλος βασιλεὺς εἰλήφει τὰς *plup.* δωρεὰς τοῦ Ἀβραμ καὶ ἐπεὶ ὁ Ἀβραμ οὐκ εἰλήφει τὰς δωρεὰς τῶν Σοδόμων,

5 ὁ θεὸς εἶπε τῷ Ἀβραμ, "μὴ ἔχε φόβον. ἕξεις τὴν ἐπιθυμίᾱν τῆς καρδίᾱς σου."

εἶπε δὲ Ἀβραμ, "ἀλλά, κύριε, ἐγὼ οὐκ ἔχω τέκνον, οὗτος ὁ ὑπηρέτης ἕξει τὸν οἶκον ἐμοῦ."

εἶπε δὲ ὁ θεός, "ἕξεις υἱόν, τὸ ἴδιον τέκνον."

10 ἐπεὶ τὴν ἐπαγγελίᾱν τέκνου εἰλήφει, *pluperfect* Ἀβραμ τῷ θεῷ ἐπίστευεν.

160. VOCABULARY.

θεός, —οῦ, ὁ: God, god, deity

πιστεύω, πιστεύσω, ἐπίστευσα, πεπίστευκα: I believe, trust (with dat. of person or thing believed to be telling the truth)

υἱός, -οῦ, ὁ: son

φόβος, -ου, ὁ: fear

161. FIRST PLUPERFECT ACTIVE. In #159 ἐμεμενήκει, he had remained, is a first pluperfect. The pluperfect has the idea of the perfect but locates it in a past context. The pluperfect indicates an action completed in a relatively remote past and leaving behind its completion a more or less lasting result in a less remote past. In ἐμεμενήκει Lot is represented as having taken up his residence in Sodom and continued it at a time earlier than that of this conversation with God.

Indicative

(ἐ)μεμενήκειν   (ἐ)μεμενήκειμεν
(ἐ)μεμενήκεις   (ἐ)μεμενήκειτε
(ἐ)μεμενήκει   (ἐ)μεμενήκεισαν

The pluperfect has no form outside the indicative.

The first pluperfect is made up of (1) augment (often not used in Hellenistic Greek), (2) reduplication (identical with that used in the perfect), (3) verb stem, (4) tense suffix (-κει-), and (5) secondary active endings (-ν, -ς, --, -μεν, -τε, -σαν).

162. SECOND PLUPERFECT ACTIVE. In #159 εἰλήφει, he had received, is a second pluperfect. The only difference between the first and second pluperfects is in the tense suffix where no κ appears in the second pluperfect.

Indicative

εἰλήφειν   εἰλήφειμεν
εἰλήφεις   εἰλήφειτε
εἰλήφει   εἰλήφεισαν

163. LIST OF SECOND PERFECTS AND PLUPERFECTS.

Present	Perfect	Pluperfect
ἀκούω	ἀκήκοα	ἠκηκόειν
---	ἐλήλυθα	ἠληλύθειν
λαμβάνω	εἴληφα	εἰλήφειν
πέμπω	πέπομφα	ἐπεπόμφειν

164. EXERCISES.

a. Translate #159.

b. Translate into Greek.

1) We had heard about the fear of Abram.
2) She had received a son.
3) Fear had remained in the village.
4) They had sent a messenger concerning their fear.
5) I had not served because you had fear.
6) Had you (sing.) believed God?
7) Abram's son's sons have believed the promise.   ἐγγονοὶ τοῦ Αβραμ ἐπίστευσαν?

c. Form the corresponding pluperfects.

1) πέπωκα ἐπεπώκειν   3) πέπομφας ἐπεπόμφεις

2) ἐληλύθασι ἐληλύθεισαν εἰλήφεισαν   4) δεδούλευκε ἐδεδουλεύκει

65

5) ἠλπίκαμεν *ἠλπίκειμεν*   9) ἀκηκόαμεν *ἠκηκόειν*

6) πεπιστεύκατε *πεπιστεύκειτε*   10) ἠλπίκατε *ἠλπίκειτε*

7) εἰλήφασι *εἰλήφεισαν*   11) ἀπέσταλκας *ἀπεστάλκει*

8) πεπώκατε *πεπώκειτε*

d. Review the kinds of action presented by tense.

Kind of action	Symbol	Tense
Progression	a line (———)	present and imperfect
Occurrence	a point (·)	aorist
Completion + result	line-point-line (——— · ———)	perfect and pluperfect

e. Associate the following English words with new Greek words in this lesson.

1) Anglophobe: one who has a fear or dislike of things English.
2) phobia: an unreasonable fear.
3) hydrophobia: fear of water.
4) theology: a systematic study of God.

LESSON 20

165. WHAT DO YOU KNOW ABOUT ABRAM?

α. τίς ἦν Αβραμ;

of a certain
υἱὸς ἀνθρώπου τινὸς ἐν τῇ Μεσοποταμίᾳ ἦν Αβραμ.

β. ἐν τίνι γῇ ἦν Αβραμ ὅτε ἦν τέκνον;

ἐν γῇ τινι, Μεσοποταμίᾳ, ἔμενεν οὗτος ὅτε ἦν τέκνον.

5   γ. τίς ἦν Σαρα;

ἡ γυνὴ ἦν αὕτη τοῦ Αβραμ.

δ. τί ἦλθεν Αβραμ ἐκ τῆς ἰδίας γῆς;

first pluperf.
εἰρήκει ὁ θεὸς αὐτῷ ἐλθεῖν ἐκ τῆς ἰδίας γῆς, τῆς Μεσοποταμίας,

καὶ εἰς ἄλλην τινὰ γῆν.

acc.   10   ε. εἰς τίνα γῆν ἦλθον Αβραμ καὶ Σαρα;

εἰς γῆν τινα μακρὰν ἦλθον. *1st. sing. +3d. plur. aor. act. or. mid.*

1st. pers. sing. ζ. μετὰ τίνος ἦλθον εἰς ταύτην τὴν γῆν;
gen.

μετὰ τοῦ Λωτ ἦλθον. *1st. sing. +3d. plur. aor. act. or mid.*

η. τί οὐκ ὁμοῦ ἔμειναν Λωτ καὶ Αβραμ;

15   ἐν τῷ αὐτῷ τόπῳ μένειν οὐκ ἴσχυον οἱ δοῦλοι αὐτῶν καὶ οἱ κάμηλοι

καὶ τὰ πρόβατα.

θ. τίνι θεῷ ἐπεπιστεύκει Αβραμ; *1st. plup.*
dat./1st. pers. sing.

66

τῷ θεῷ τῆς ἀληθείας ἐπεπιστεύκει Αβραμ, ἀλλὰ οἱ ἄνθρωποι ἐν τῇ

Μεσοποταμίᾳ οὐκ ἐπεπιστεύκεισαν τῇ ἀληθείᾳ περὶ τοῦ θεοῦ.

166. VOCABULARY.

τίς, τί: who? which? what? (τί may mean "why?")

τις, τι: (masc. and fem.) one, anyone, someone, a certain; (neut.)
anything, something

167. INTERROGATIVE PRONOUN AND ADJECTIVE.

Masc. & Fem.		Neuter
	Singular	
τίς		τί
τίνος		τίνος
τίνι		τίνι
τίνα		τί
	Plural	
τίνες		τίνα
τίνων		τίνων
τίσι		τίσι
τίνας		τίνα

The interrogative pronoun and adjective always has an acute accent.

Used as a pronoun τίς in any of its forms serves as a substantive.

τίς ἦν Αβραμ;
Who was Abram?

Used as an adjective τίς in any of its forms modifies a noun.

τίς γυνὴ ἦν ἡ Μαρίᾱ;
Which woman was Mary?

168. INDEFINITE PRONOUN AND ADJECTIVE.

Masc. & Fem.		Neuter
	Singular	
τις		τι
τινός		τινός
τινί		τινί
τινά		τι
	Plural	
τινές		τινά
τινῶν		τινῶν
τισί		τισί
τινάς		τινά

The indefinite pronoun and adjective is enclitic in all its forms and
subject to the restrictions of that class of words, as will be explained in #170. Except for its accent the indefinite τις is declined
just like the interrogative τίς.

Used as a pronoun τις in any of its forms serves as a substantive.

ἦν τις ἐν τῇ κώμῃ.
Someone was in the village.

Used as an adjective τὶς in any of its forms modifies a noun.

ἦν ὑπηρέτης τις ἐν κώμῃ τινί.
There was a certain attendant in a certain village.

169.　PROCLITICS.　Certain Greek words such as αἱ, εἰς, ἐκ, ἐν, ἡ, ὁ, οἱ, οὐ, οὐκ, and οὐχ have no accents of their own and are each pronounced with the word immediately following.

ὁ δοῦλος οὐκ ἦν ἡ ἀδελφή.
The slave was not the sister.

These words are called proclitics.　(Cf. προκλίνειν, to lean forward.)

170.　ENCLITICS.　Certain Greek words, such as the forms of the indefinite τὶς in most instances do not retain their own accent, but are each pronounced with the word immediately preceding.

ἀδελφή τις ἦν.
There was a certain sister.

These words are called enclitics.　(Cf. ἐγκλίνειν, to lean on.)

a.　The accent of the enclitic is retained in the following situations:

1)　If it contains two syllables and follows a word with an acute on the penult.

κώμῃ τινί, for a certain village

2)　If it contains two syllables and follows a proclitic.

ἐν τινί κώμῃ, in a certain village

3)　When it is emphasized, as at the beginning of a sentence.

τὶς ἦν ἐν τῇ κώμῃ, someone was in the village

b.　The accent of the enclitic is placed as an acute on the ultima of the preceding word in the following situations:

1)　When the preceding word is proclitic (except in the situation described above).

εἴς τι σπήλαιον, into a certain cave

2)　When the preceding word is accented on the antepenult.

ἀλήθειά τις, a certain truth

3)　When the preceding word is accented with a circumflex on the penult.

κῶμαί τινες, certain villages

c.　In the remaining instances the accent of the enclitic is lost altogether:

1)　When it consists of one syllable and follows a word accented with an acute on the penult.

τόπος τις, a certain place

2)　When it follows a word accented on the ultima. (If the accent of the preceding word is an acute, it remains an acute before the enclitic contrary to the general principle.)

ἀδελφή τις, a certain sister
ἀδελφάς τινας, certain sisters
ἀδελφῆς τινος, of a certain sister

171. EXERCISES.

a. Translate #165.

b. Put correct accents and breathings on the following words.

1) ἄνθρωποί τινες ἦσαν υἱοί.

τίς
to whom, sing. 2) τίς θεραπεύσει κακὴν κώμην;

3) *τίνι* τίνι επεμψατε τον γεωργον;

4) ἀκούσομεν τὸν ἄγγελόν τινος. *a certain*

5) τί βλεπομεν τον τοπον;

c. Ask a question in Greek beginning with each of the following words.

1) τίς *ἦν ἐν τῷ οἴκῳ;*   5) τινά *εἰς τὴν κώμην;*
2) τίνος *ἐν τῷ κήπου;*   6) τινῶν *δωρεὰ ἐστιν;*
3) τίνι *εἰς τὴν κῆπον;*   7) τισί *δώσεις δωρεάν;*
4) τίνα *δώσομεν τὸ δῶρον;*   8) τί *εἰ ὧδε; ὧδε;*

d. The following table indicates shift, loss, or preservation of accent on enclitics.

Description of word preceding enclitic	Effect on accent of	
	monosyllabic enclitic	dissyllabic enclitic
Acute on antepenult	Shifted	Shifted
Circumflex on penult	Shifted	Shifted
Acute on penult	Lost	Kept
Acute or circumflex on ultima	Lost	Lost
Proclitic	Shifted	Kept
Enclitic	Lost	Lost
No word	Kept	Kept

e. Translate into English.

1) τίνων τὴν δωρεὰν ἀπεστάλκειν; *whose gifts did we send*

2) τίσι δωρεὰς πέμψομεν; *to whom will we send the gifts?*

3) τίνας δωρεὰς ἐλπίεττε λαβεῖν; *whose gift do you hope to take?*

4) τίνα βλέπετε ἐν τῷ σπηλαίῳ; *whom did you see in the cave?*

5) τίνες οἴσουσί τινα εἰς τὸ σπήλαιον; *who were the ones carried into the cave?*

6) τίνων ἡ χρείᾱ ἦν μικρά; *whose need was small?*

7) ἐν τίσι κώμαις ἠσθίομεν; *in what villages did we eat?*

8) τίνας ἀδελφὰς εἴληφας; *what sisters did you take*

9) τίνες ἦσαν αἱ ἀδελφαὶ ἐν τῇ Μεσοποταμίᾳ; *who were the sisters in Mesopotamia*

what place do they 10) τίνας τόπους ἐλπίζουσι βλέψαι; *expect to see?*

f. Translate the English in parentheses by one Greek word.

1) ἀπεστάλκειν τὴν δωρεᾶν (belonging to certain men). *τινῶν*
2) πέμψομεν δωρεάς (to certain women). *τισί*

69

3) δωρεᾶς (some) ἐλπίεττε λαβεῖν.
4) βλέπετέ (certain things) ἐν τῷ σπηλαίῳ;
5) τίνα οἴσουσί (some people) εἰς τὸ σπήλαιον;
6) ἡ χρείᾱ (of some persons) μικρὰ ἦν.
7) ἠσθίομεν ἔν (certain) κώμαις.
8) πέπομφάς (certain) ἀδελφάς.
9) ἦσάν (certain) ἀδελφαὶ ἐν τῇ Μεσοποταμίᾳ.
10) ἐλπίζουσι βλέψαι τόπους (certain).
11) ἐφάγετε πρόβατά (some).
12) ἤγαγον τέκνα (certain) εἰς τὸν οἶκον.

LESSON 21

172. JOSEPH'S FUTURE IN EGYPT.

ὅτε ᾿Ιωσὴφ ἔρχεται εἰς τὴν γῆν Αἰγύπτου, γενήσεται δοῦλος Αἰγυπτίου τινὸς ἀλλὰ οὐ μένει ἐν τῷ οἴκῳ τούτου. μετὰ δὲ τοῦτο
᾿Ιωσὴφ γενήσεται ὑπηρέτης τοῦ Φαραώ. τότε ἑπτὰ ἔτη ᾿Ιωσὴφ καὶ οἱ δοῦλοι τοῦ Φαραὼ συνάξουσι σῖτον. ὅτε δὲ μετὰ τὰ ἑπτὰ ἔτη σῖτος οὐκέτι
5 ἔσται τοῖς γεωργοῖς τῆς γῆς Αἰγύπτου, τότε ᾿Ιωσήφ, ὁ ὑπηρέτης τοῦ
Φαραώ, ἕξει σῖτον τοῖς Αἰγυπτίοις καὶ τοῖς ἄλλοις.

ἐλεύσονται γὰρ ἐκ ἄλλων τόπων εἰς ταύτην τὴν γῆν. οὗτοι δὲ
λήμψονται σῖτον καὶ ἐροῦσι, "νῦν φαγόμεθα. νῦν οὐκ ἀποθανούμεθα."
καὶ οἱ ἀδελφοὶ τοῦ ᾿Ιωσὴφ ἐλεύσονται ὅτι ἕξουσι χρείᾱν σίτου.
10 ἐπιγνώσεται οὖν ἐκείνους οὗτος. ἀλλὰ ἐκεῖνοι τὸν ἀδελφὸν ᾿Ιωσήφ, τὸν
ὑπηρέτην τοῦ Φαραώ, οὐκ ἐπιγνώσονται.

ὅτε ἐκεῖνοι ἐλεύσονται ἐκ τῆς Αἰγύπτου ἐνεγκεῖν τὸν σῖτον πρὸς
τὰ τέκνα εἰς τὴν ἄλλην γῆν, τότε ὁ ᾿Ιωσήφ, ὁ ὑπηρέτης τοῦ Φαραώ,
λήμψεταί τινα τῶν ἀδελφῶν καὶ ἕξει αὐτόν. καὶ τότε ἐροῦσιν οἱ ἀδελ-
15 φοί, "τοῦτο γίνεται ὅτι ἐπέμψαμεν ᾿Ιωσὴφ δοῦλον εἰς τὴν Αἴγυπτον."
οἱ ἄλλοι οὖν ἐλεύσονται ἐκ τῆς Αἰγύπτου εἰς τὴν ἄλλην γῆν.

173. VOCABULARY.

ἀποθνῆσκω, ἀποθανοῦμαι, ἀπέθανον: I die

γίνομαι, γενήσομαι, (aor. later), γέγονα: I come into being, am
    born, am made, am ordained, become, come to pass, happen

ἐπιγινώσκω, ἐπιγνώσομαι, (aor. later), ἐπέγνωκα: I observe, perceive,
recognize, know

ἑπτά (indecl.): seven

ἑπτὰ ἔτη (neut. nom. or acc. pl.): seven years, for seven years

ἔρχομαι, ἐλεύσομαι, ἦλθον, ἐλήλυθα: I come, go

ἐσθίω, φάγομαι, ἔφαγον: I eat

ἔσομαι: I shall be

ἔτη (neut. nom. or acc. pl.): years

'Ιωσήφ (indecl.), ὁ: Joseph

λαμβάνω, λήμψομαι, ἔλαβον, εἴληφα: I take, receive, seize

σῖτος, -ου, ὁ: wheat, corn, grain, food

συνάγω, συνάξω, συνήγαγον, ---: I gather, bring together

174. MIDDLE VOICE: ITS MEANING.

a. In defective verbs. A Greek verb which has all the forms that
theoretically belong to it has three voices---active, middle, and
passive. In all the lessons before this one verbs have been in
the active voice. With the story in #172 middle forms have been
introduced. Later, passive forms will be used. Now some Greek
verbs have in use only a part of the forms that are theoretically
possible. A verb may, for instance, use a middle future like
λήμψομαι in λαμβάνω without ever using a corresponding active
form. λαμβάνω, then, is said to be defective in the future tense.
But the meaning of the future of λαμβάνω is not influenced at all
by the use of middle forms. λήμψομαι means "I shall take." Besides the future of λαμβάνω this lesson introduces several other
examples of defective verbs. We find γίνομαι and ἔρχομαι defective
in their present and future. We also find ἀποθνήσκω, εἰμί, ἐπιγινώσκω, and ἐσθίω defective in the future. Further notice will
be taken of ἀποθνήσκω and ἐσθίω.

b. In complete verbs. When a Greek verb is not defective, the middle
forms convey meanings different from those conveyed by active
forms. The action of the verb is presented by the middle as being
performed by the subject and as taking effect on the subject or on
something more or less closely related to the subject. At any
rate, the subject is shown to be more involved in the action of the
verb than is the subject of an active form. None of this kind of
middle was used in #172, but it will appear in the exercises.

βλεπόμεθα, we see ourselves.

πέμψεται τὸν ἄγγελον, he will send his own messenger (or)
he will send the messenger for himself.

175. MIDDLE VOICE: ITS FORMS.

a. Present Middle Indicative: ἔρχομαι

ἔρχομαι	ἐρχόμεθα
ἔρχῃ	ἔρχεσθε
ἔρχεται	ἔρχονται

To the verb stem ἐρχ- are added (1) the tense suffix which is here
the variable vowel -ο/ε- and (2) the primary middle personal endings.

71

These primary middle personal endings are:

-μαι	-μεθα
-σαι	-σθε
-ται	-νται

The second singular -σαι appears unchanged only in the perfect (to be given later). Elsewhere (except #177, 417, 418) the -σ- has been lost, resulting in the contracted ending -ῃ.

b. Present Middle Infinitive of ἔρχομαι: ἔρχεσθαι.

This form is composed of the verb stem plus the tense suffix plus the middle infinitive ending.

c. Future Middle Indicative: ἔρχομαι.

ἐλεύσομαι	ἐλευσόμεθα
ἐλεύσῃ	ἐλεύσεσθε
ἐλεύσεται	ἐλεύσονται

To the verb stem ἐλευ- are added (1) the tense suffix -σο/ε- and (2) the primary middle personal endings. ἐλεύσῃ represents a shortening of ἐλεύσεσαι by the loss of the second -σ- and by the contraction of -ε- and -αι.

d. Future Middle Indicative: εἰμί.

ἔσομαι	ἐσόμεθα
ἔσῃ	ἔσεσθε
ἔσται	ἔσονται

The third singular form ἔσται has lost the -ε- before the -τ-.

176. MIDDLE OF LIQUID AND NASAL FUTURES.

Indicative

ἀποθανοῦμαι	ἀποθανούμεθα
ἀποθανῇ	ἀποθανεῖσθε
ἀποθανεῖται	ἀποθανοῦνται

These forms represent shortenings of the following, which are <u>not</u> in use:

ἀποθανέσομαι	ἀποθανεσόμεθα
ἀποθανέσεσαι	ἀποθανέσεσθε
ἀποθανέσεται	ἀποθανέσονται

The -σ- in the tense suffix (and in the second singular both -σ-'s) drops out and the vowel thus brought together are contracted.

ε+ο=ου	ε+ε=ει	ε+αι=ῃ

177. FUTURE OF ἐσθίω AND πίνω.

φάγομαι	φαγόμεθα	πίομαι	πιόμεθα
φάγεσαι	φάγεσθε	πίεσαι	πίεσθε
φάγεται	φάγονται	πίεται	πίονται

These forms have no sign of the future tense, and yet they are future.

178. EXERCISES.

a. Translate #172.

b. Translate the following expressions which contain verbs with middle meanings. *fut. act. or mid.*

1) πιστεύσεσθε; *fut. act. or mid. 2 per. pl. ὁμεθα οντ̓αι σομαι ση σεται*

2) οὐ φονευόμεθα. *pres. act. or mid. 1 per. pl.*

3) διώκονται περὶ τὸν οἶκον. *fut. mid. ind. 3 per. pl.*

4) ἀκούῃ, τέκνον; *fut. act. or mid.*

5) οἱ κάμηλοι ἀπολοῦνται. *fut. mid. ind. 3 per. pl.*

6) βλέπεσθε, ὑπηρέται. *fut. mid. ind. 2 per. pl.*

7) ἐσθίεσθε τὸν σῖτον, ἄνθρωποι. *fut. mid.*

8) ἰσχύσουσι πέμπεσθαι τὰ τέκνα. *pres. mid. inf.*

9) θεραπεύσομαι. *fut. mid. ?*

10) πῶς φέρεσθε; *mid. ?*

c. Translate into Greek, distinguishing between what should be expressed by an active and what by a defective middle.

1) I am coming. *ἔρχομαι*
2) Will you be eating, Philip? *φαγεσαι, Φιλιππε;*
3) Can you eat yourselves, slaves? *ἐσθίεσθε, δοῦλοι;*
4) We shall become noble. *ἐσόμεθα καλόν; ἐσεσθε καλόν; θερου*
5) How will you become noble? *πῶς ἐσῃ;*
6) Perhaps noble slaves will become free men. *ταχα ἔσονται καλοι δοῦλοι ἐλεύ⁵*
7) We shall come into the garden. *ἐρχομεθα εἰς τὸν κηπον*
8) Will you die? No, you will not die, Mark. *ἀποθανῃ; οὐ ἀποθανῃ, Μαρκε.*
9) Mary, you will recognize Lazarus. *Μαρια, ἐπιγνωσῃ Λαζαρον*
10) He will be in the Jordan. *ἔσται εἰς τὸν Ἰορδανην*
11) Mary will not die. *Μαρια οὐκ ἀποθανεῖται.*
12) Mary and Mark will not die. *Μαρια και Μαρκε οὐκ ἀποθανεῖσθε.*
13) Mary and Mark, you will not die. *ἀποθανοῦνται*

d. Translate the following middles, some of which are defective.

1) λημψόμεθα σῖτον; *shall we eat grain!*

2) τίς ἐπιγνώσεται τὰ τέκνα μετὰ ἑπτὰ ἔτη; *who will recognize the children after 7 yrs?*

3) φάγεσαι ἄρτον ἑπτὰ ἔτη. *you will eat bread for 7 yrs.*

4) ἐλεύσεσθε ἐκ τῆς γῆς ἐκείνης καὶ εἰς ταύτην. *you will depart out of this land and into the other*

5) ἔρχῃ εἰς τοῦτον τὸν οἶκον; *you will go into this house*

6) γενήσομαι βασιλεύς; *will I become king?*

7) οὐκ ἀποθανούμεθα μετὰ ἑπτὰ ἔτη. *we shall not die after 7 yrs.*

8) γίνεταί τις δοῦλος; *will someone become slave?*

9) συνάξῃ κακοὺς εἰς τὴν Αἴγυπτον. *bring together the bad ones into Egypt.*

10) οἱ κακοὶ ὑπηρέται συνάγονται. *they brought the bad ones together*

11) ἰσχύσετε συνάγεσθαι; *will you be able to gather?*

perfect 12) γέγονα καλός, ἀλλὰ ἀποθανοῦμαι. *I became well, but I shall die*

13) μετὰ ἑπτὰ ἔτη ἐπιγνώσῃ τὸν ἀδελφὸν σου. *after 7 yrs. you will recognize yr. b.*

73

def. v. mid. voice 14) φάγεσθε σῖτον· ἐγὼ δὲ ἀρνίον φάγομαι. *fut. of ἐσθίω, 1st. per. sing.*

εἴωθε οὐμεθα 15) πῶς ἀποθανοῦνται οἱ Αἰγύπτιοι; *mid. voice, fut. of liqu. + nasal verbs, 3per. plu.*
οὖμαι ῆ εἶται liqu. + nasal

e. Conjugate, making necessary changes.

fut. of ἔρχομαι 1) ἐλεύσομαι εἰς τὴν γῆν ταύτην;   5) ἔσομαι ὑπηρέτης.
def. v. pl. ind. mid. 1 st.
per. sing.
fut. mid. ind. 2) ἐπιγνώσομαι τοῦτον τὸν τόπον.   6) φάγομαι καλὸν ἄρτον.
pres. mid. ind. 3) ἔρχομαι πρὸς τὸν κύριον.   7) οὐ πίομαι σῖτον.
liqu. + nasal mid. fut. 4) ἀποθανοῦμαι ἐν ἐκείνῳ τῷ οἴκῳ.

f. Give one correct possible location for each ending.

1) -ῃ   6) ἐλεύ-σεται   11) -ούμαι
2) -εῖται   7) -ομαι   12) -όμεθα
3) -εσαι   8) ἐλεύ-σομαι   13) -εῖσθε
4) -σῃ   9) ἐλευ-σόμεθα   14) -οῦνται
5) -εται   10) -ούμεθα

g. Associate the following English words with Greek words in the vocabulary of this lesson.

1) **genesis**: a coming into being.
2) **heptagon**: a seven-sided geometric figure.
3) **bacteriophage**: something that eats bacteria.
4) **etesian winds**: winds that blow each year at a certain season.
5) **sitophobia**: fear or dislike of food.

LESSON 22

179. I NEED TO LEARN EGYPTIAN.

ὁ Αἰγύπτιος διδάσκαλος: "τίς εἶ σὺ ἐκεῖ ἐν τοῖς μαθηταῖς ἐμοῦ;"

ὁ μαθητὴς Ἰωσήφ: "δοῦλος ἐγὼ εἰμι ἐν τῷ οἴκῳ Αἰγυπτίου ἐλευθέρου.

δοῦλός εἰμι σήμερον, ἀλλ' αὔριον ἐλεύθερος γίνεσθαι ἐλπίζω."

ὁ διδάσκαλος: "τί εἶ σὺ ὧδε ἐν τῇ σχολῇ ταύτῃ;"

5   ὁ μαθητής: "τὴν γλῶσσαν τὴν Αἰγυπτίαν μανθάνειν θέλω λίαν. ὅτε
     ἐλεύθερος ἔσομαι, λέγειν ὑμῖν Αἰγυπτίοις ἐν ταῖς συναγωγαῖς ὑμῶν
     χρείαν ἕξω. ἀλλ' ὅτε ἦν ἐγὼ μικρὸν τέκνον, τὴν Αἰγυπτίαν γλῶσσαν
     οὐκ ἔμαθον. διὰ τοῦτο, διδάσκαλε, ὧδέ εἰμι."

     ὁ διδάσκαλος: "οὐ θέλεις οὖν τὴν γλῶσσαν τὴν Ἑλληνικὴν μαθεῖν."

10   ὁ μαθητής: "οὐχί. τίς ἡμῶν ἐν τῇ Αἰγύπτῳ τὴν Ἑλληνικὴν γλῶσσαν
     λέγειν χρείαν ἔχει; οὗτοι οἱ ἄλλοι μαθηταί σου ταύτην τὴν γλῶσσαν
     μαθεῖν οὐ θελήσουσι."

     ὁ διδάσκαλος: "ἐχθὲς ἦν ἐν ἡμῖν μαθητής τις καὶ τὴν Ἑλληνικὴν
     γλῶσσαν μανθάνειν ἤθελε. ἀλλ' ἐκεῖνος νῦν ποῦ ἐστιν; οὐ βλέπω
15   ἐκεῖνον ἐν τῇ σχολῇ ὧδε. μαθηταί μου, ποῦ ἐστιν ὁ μικρὸς μαθητὴς
     τῆς Ἑλληνικῆς γλώσσης;"

     οἱ ἄλλοι μαθηταί: "σοί, διδάσκαλε καλέ, λέγειν οὐ δυνατοί ἐσμεν
     ἡμεῖς. οὐ σήμερον ἐβλέψαμεν αὐτὸν ἡμεῖς. οὐ διὰ τοῦ κήπου τῆς
     σχολῆς ἡμῶν ἦλθε σήμερον. τάχα εἰς ἄλλην σχολὴν ἦλθεν."

20   ὁ διδάσκαλος: "τάχα, ἀλλ' ἦν λίαν μικρός. τέκνον μικρὸν ἦν.
     δοῦλε καλὲ Ἰωσήφ, μετὰ ἐμοῦ οὖν σὺ θέλεις τὴν Αἰγυπτίαν γλῶσσαν
     μανθάνειν; καλὸν ἐστιν. διὰ τὴν χρείαν σου δυνατὸς διδάσκειν
     σε ἐγὼ ἔσομαι. διὰ δὲ τὸ αὐτὸ δυνατὸς ἀκούειν ἐμὲ σὺ ἔσῃ.
     μένε μετὰ ἡμῶν ὧδε."

180. VOCABULARY.

ἀλλ': ἀλλά with the final vowel elided

αὔριον: tomorrow, on the next day

γλῶσσα, -ης, ἡ: tongue, language (#105)

διά: (with gen.) through, by; (with acc.) because of, on account of

διὰ τὸ αὐτό: for the same reason

διδάσκαλος, -ου, ὁ: teacher

διδάσκω, διδάξω, ἐδίδαξα, --- : I teach (frequently used with a
                 double accusative, one of the person taught and one
                 of the subject matter taught)

δυνατός, -ή, -όν: able, capable, strong, powerful, possible

εἰμί, ἔσομαι, --- , --- : I am

ἐκεῖ: there

Ἑλληνικός, -ή, -όν: Greek

ἐχθές: yesterday

θέλω, θελήσω, ἠθέλησα: I will, am willing, wish, desire
(imperfect ἤθελον)

λίαν: exceedingly, very, **very** much

μαθητής, -οῦ, ὁ: disciple, student, pupil

μανθάνω, --- , ἔμαθον, μεμάθηκα: I learn

ποῦ: where?

συναγωγή, -ῆς, ἡ: assembly, synagogue

σχολή, -ῆς, ἡ: school

ὧδε: here

181. PERSONAL PRONOUNS. In addition to the personal pronouns presented in #127, notice below the unaccented, slightly less emphatic, enclitic forms for the first and second persons, and the words used for the third person.

First Person

Singular		Plural	
ἐγώ	(I)	ἡμεῖς	(we)
ἐμοῦ, μου	(of me)	ἡμῶν	(of us)
ἐμοί, μοι	(for me)	ἡμῖν	(for us)
ἐμέ, με	(me)	ἡμᾶς	(us)

Second Person

σύ	(you)	ὑμεῖς	(you)
σοῦ, σου	(of you)	ὑμῶν	(of you)
σοί, σοι	(for you)	ὑμῖν	(for you)
σέ, σε	(you)	ὑμᾶς	(you)

Third Person

The demonstratives οὗτος and ἐκεῖνος, and αὐτός may be used as personal pronouns in all their forms.

182. CONJUGATION OF εἰμί: I am.

Present Indicative

εἰμί	ἐσμέν
εἶ	ἐστέ
ἐστί(ν)	εἰσί(ν)

All these forms except the second singular, εἶ, are enclitic.

Present Imperative

ἴσθι	ἔστε
ἔστω	ἔστωσαν

Present Infinitive: εἶναι

Imperfect Indicative

ἤμην	ἦμεν or ἤμεθα
ἦς	ἦτε
ἦν	ἦσαν

The forms ἤμην and ἤμεθα are middle without influencing the meaning.

Future Indicative

ἔσομαι	ἐσόμεθα
ἔσῃ	ἔσεσθε
ἔσται	ἔσονται

This verb is defective in the future.

This verb is a -μι verb (so designated from the ending in the form εἰμί). Other verbs of this type will be met, but this is the one most frequently used. The peculiarities of -μι verbs appear in the present, imperfect, and aorist. But εἰμί has no tenses except the present, imperfect, and future.

183. CASE: ACCUSATIVE OF DOUBLE DIRECT OBJECT. In the sentence διδάσκομεν ὑμᾶς τὴν γλῶσσαν τὴν Ἑλληνικήν, "we teach you the Greek language," both ὑμᾶς and γλῶσσαν are accusative direct objects of διδάσκομεν. The one represents the persons, the other the subject matter directly affected by the action of the verb. This construction is used with other verbs besides διδάσκω.

184. EXERCISES.

a. Translate #179.

b. Conjugate the verbs in the following patterns, changing everything that needs to be changed for each new form.
   For example: σὺ ἴσθι δυνατός
   οὗτος ἔστω δυνατός
   ὑμεῖς ἔστε δυνατοί
   οὗτοι ἔστωσαν δυνατοί

   1) ὁ διδάσκαλός εἰμι σήμερον.
   2) ἐγὼ οὐκ ἔσομαι ἄγγελος αὔριον.
   3) δοῦλος ἐκεῖ ἤμην ἐγὼ ἐχθές.
   4) ἐν τῇ σχολῇ διὰ τὸ αὐτό εἰμι.
   5) ἴσθι μαθητὴς καλός.
   6) Πέτρε, ἴσθι ὧδε αὔριον.

c. Translate into Greek.

   1) Be a good child, Mary.
   2) Yes, let Mary be good.
   3) Be good children, Mary and Sarai.
   4) Yes, let Mary and Sarai be good.
   5) Do you want to be good, my child?
   6) I do not want to be good today, but I shall want to be good tomorrow.
   7) Mary and Sarai wanted to be good yesterday.
   8) Where is Lazarus?
   9) I am here to learn.
   10) Where are Peter and Philip?
   11) They are not here for the same reason.
   12) Peter and Philip, where are you?
   13) Peter is in the school.
   14) Philip was there yesterday, but he was not happy.
   15) Let them be in the same school tomorrow.

d. Associate the following English words with new Greek words in this lesson.

1) glossal: related to the tongue.
2) didactic: related to teaching.
3) dynamo: a machine capable of producing electrical power.
4) mathematics: a science made up of things learned and therefore known about exact quantitative relationships.
5) glossectomy: a surgical removal of the tongue.
6) chrestomathy: a collection of passages useful for learning a
language.
7) Hellenic: related to Classical Greek culture.
8) scholar: one who goes to school.
9) synagogue: a place where Jews gather together for worship.

LESSON 23

185. RELUCTANTLY JACOB LETS BENJAMIN GO TO EGYPT.

ἐπεὶ εἶχε Ἰακὼβ πάλιν χρείᾱν σίτου, εἶπε τοῖς υἱοῖς, "ἐρχέσθωσαν

οἱ υἱοί μου εἰς τὴν Αἴγυπτον πάλιν. ἐνεγκέτωσαν σῖτον καὶ φαγόμεθα

καὶ οὐκ ἀποθανούμεθα."

οἱ δὲ υἱοὶ ἐμνημόνευσαν τοῦ κυρίου τῆς Αἰγύπτου καὶ εἶπον τῷ

5 Ἰακὼβ, "ἡμεῖς οὐκ ἐσόμεθα δυνατοὶ βλέψαι τὸν κύριον τῆς Αἰγύπτου.

ἐρχέσθω οὖν ὁ Βενιαμίν, ὁ νεώτερος υἱός σου, σὺν ἡμῖν. ὁ γὰρ κύριος

ἐκείνης τῆς γῆς ἡμῖν εἴρηκε, 'ἔρχεσθε μετὰ τοῦ ἀδελφοῦ ὑμῶν τοῦ νεω-

τέρου, ἢ οὐ βλέψετε ὑμεῖς ἐμέ.'"

τότε οὖν ἐμνημόνευεν Ἰακὼβ ὅτι πάλαι ἡ γυνὴ Ῥαχὴλ ἔσχε υἱούς,

10 Ἰωσὴφ καὶ Βενιαμίν, τὸν νεώτερον. ἀλλὰ πάλαι Ῥαχὴλ ἀπέθανε καὶ ὁ

Ἰωσὴφ ἀπεληλύθει, καὶ πάλαι ὁ Ἰακὼβ εἰρήκει, "ἀπέθανε Ἰωσήφ, καὶ

αὐτὸν οὐ βλέψω πάλιν."

εἶπεν δὲ Ἰακὼβ πρὸς τοὺς υἱούς, "οὐκ ἐλεύσεται Βενιαμίν, ὁ νεώ-

τερος υἱὸς τῆς Ῥαχήλ."

15 ἀλλ' εἶπεν ὁ Ἰούδας πρὸς Ἰακώβ, "ἐγὼ ἄξω αὐτὸν πρὸς σε πάλιν."

ὅτι οὖν εἶπε τοῦτο ὁ Ἰούδας καὶ ὅτι ἦν οὐ μικρᾷ χρείᾱ σίτου,

εἶπεν Ἰακώβ, "ἐρχέσθω Βενιαμὶν μετὰ τῶν ἄλλων υἱῶν."

ἡ δὲ καρδίᾱ τοῦ Ἰακὼβ οὐκ ἦν μακαρίᾱ ὅτε ἀπῆλθεν ὁ υἱὸς ὁ νεώ-

τερος τῆς Ῥαχήλ.

186. VOCABULARY.

ἀπέρχομαι, ἀπελεύσομαι, ἀπῆλθον, ἀπελήλυθα: I go **away**, depart from

Βενιαμίν (indecl.), ὁ: Benjamin

Ἰακώβ (indecl.), ὁ: Jacob

Ἰούδας, -α, (-ᾳ, -αν, -α), ὁ: Judah, Judas

νεώτερος, -ᾱ, -ον: newer, younger, (or in harmony with Hellenistic
usage) youngest

πάλαι: long ago, of old, in past time

Ῥαχήλ (indecl.), ἡ: Rachel

187. PRESENT MIDDLE IMPERATIVE.

a. In defective verbs.

ἔρχου: go
ἐρχέσθω: let him go
ἔρχεσθε: go
ἐρχέσθωσαν: let them go

These forms, although middle in spelling, are active in meaning
since ἔρχομαι is a defective verb.

b. In complete verbs

δουλεύου: **serve yourself**
δουλευέσθω: let him **serve himself**
δουλεύεσθε: **serve yourselves**
δουλευέσθωσαν: let them serve themselves.

These forms carry distinct middle meanings.

188. EXERCISES.

a. Translate #185 into English.

b. Translate into Greek.

1) Go away, Benjamin, son of Rachel. *ἀπέρχου, Βενιαμίν, υἱὸς Ῥαχήλ.*
2) Let Judah come again. *ἐρχέσθω Ἰούδας πάλιν.*
3) Judah and Benjamin, stop departing. *Ἰούδας καὶ Βενιαμίν, οὐκ ἀπέρχεσθε*
4) Rachel went away long ago to another land. *Ῥαχὴλ ἀπῆλθε πάλαι εἰς ἄλλην γῆν.*
5) Let Rachel serve herself. *8 οὐκ ἀπέρχου! Ῥαχήλ.*
6) Serve yourselves, sons of Judah. *δουλεύεσθε, υἱοὶ Ἰούδας.*
7) Long ago Jacob said, "Go away to Egypt, Judah." *πάλαι Ἰακὼβ εἶπεν, ἀπέρχου*
8) Do not go away, Rachel. *δουλευέσθω Ῥαχήλ! 75. [εἰς τὴν Αἴγυπτον, Ἰούδας.*
9) Let the Egyptians go away. *ἐρχέσθωσαν οἱ Αἰγύπτιοι.*
10) Become a strong man. *ἔση Ἰυνατός·*

c. Locate by giving (1) tense, (2) mood, (3) voice, (4) person,
(5) number, and (6) first principal part.

ἄγω · ἄξω · ἤγαγον	1)	*pres. impv. act.* συνάγεσθε *2 pers. plur.*	*ἀποστέλλω* 6)	*pres. impv. mid. 3p. pl.* ἀποστέλλεσθε
ἄγω · ἄξω · ἤχθην				
ἔρχομαι	2)	*pres. impv. mid. 3p. pl.* ἐρχέσθωσαν	*ἀποκτείνω* 7)	*pres. impv. mid. 3p. pl.* ἀποκτεινέσθωσαν
ἀπέρχομαι	3)	*pres. impv. mid. 2p. sın.* ἀπέρχου		8)	*Fut. mid. ind. 3p. sing.* φάγεται
			φάγομαι	
γίνομαι	4)	*pres. impv. mid. 3p. pl.* γινέσθωσαν	*ἐλεύσομαι* 9)	*Fut. ind. mid. 2p. sing.* ἐλεύσῃ
λαμβάνομαι	5)	*pres. impv. mid. 2p. pl.* λήμψεσθε	*ἐπιγινώσκω* 10)	*aor. impv. mid. 3p. sing.* ἐπιγινωσκέσθω

79

d. Associate the following English words with the new Greek words presented recently.

    1) <u>Jacobite</u>: a supporter in England of James II (in Latin, <u>Jacobus</u>, derived from Greek).
    2) <u>paleo</u>: a prefix used in technical scientific terms to mean "related to the distant past, <u>long ago</u>."

LESSON 24

189. TABLE OF SOME RELATED GROUPS OF VERB ENDINGS. (Full inflections are given in the appendix, #412 forward.)

Indicative Active				Indicative Middle		
Perf. (1st)	Perf. (2nd)	Plperf. (1st)	Plperf. (2nd)	Pres.	Future (usual)	Future (liq. & nasal)
-κα	-α	-κειν	-ειν	-ομαι	-σομαι	-οῦμαι
-κας	-ας	-κεις	-εις	-ῃ	-σῃ	-ῇ
-κε	-ε	-κει	-ει	-εται	-σεται	-εῖται
-καμεν	-αμεν	-κειμεν	-ειμεν	-όμεθα	-σόμεθα	-ούμεθα
-κατε	-ατε	-κειτε	-ειτε	-εσθε	-σεσθε	-εῖσθε
-κᾶσι	-ᾶσι	-κεισαν	-εισαν	-ονται	-σονται	-οῦνται
Infinitive Active				Infinitive Middle		
-κέναι	-έναι	None	None	-εσθαι	Rare -σεσθαι	Rare -εῖσθαι
Imperative Active				Imperative Middle		
None	None	None	None	-ου -έσθω -εσθε -έσθωσαν	None	None

190. LOCATION DRILL. Locate the following verb forms by giving (1) tense, (2) mood, (3) voice, (4) person, (5) number, and (6) first principal part.

a. ἀποθανοῦνται

b. ἔστε

c. ἐστέ

d. φάγεται

e. ἔρχῃ

f. ἐλεύσεσθε

g. ἔσται

h. ἀπελήλυθας

i. πιστευσόμεθα

j. ἴσθι

k. εἰρήκειτε

n. ἐσθίειν

l. δουλεύσουσι

o. ἀπέστειλαν

m. λεγέτω

p. ἔσθιε

191. VOCABULARY. Review thoroughly the vocabulary introduced since Lesson 18.

NOUNS	VERBS	ADVERBS
Βενιαμίν	ἀπέρχομαι	αὔριον
γλῶσσα	ἀποθανοῦμαι	διὰ τὸ αὐτό
διδάσκαλος	γίνομαι	ἐκεῖ
ἔτη	διδάσκω	ἐχθές
θεός	ἐπιγινώσκω	λίαν
Ἰακώβ	ἔρχομαι	πάλαι
Ἰούδας	ἔσομαι	ποῦ
Ἰωσήφ	θέλω	ὧδε
μαθητής	λήμψομαι	
Ῥαχήλ	μανθάνω	PREPOSITION
σῖτος	πιστεύω	
συναγωγή	συνάγω	διά
σχολή		
υἱός		ADJECTIVES
φόβος		
	PRONOUNS	δυνατός
CONJUNCTION		Ἑλληνικός
	τίς	ἑπτά
ἀλλ'	τὶς	νεώτερος

192. INTERROGATIVES AND INDEFINITES. Use the form of τίς or τὶς suitable for each of the following situations.

a. (Who) διδάξει ἡμᾶς τὴν γλῶσσαν Ἑλληνικήν;

b. ἐμάθετε γλῶσσαν (a certain).

c. υἱός (of someone) οὐκ ἔστι δίκαιος.

d. (To whom) ἀποστελεῖς τοῦτον τὸν ἄγγελον;

e. ἀπὸ (what) κώμης ἀπήλθομεν;

f. τεθεράπευκε ὁ Ἑλληνικὸς ὑπηρέτης (anybody) ἐν ἐκείνῳ τῷ οἴκῳ;

193. PROCLITICS AND ENCLITICS. By reference to #169 and #170 and vocabulary lists accent the following groups of words.

a. τις ἐστιν οὑτος;

b. τινος ἠν ἐκεινη ἡ ἀδελφη;

c. λεγετε τινι φαγειν τουτο το ὀψαριον.

d. βλεπομεν το ἀρνιον τινος ἐν τῳ κηπῳ.

e. ὁ δουλος τεθεραπευκε τινα τεκνα.

194. BENJAMIN FRAMED.

ὅτε πάλιν εἰς τὴν Αἴγυπτον ἤρχοντο οἱ υἱοὶ τοῦ Ἰακώβ, ὁ Ἰωσὴφ ἔβλεψεν αὐτούς, τοὺς ἄλλους καὶ τὸν ἴδιον ἀδελφόν, Βενιαμίν.

ἐνετείλατο οὖν τῷ ἰδίῳ ὑπηρέτῃ, "ἐρχέσθωσαν εἰς τὸν οἶκόν μου οὗτοι, μετ' ἐμοῦ γὰρ φάγονται ἄρτον σήμερον."

5   ἐσχήκει δὲ ὁ Ἰωσὴφ τῶν ἰδίων ἀδελφῶν τινα ὅτε ἐκεῖνοι πρὸς Ἰακὼβ ἤρχοντο καὶ ἔμενον ἐκεῖ καὶ ἦγον Βενιαμὶν εἰς τὴν Αἴγυπτον. ναί, υἱός τις τοῦ Ἰακὼβ ἐμεμενήκει ἐν τῇ Αἰγύπτῳ μετὰ τοῦ Ἰωσήφ. τοῦτον τὸν ἀδελφὸν ἤγαγε πρὸς τοὺς ἄλλους ὁ Ἰωσὴφ καὶ εἶπεν αὐτοῖς ὅτε ἔβλεπε τὸν Βενιαμίν, "οὗτός ἐστιν ὁ ἀδελφὸς ὑμῶν ὁ νεώτερος;"

10   καὶ εἶπον, "ναί."

ἐπεὶ οὖν ἔφαγον ἄρτον ὁμοῦ, ἐνετείλατο τῷ ἰδίῳ ὑπηρέτῃ ὁ Ἰωσήφ, "σχέτωσαν σῖτον οὗτοι. τὸ δὲ ἀργύριον ἑκάστου εἰς τὸν σῖτον βάλε. καὶ εἰς τὸν σῖτον τοῦ νεωτέρου βάλε τὸ ἀργύριον αὐτοῦ καὶ τὸ ἀργυρίου ποτήριον ἐμοῦ." ταῦτα δὲ ἔβαλεν ὁ ὑπηρέτης ποῦ ἐνετείλατο ὁ Ἰωσήφ.

15   αὔριον οὖν ἐκ τῆς γῆς Αἰγύπτου οἱ ἀδελφοὶ ἤρχοντο. ἀλλὰ τότε ὁ Ἰωσὴφ τῷ ἰδίῳ ὑπηρέτῃ εἶπεν, "ἐντέλλομαί σοι διῶξαι τοὺς ἀνθρώπους τούτους. καὶ ἐρεῖς αὐτοῖς, 'τί ἐλάβεσθε τὸ ἀργυρίου ποτήριον τοῦ κυρίου ἐμοῦ; ἐγένεσθε κακοί.'"

ἐδίωξεν οὖν ὁ ὑπηρέτης τοὺς υἱοὺς τοῦ Ἰακώβ, καὶ εἶπεν αὐτοῖς, 20   "τί ἐλάβεσθε τὸ ἀργυρίου ποτήριον;"

οὗτοι δὲ ἔλεγον, "οὐχί. οὐκ ἐλαβόμεθα ἐκεῖνο τὸ ποτήριον. βλέπε τὸν σῖτον ἑκάστου ἡμῶν. οὐ βλέψεις αὐτὸ ἐν τῷ σίτῳ τινὸς ἡμῶν."

"βλέψω," εἶπεν ὁ Αἰγύπτιος, "ἐν τῷ σίτῳ ἑκάστου ὑμῶν."

"τὸ ποτήριόν τις ἕξει; οὗτος ἀποθανέτω, καὶ οἱ ἄλλοι ἀδελφοὶ 25   ἔστωσαν δοῦλοι τοῦ κυρίου σου." ταῦτα ἔλεγον πολλάκις, οὐ γὰρ μακάριοι ἦσαν.

ἔβλεψεν οὖν ὁ ὑπηρέτης τὸν σῖτον ἑκάστου. καὶ τὸ ποτήριον ἦν ἐν τῷ σίτῳ τοῦ νεωτέρου, τοῦ Βενιαμίν. μετὰ τοῦτο οἱ ἀδελφοὶ ἦλθον πάλιν πρὸς τὸν Ἰωσήφ.

195. VOCABULARY.
ἀργύριον, -ου, τό: silver, money
βάλλω, βαλῶ, ἔβαλον, βέβληκα: I throw, cast, put

ἕκαστος, -η, -ον: each, every

ἐντέλλομαι, ἐντελοῦμαι, ἐνετειλάμην: I order, command (with dat. of person and an infinitive)

μετ': μετά with final vowel elided

196. MORE MIDDLE FORMS.

Imperfect Middle Indicative of ἔρχομαι

ἠρχόμην	ἠρχόμεθα
ἤρχου	ἤρχεσθε
ἤρχετο	ἤρχοντο

First Aorist Middle Indicative of δουλεύω

ἐδουλευσάμην	ἐδουλευσάμεθα
ἐδουλεύσω	ἐδουλεύσασθε
ἐδουλεύσατο	ἐδουλεύσαντο

Second Aorist Middle Indicative of γίνομαι

ἐγενόμην	ἐγενόμεθα
ἐγένου	ἐγένεσθε
ἐγένετο	ἐγένοντο

Liquid Aorist Middle Indicative of ἐντέλλομαι

ἐνετειλάμην	ἐνετειλάμεθα
ἐνετείλω	ἐνετείλασθε
ἐνετείλατο	ἐνετείλαντο

197. SECONDARY MIDDLE ENDINGS.

In all the paradigms just presented the secondary middle endings have been used.

-μην	-μεθα
-σο	-σθε
-το	-ντο

The second singular -σο appears unchanged only in the pluperfect (to be given later). Elsewhere the -σ- has been lost and a contraction of vowels has occurred.

	Assumed earlier form	Form in actual use
Imperfect	ἤρχεσο	ἤρχου
1st Aorist	ἐδουλεύσασο	ἐδουλεύσω
2nd Aorist	ἐγένεσο	ἐγένου
Liquid Aorist	ἐνετείλασο	ἐνετείλω

198. EXERCISES.

a. Translate #194.

b. Locate.

1) ἐγίνετο

2) ἐνετείλω

3) ἐβάλου

4) ἀπεστελλόμην

5) ἐροῦμεν

6) ἀπελύσω

7) ἐθεραπεύσασθε

8) πιστεύεσθαι

9) βεβλήκατε

10) βαλοῦνται

11) φάγεσθε

12) βαλοῦσι

13) ἐνετείλαντο

14) ἐθεραπεύσαντο

15) ἐβάλοντο

c. Write a synopsis of ἀπολύω (1) in the third person singular and
(2) in the second person singular. A synopsis is a set of forms
representing the behavior of a verb throughout its conjugation.
Instead of a full inflection, one form is taken as a sample from
each set of six (as in the indicative) or of four (as in the imperative). The following is a synopsis of ἀκούω in the third
plural present and imperfect.

	Active	Middle
Present Indicative:	ἀκούουσι	ἀκούονται
Present Imperative:	ἀκουέτωσαν	ἀκουέσθωσαν
Imperfect Indicative:	ἤκουον	ἠκούοντο

Do this for all tenses, moods, and voices which you have had.

LESSON 26

199. "I AM YOUR BROTHER."

πάλιν οὖν ἦλθεν ὁ Ἰούδας σὺν τοῖς ἑαυτοῦ ἀδελφοῖς πρὸς Ἰωσήφ.
εἶπε δὲ αὐτοῖς Ἰωσήφ, "τί τοῦτο τὸ ποτήριον ἑαυτοῖς ἐλάβετε;"

εἶπε δὲ Ἰούδας, "τί ἐρῶ τῷ κυρίῳ ἐμαυτοῦ; ὁ δὲ θεὸς ἔβλεψεν
ὅτι κακοί εἰσιν οἱ δοῦλοί σου. δοῦλοι σοῦ γὰρ γενησόμεθα, ἡμεῖς καὶ
5   Βενιαμίν."

εἶπε δὲ οὕτως Ἰωσήφ, "οὐ γενήσεσθε ὑμεῖς δοῦλοι ἐμοῦ, ἀλλ'
οὗτος ὁ ἄνθρωπος. ἀντὶ ὑμῶν, ἕξω τοῦτον. οὗτος ἔσται δοῦλος ἐμοῦ.
ὑμεῖς δὲ ἐλεύθεροι ἔσεσθε."

τότε δὲ αὐτῷ Ἰούδας οὕτως εἶπεν, "ὁ κύριος ἐμοῦ ἀκουσάτω τοῦ
10   δούλου ἑαυτοῦ. πάλαι εἴπομεν οὕτως τῷ ἑαυτῶν κυρίῳ. 'ἔχομεν πατέρα
πρεσβύτερον, καὶ οὗτος ἔχει ἄλλον υἱὸν νεώτερον. πάλαι εἶχε καὶ ἄλλον
υἱόν, οὗτος δὲ ἀπέθανεν.' εἶπες δὲ ἡμῖν, 'ὁ νεώτερος υἱὸς ἐλθέτω σὺν
ὑμῖν πρὸς ἐμέ.' καὶ εἴπομεν τῷ κυρίῳ ἑαυτῶν, 'ὁ πατὴρ ὁ πρεσβύτερος

84

οὐκ ἔσται δυνατὸς ἀποστεῖλαι τὸν ἑαυτοῦ υἱὸν τὸν νεώτερον. ὅτε γὰρ ὁ
15 πατὴρ ἀποστελεῖ τοῦτον, ὁ πατὴρ ὁ πρεσβύτερος ἀποθανεῖται.' νῦν δὲ
ἐληλύθαμεν μετὰ τοῦ νεωτέρου υἱοῦ, τοῦ ἀδελφοῦ ἑαυτῶν, ὅτι ἐνετείλω
ἡμῖν. ἀλλ' ὅτε ἐλευσόμεθα πάλιν πρὸς τὸν πατέρα ἑαυτῶν καὶ οὗτος οὐ
βλέψει τὸν νεώτερον μεθ' ἡμῶν, ὁ πατὴρ ἡμῶν ἀποθανεῖται. νῦν οὖν
μενῶ ἐγὼ ἀντὶ τοῦ νεωτέρου Βενιαμὶν τοῦ ἀδελφοῦ ἐμοῦ. ἐκεῖνος δὲ ἀπ-
20 ερχέσθω πάλιν πρὸς τὸν πατέρα ἀντὶ ἐμοῦ. πῶς γὰρ βλέψω τὸν πατέρα ὅτε
οὐκ ἄξω πάλιν Βενιαμίν;"

τότε οὖν εἶπεν ὁ Ἰωσὴφ πρὸς τοὺς ἑαυτοῦ ἀδελφούς, "ἐγώ εἰμι
Ἰωσήφ. ἐπιγινώσκετε ἐμέ; ἔστε μακάριοι, ἐμὲ γὰρ ἀπέστειλεν ὁ θεὸς
εἰς ταύτην τὴν γῆν. χρεῖα σίτου ἔσται μακρά. νῦν οὖν οὐχ ὑμεῖς με
25 ἀπεστάλκατε ὧδε, ἀλλ' ὁ θεός. καὶ διὰ τὸν θεὸν ἐγενόμην ὁ κύριος τῆς
γῆς Αἰγύπτου. μὴ μένετε οὖν ἀλλ' ἔρχεσθε πρὸς τὸν πατέρα ἡμῶν τὸν
πρεσβύτερον καὶ λέγετε αὐτῷ, 'οὕτως λέγει ὁ υἱὸς σοῦ Ἰωσήφ, "διὰ τὸν
θεὸν ἐγενόμην ὁ κύριος τῆς γῆς Αἰγύπτου. ἐλθέ, σὺ γὰρ ἔσῃ πρὸς ἐμοί,
σὺ καὶ οἱ υἱοὶ σεαυτοῦ καὶ οἱ υἱοὶ τῶν υἱῶν σεαυτοῦ καὶ τὰ πρόβατά
30 σου." '"

200. VOCABULARY.

ἀντί: (with gen.) instead of, in place of, in exchange for, in return
for, against

ἑαυτοῦ, -ῆς, -οῦ: of himself, herself, itself; (pl.) of ourselves,
yourselves, themselves

ἐμαυτοῦ, -ῆς: of myself

μεθ' ἡμῶν: μετὰ ἡμῶν: with us (Before a following vowel the α in
μετά is elided. When this following vowel is
rough, the -τ- may be changed to -θ.)

οὕτως: thus, so

πατέρα (acc. sing.): father

πατήρ (nom. sing.): father

πρεσβύτερος, -ᾱ, -ον: elder

σεαυτοῦ, -ῆς: of yourself

201. REFLEXIVE PRONOUNS: THEIR USE. A reflexive pronoun refers to the
subject of the clause in which it stands.

βλέπω {ἐμαυτόν / ἐμαυτήν}	(=βλέπομαι)	I see myself.
βλέπεις {σεαυτόν / σεαυτήν}	(=βλέπῃ)	You see yourself.
βλέπει ἑαυτόν	(=βλέπεται)	He sees himself.
βλέπει ἑαυτήν	(=βλέπεται)	She sees herself.
βλέπει ἑαυτό	(=βλέπεται)	It sees itself.

βλέπομεν	{ἑαυτούς ἑαυτάς}	(=βλεπόμεθα)	We see ourselves.
βλέπετε	{ἑαυτούς ἑαυτάς}	(=βλέπεσθε)	You see yourselves.
βλέπουσι	{ἑαυτούς ἑαυτάς ἑαυτά}	(=βλέπονται)	They see themselves.
ἀκούω	{ἐμαυτοῦ ἐμαυτῆς}	(=ἀκούομαι)	I hear myself.
πιστευεις	{σεαυτῷ σεαυτῇ}	(=πιστεύῃ)	You believe yourself.

202. REFLEXIVE PRONOUNS: THEIR FORMS.

a. First Person.

| | Singular | | Plural | | |
	Masc.	Fem.	Masc.	Fem.	Neut.
N.	--	--	--	--	--
G.A.	ἐμαυτοῦ	ἐμαυτῆς	ἑαυτῶν	ἑαυτῶν	ἑαυτῶν
L.I.D.	ἐμαυτῷ	ἐμαυτῇ	ἑαυτοῖς	ἑαυταῖς	ἑαυτοῖς
Acc.	ἐμαυτόν	ἐμαυτήν	ἑαυτούς	ἑαυτάς	ἑαυτά

b. Second Person

| | Singular | | Plural | | |
	Masc.	Fem.	Masc.	Fem.	Neut.
N.	--	--	--	--	--
G.A.	σεαυτοῦ	σεαυτῆς	ἑαυτῶν	ἑαυτῶν	ἑαυτῶν
L.I.D.	σεαυτῷ	σεαυτῇ	ἑαυτοῖς	ἑαυταῖς	ἑαυτοῖς
Acc.	σεαυτόν	σεαυτήν	ἑαυτούς	ἑαυτάς	ἑαυτά

c. Third Person

| | Singular | | | Plural | | |
	Masc.	Fem.	Neut.	Masc.	Fem.	Neut.
N.	--	--	--	--	--	--
G.A.	ἑαυτοῦ	ἑαυτῆς	ἑαυτοῦ	ἑαυτῶν	ἑαυτῶν	ἑαυτῶν
L.I.D.	ἑαυτῷ	ἑαυτῇ	ἑαυτῷ	ἑαυτοῖς	ἑαυταῖς	ἑαυτοῖς
Acc.	ἑαυτόν	ἑαυτήν	ἑαυτό	ἑαυτούς	ἑαυτάς	ἑαυτά

NOTE. These reflexive pronouns are combinations of αὐτός and the
personal pronoun stems ἐμ- (found in ἐμοῦ, ἐμοί, and ἐμέ),
σε- (found in σέ, the accusative of σύ), and ἑ- (found in ἕ,
a third singular accusative pronoun not used in the New Testament.)

203. EXERCISES.

a. Translate #199.

b. Translate orally into Greek in two ways (1) by an active form and a reflexive pronoun, and (2) by a middle form alone.

1) I teach myself.
2) We taught ourselves.
3) They will teach themselves.
4) She believes herself (dat.).
5) You hear yourself (gen.).
6) We have heard ourselves (gen.).

c. Using the expressions with βλέπω in #201 as patterns, conjugate the following.

1) θεραπεύσω ἐμαυτήν ἀντὶ σοῦ.

2) ἐδούλευον ἐμαυτῷ ἀντὶ ἐκείνου.

3) ἀκήκοα ἐμαυτῆς ἀντὶ αὐτῆς.

4) ἐρῶ ἐμαυτῇ ἀντὶ ὑμῶν.

LESSON 27

204. "UNTO YOU IS BORN . . ."

πάλαι ἀπέστειλεν ὁ θεὸς τὸν ἑαυτοῦ υἱὸν γενέσθαι τέκνον ἐν ἀνθρώποις. ἐν Βηθλεὲμ οὖν οὗτος ὁ υἱὸς ἐγένετο τὸ τέκνον τῆς Μαρίας.

εἰρήκει γὰρ ὁ θεὸς τῇ Μαρίᾳ, "γενοῦ ἡ μήτηρ τοῦ υἱοῦ ἐμοῦ." καὶ
εἰρήκει ἡ Μαρία, "τοῦτο γενέσθω." ἡ δὲ Μαρία ἡ μήτηρ τοῦ κυρίου ἡμῶν
5   ἐγένετο.

μετὰ ταῦτα ἄγγελοί τινες ἦλθαν πρὸς ἀνθρώπους τινὰς μετὰ τῶν προβάτων ἐν τῇ γῇ τῆς Βηθλεέμ. εἶπαν δὲ τοῖς ἀνθρώποις περὶ τοῦ μικροῦ
τέκνου ἐν Βηθλεέμ.

οἱ δὲ ἄγγελοι ἐνετείλαντο αὐτοῖς, "μακάριοι γένεσθε διὰ τοῦτο τὸ
10   τέκνον. οἱ ἄνθρωποι τῆς Βηθλεὲμ μακάριοι γενέσθωσαν καὶ δεξάσθωσαν τὸ
τέκνον. ἕκαστος ἐν Βηθλεὲμ δεξάσθω αὐτό."

διὰ τοὺς ἀγγέλους ὁ φόβος τοὺς ἀνθρώπους ἔλαβεν, ἀλλὰ μετὰ μικρὸν
χρόνον ἀπῆλθαν ἀπὸ τῶν ἑαυτῶν προβάτων εἰς τὴν Βηθλεέμ. ἐκεῖ δὲ
ἔβλεψαν τὸ τέκνον Μαρίας, τὸν υἱὸν τοῦ θεοῦ. ἐγένοντο λίαν μακάριοι.
15   μετὰ ταῦτα ἦλθον ἄλλοι ἀπὸ γῆς τινος μακρᾶς εἰς Ἱεροσόλυμα.

οὗτοι καὶ ἤθελον βλέπειν τὸ αὐτὸ τέκνον ἐν Βηθλεὲμ ὅτι περὶ αὐτοῦ ἠκηκόεισαν ἐν τῇ ἑαυτῶν γῇ. ἔφερον οὖν δωρεὰς καλὰς ἐκ τοῦ ἑαυτῶν πλούτου. ἐκ Ἰεροσολύμων εἰς Βηθλεὲμ ἦλθον. ἐκεῖ δὲ ἔβλεψαν τὸ μικρὸν τέκνον τῆς Μαρίας οὗτοι.

20 τότε δὲ εἶπαν τάχα, "δέξαι, Μαρίᾱ, ταύτᾱς τὰς δωρεάς. ἐγένου ἡ μήτηρ τούτου τοῦ τέκνου. αὗται γενέσθωσαν ὁ πλοῦτος τοῦ τέκνου. σὺ καὶ Ἰωσήφ, δέξασθε ταύτᾱς."

ἀλλά τις βασιλεὺς ἠκηκόει ὅτι τὸ μικρὸν τέκνον ἔσται ἄλλος βασιλεύς. ἐκεῖνος οὖν ἤθελεν τοῦτο ἀποκτεῖναι.

25 ἐνετείλατο οὖν ὁ θεὸς τῷ Ἰωσήφ, "ἀπέρχου ἀπὸ τῆς Βηθλεὲμ εἰς τὴν γῆν Αἰγύπτου, καὶ ἀπερχέσθωσαν μετὰ σοῦ ἡ μήτηρ καὶ τὸ τέκνον. μένε δὲ ἐκεῖ μετὰ τῆς Μαρίᾱς καὶ τοῦ τέκνου. ὅτε οὗτος ὁ κακὸς βασιλεὺς ἀποθανεῖται, ἐντελοῦμαί σοι ἐλθεῖν πάλιν εἰς ταύτην τὴν γῆν."

τὸ τέκνον οὖν ὁ κακὸς βασιλεὺς οὐκ ἀπέκτεινεν.

205. VOCABULARY.

Βηθλεὲμ (indecl.), ἡ: Bethlehem

δέχομαι, ---, ἐδεξάμην: I receive, accept, welcome

Ἰεροσόλυμα, -ων, τά: Jerusalem

μήτηρ (nom. sing.), ἡ: mother

206. AORIST MIDDLE IMPERATIVES.

a. First Aorist.

δέξαι	δέξασθε
δεξάσθω	δεξάσθωσαν

b. Second Aorist.

γενοῦ	γένεσθε
γενέσθω	γενέσθωσαν

c. Liquid Aorist.

ἔντειλαι	ἐντείλασθε
ἐντειλάσθω	ἐντειλάσθωσαν

207. AORIST MIDDLE INFINITIVES.

a. First Aorist: δέξασθαι.

b. Second Aorist: γενέσθαι.

c. Liquid Aorist: ἐντείλασθαι.

208. EXERCISES.

a. Translate #204.

b. Use aorist imperatives to translate the following underlined expressions.

1) <u>Start welcoming</u> Mary, shepherds.
2) <u>Start healing yourself</u>, doctor.
3) <u>Command little Joseph once for all</u> to be quiet, Peter.
4) <u>Let</u> the men <u>command</u> the children to go home.

c. Use present imperatives to translate the following underlined expressions.

1) <u>Keep on welcoming</u> the strangers, my friends.
2) <u>Let the mother always go away</u> after class.
3) <u>Let them send themselves forth</u> every week.
4) Disciples, <u>teach yourselves</u> by reading carefully whenever your instructor is absent.

d. Translate.

1) καλοὶ γενέσθωσαν ὁ βασιλεὺς καὶ οἱ ἄλλοι ἐν τοῖς Ἱεροσολύμοις.

2) οἱ κακοὶ τῶν Ἱεροσολύμων δεξάσθωσαν τὸν υἱὸν τοῦ θεοῦ.

3) ἄγγελε, ἔντειλαι τοῖς δούλοις ἐκείνοις δεξάσθαι τὰς δωρεὰς ταύτᾱς.

4) υἱέ, γενοῦ ἄνθρωπος.

5) ὁ πατὴρ καὶ ἡ μήτηρ θελέτωσαν δεξάσθαι τὰ τέκνα.

6) ἐντείλασθε τοῖς καμήλοις μεῖναι ὧδε.

7) ὁ βασιλεὺς γενέσθω μαθητὴς τοῦ διδασκάλου ἐν Ἱεροσολύμοις.

8) βλεψάσθω ἡ μήτηρ.

9) γένεσθε μακάριοι ὅτε ἀκούσετε τῶν ἀγγέλων.

10) Πέτρε, θέλεις γενέσθαι καλός;

11) δέξαι τὰ τέκνα ταῦτα, Φίλιππε.

12) γενοῦ καλὸς ὑπηρέτης, υἱέ.

13) ἔρχου νῦν, δοῦλε.

14) ἐντειλάσθω ἡ μήτηρ τοῖς τέκνοις φαγεῖν.

209. MOSES, A MAN WITH A PAST.

ὁ Μωυσῆς ἦν πρὸ Φαραὼ καὶ ἕτοιμος ἦν εἰπεῖν, "ὁ θεὸς ἐντέλλεται τῷ 'Ισραὴλ ἐλθεῖν ἐκ ταύτης τῆς γῆς." τί οὖν ἦν Μωυσῆς ἐκεῖ; τί ἐγένετο τούτῳ πρὸ ἐκείνου τοῦ χρόνου;

πάλαι ἀπέκτεινε Μωυσῆς Αἰγύπτιόν τινα καὶ ἐδεδίωκτο ὑπὸ τῶν δού-
5   λων τοῦ Φαραώ. ἀλλὰ Μωυσῆς ἠληλύθει ἐκ τῆς Αἰγύπτου εἰς γῆν μακράν. ἐκεῖ ἔβλεψεν ἑπτὰ ἀδελφὰς μετὰ τῶν προβάτων αὐτῶν. τούτων δὲ τῶν ἑπτὰ ἀδελφῶν ὁ πατὴρ ἐδέδεκτο Μωυσῆν. τῶν ἀδελφῶν τις ἐγεγένητο ἡ γυνὴ τοῦ Μωυσέως.

μετὰ δὲ μακρὰ ἔτη Μωυσῆς ἀπέσταλτο ὑπὸ τοῦ θεοῦ πάλιν εἰς τὴν
10   Αἴγυπτον, ὁ ἀδελφὸς αὐτοῦ ἐδέδεκτο αὐτόν, καὶ ὁμοῦ οὗτοι ἠληλύθεισαν πάλιν εἰς τὴν Αἴγυπτον.

τότε οἱ υἱοὶ τοῦ 'Ισραὴλ συνηγμένοι ἦσαν πρὸ τοῦ Μωυσέως, καὶ αἱ ἐπαγγελίαι τοῦ θεοῦ εἰρημέναι ἦσαν τούτοις.

νῦν οὖν Μωυσῆς καὶ ὁ ἴδιος ἀδελφὸς ἦσαν ἕτοιμοι λέγειν πρὸ τοῦ
15   Φαραώ, "ἐλθέτω ὁ λαὸς ἐκ τῆς γῆς σου. ἡμεῖς πρὸς σὲ ἀπεστάλμεθα ὑπὸ τοῦ θεοῦ τοῦ 'Ισραήλ. ὁ γὰρ λαὸς τοῦ 'Ισραὴλ ἀπέσταλται ἐκ τῆς γῆς."

210. VOCABULARY.

γράφω, --- , ἔγραψα, γέγραφα, γέγραμμαι: I write

'Ισραὴλ (indecl.), ὁ: Israel

λαός, -οῦ, ὁ: people

Μωυσῆς, Μωυσέως, Μωυσεῖ, Μωυσῆν, ὁ: Moses

πείθω, πείσω, ἔπεισα, πέποιθα, πέπεισμαι: I persuade; (mid.) I be-
                lieve, obey (dat. of dir. obj. with mid.)

πρό: (with abl.) before, in front of, earlier than, preferable to,
     in lieu of

ὑπό: (with abl.) by; (with gen.) under; (with acc.) under

211. LIST OF PERFECT AND PLUPERFECT MIDDLE OR PASSIVE INDICATIVES USED IN
                                                                    #209.
ἀπεστάλμεθα (ἀποστέλλω): we have been sent

ἀπέσταλται (ἀποστέλλω): it has been sent

ἀπέσταλτο (ἀποστέλλω): he had been sent

ἐγεγένητο (γίνομαι): she had become

ἐδέδεκτο (δέχομαι): he had welcomed

ἐδεδίωκτο (διώκω): he had been pursued closely

εἰρημέναι ἦσαν (λέγω): they had been spoken

ἐπέπειστο (πείθω): he had obeyed

συνηγμένοι ἦσαν (συνάγω): they had been gathered together

212. PASSIVE VOICE: ITS MEANING.

    a. In defective verbs. In #174 it has been explained that some verbs have middle forms with active meanings. There are also Greek verbs having passive forms with active meanings. This will be clearer when the future and aorist passive have been introduced.

    b. In complete verbs. When a Greek verb is not defective, the passive forms have meanings different from the meanings of active and middle forms. The action of a passive form is presented as taking effect on the subject but as being performed usually by some agent other than the subject.

213. IDENTITY OF SOME MIDDLE AND PASSIVE FORMS. The middle forms of the present, imperfect, perfect, and pluperfect tenses are identical with the passive forms of these tenses. The following examples illustrate both the forms and meanings of the three voices.

Present

Active	βλέπω	I see
Middle	βλέπομαι	I see myself
Passive	βλέπομαι	I am seen

Imperfect

Active	ἐθεράπευε	he was healing
Middle	ἐθεραπεύετο	he was healing himself
Passive	ἐθεραπεύετο	he was being healed

Perfect

Active	εἰλήφαμεν	we have taken
Middle	εἰλήμμεθα	we have taken for ourselves
Passive	εἰλήμμεθα	we have been taken

Pluperfect

Active	ἐπεγνώκειτε	you had recognized
Middle	ἐπέγνωσθε	you had recognized yourselves
Passive	ἐπέγνωσθε	you had been recognized

214. PERFECT MIDDLE AND PASSIVE INDICATIVE AND INFINITIVE OF OMEGA VERBS.

    a. Indicative of θεραπεύω.

τεθεράπευμαι	τεθεραπεύμεθα
τεθεράπευσαι	τεθεράπευσθε
τεθεράπευται	τεθεράπευνται

To the verb stem -θεραπευ- is prefixed the reduplication τε-
(the smooth form of the initial consonant since the Greeks disliked
rough consonants in successive syllables). No tense suffix is used
here. Directly to the reduplicated verb stem are added the primary
middle endings. Of course, other forms of reduplication may be
used as in ἀπέσταλμαι the perfect middle of ἀποστέλλω.

b. Infinitive of θεραπεύω: τεθεραπεῦσθαι.

This form is composed of reduplication plus the verb stem plus the
middle infinitive ending. Notice the accent.

215. PLUPERFECT MIDDLE AND PASSIVE INDICATIVE OF OMEGA VERBS.

ἐτεθεραπεύμην	ἐτεθεραπεύμεθα
ἐτεθεράπευσο	ἐτεθεράπευσθε
ἐτεθεράπευτο	ἐτεθεράπευντο

The initial ἐ-, the augment, may be omitted in the pluperfect in
Hellenistic Greek.

216. PERFECT MIDDLE AND PASSIVE SYSTEM OF VERBS WITH STEMS ENDING IN A
MUTE OR LIQUID. The perfect middle and passive system includes
the perfect and pluperfect tenses. The personal endings used in
these tenses can be added without complication to stems terminating
in a vowel, for example: τεθεράπευ-ται, ἐτεθεραπεύ-μεθα.

But verbs whose stems end with a consonant deviate from the pattern
of θεραπεύω. Certain changes in spelling occur where the personal
endings touch the rest of the verb. Some combinations of consonants
were more pleasing to the ancient Greeks or were easier for them to
pronounce than others. The less agreeable combinations were often
modified to make more acceptable sounds. Notice the various spellings
of the prefix in in the following English words: inability, impossible
illogical, irregular. In the third plural we find not merely a
modification but an outright substitution.

In the paradigms that follow, the unacceptable regular formation is
placed in parentheses after the form in use.

a. Paradigms of γράφω to illustrate the formation of verbs whose
stems end in π, β, or φ.

  1) Perfect Indicative Middle and Passive.

γέγραμμαι	(γέγραφμαι)
γέγραψαι	(γέγραφσαι)
γέγραπται	(γέγραφται)
γεγράμμεθα	(γεγράφμεθα)
γέγραφθε	(γέγραφσθε)
γεγραμμένοι εἰσί	(γέγραφνται)

  2) Perfect Infinitive Middle and Passive.

  γεγράφθαι   (γεγράφσθαι)

  3) Pluperfect Indicative Middle and Passive.

ἐγεγράμμην	(ἐγεγράφμην)
ἐγέγραψο	(ἐγέγραφσο)
ἐγέγραπτο	(ἐγέγραφτο)
ἐγεγράμμεθα	(ἐγεγράφμεθα)
ἐγέγραφθε	(ἐγέγραφσθε)
γεγραμμένοι ἦσαν	(ἐγέγραφντο)

b. Paradigms of διώκω to illustrate the formation of verbs whose stems end in κ, γ, or χ.

1) Perfect Indicative Middle and Passive.

δεδίωγμαι   (δεδίωκμαι)
δεδίωξαι   (δεδίωκσαι)
δεδίωκται   (same form)
δεδιώγμεθα   (δεδιώκμεθα)
δεδίωχθε   (δεδίωκσθε)
δεδιωγμένοι εἰσί   (δεδίωκνται)

2) Perfect Infinitive Middle and Passive.

δεδιῶχθαι   (δεδιῶκσθαι)

3) Pluperfect Indicative Middle and Passive.

ἐδεδιώγμην   (ἐδεδιώκμην)
ἐδεδίωξο   (ἐδεδίωκσο)
ἐδεδίωκτο   (same form)
ἐδεδιώγμεθα   (ἐδεδιώκμεθα)
ἐδεδίωχθε   (ἐδεδίωκσθε)
δεδιωγμένοι ἦσαν   (ἐδεδίωκντο)

c. Paradigms of πείθω to illustrate the formation of verbs whose stems end in τ, δ, or θ.

1) Perfect Indicative Middle or Passive.

πέπεισμαι   (πέπειθμαι)
πέπεισαι   (πέπειθσαι)
πέπεισται   (πέπειθται)
πεπείσμεθα   (πεπείθμεθα)
πέπεισθε   (πέπειθσθε)
πεπεισμένοι εἰσί   (πέπειθνται)

2) Perfect Infinitive Middle and Passive.

πεπεῖσθαι   (πεπεῖθσθαι)

3) Pluperfect Indicative Middle and Passive.

ἐπεπείσμην   (ἐπεπείθμην)
ἐπέπεισο   (ἐπέπειθσο)
ἐπέπειστο   (ἐπέπειθτο)
ἐπεπείσμεθα   (ἐπεπείθμεθα)
ἐπέπεισθε   (ἐπέπειθσθε)
πεπεισμένοι ἦσαν   (ἐπέπειθντο)

d. Paradigms of ἐντέλλομαι to illustrate the formation of verbs whose stems end in λ, μ, ν, or ρ.

1) Perfect Indicative Middle and Passive

ἐντέταλμαι   ⎫
ἐντέταλσαι   ⎬
ἐντέταλται   ⎪   (same forms)
ἐντετάλμεθα ⎭
ἐντέταλθε   (ἐντέταλσθε)
ἐντεταλμένοι εἰσί   (ἐντέταλνται)

2) Perfect Infinitive Middle and Passive

ἐντετάλθαι   (ἐντετάλσθαι)

3) Pluperfect Indicative Middle and Passive: (No forms in the
                                               New Testament).

93

217. AUGMENT IN THE PLUPERFECT. The pluperfect occurs either with or without augment in the Greek of the New Testament period (#161). The paradigms just presented have uniformly included augment. Exercises, however, will give both augmented and unaugmented forms.

218. SUMMARY OF CONSONANT CHANGES ILLUSTRATED IN #216.

Final stem consonant	Initial terminal consonant	Result of change
π β φ } +	μ_____ σ + vowel_____ σ + θ_____ τ_____	μμ ψ + vowel φθ πτ
κ γ χ } +	μ_____ σ + vowel_____ σ + θ_____ τ_____	γμ ξ + vowel χθ κτ
τ δ θ } +	μ_____ σ + vowel_____ σ + θ_____ τ_____	σμ σ + vowel σθ στ

219. PERIPHRASTIC THIRD PLURAL IN THE PERFECT AND PLUPERFECT INDICATIVE MIDDLE AND PASSIVE. Forms like δεδιωγμένοι ἦσαν and πεπεισμένοι εἰσί are made up of perfect middle or passive participles and the third plural indicative of εἰμί in the present for the perfect and in the imperfect for the pluperfect. The participle agrees with the subject and therefore has different endings to modify nouns of different gender. These combinations are called periphrastics.

αἱ ἀδελφαί δεδιωγμέναι εἰσί.
The sisters have been closely pursued, (or)
The sisters have closely pursued each other.

οἱ δοῦλοι πεπεισμένοι ἦσαν.
The slaves had been persuaded, (or)
The slaves had persuaded one another.

Notice that the participle can **never** have augment **at any time**. (#96)

220. ABLATIVE OF AGENT. The ablative case is used with the prepositions ἀπό, ἐκ, παρά, and ὑπό to indicate the person by whom an action is performed. This construction is used with the passive voice.

διωκόμεθα ὑπό τοῦ ἐχθροῦ.
We are being pursued by the enemy.

221. LIST OF VERBS WITH PERFECT MIDDLE AND PASSIVE SYSTEMS.

Present Active	Perfect Middle and Passive
ἀπολύω	ἀπολέλυμαι
ἀποστέλλω	ἀπέσταλμαι
βάλλω	βέβλημαι
γίνομαι	γεγένημαι
γράφω	γέγραμμαι
δέχομαι	δέδεγμαι
διώκω	δεδίωγμαι
ἐντέλλομαι	ἐντέταλμαι
θεραπεύω	τεθεράπευμαι
λαμβάνω	εἴλημμαι

Present Active | Perfect Middle and Passive

λέγω   εἴρημαι
πείθω   πέπεισμαι
πιστεύω   πεπίστευμαι
συνάγω   συνῆγμαι

222. EXERCISES.

a. Translate #209.

b. Locate by giving (1) **tense**, (2) mood, (3) voice, (4) person, (5) number, and (6) first principal part.

1) ἀπολέλυνται   7) ἐνετείλω

2) βεβλημένοι ἦσαν   8) εἰρημένοι εἰσί

3) δεδίωχθε   9) ἠγάγετε

4) πεπίστευσαι   10) πεπεισμέναι ἦσαν

5) πέπειστο   11) ἐπεπίστευντο

6) δεδέγμην

c. Translate in two ways if possible.

1) ἐδεδέγμεθα   6) πεπίστευνται

2) εἰρημένοι ἦσαν   7) ἐτεθεράπευντο

3) πέπεισο   8) ἀπολέλυνται

4) συνῆκται   9) ἐπεπίστευντο

5) ἀπελέλυντο   10) τεθεράπευνται

d. Translate.

1) Ἑπτὰ ἔτη ἐν Αἰγύπτῳ Μωυσῆς μεμενήκει καὶ ἑπτὰ ἔτη ἐν γῇ τινι μακρᾷ.

2) οὐκ ἦν Μωυσῆς ἕτοιμος λέγειν τῷ λαῷ τοῦ Ἰσραήλ.

3) ὅτε ἐκ τῆς μακρᾶς γῆς εἰς τὴν Αἴγυπτον λέγειν πρὸ τοῦ Φαραὼ Μωυσῆς ἐληλύθει, οὐκ ἦν ἕτοιμος ὁ Φαραὼ ἐντείλασθαι τῷ λαῷ ἔρχεσθαι ἐκ τῆς γῆς.

4) ὁ λαὸς ἀπέσταλται ὑπὸ τοῦ θεοῦ.

5) πρὸ τούτου τοῦ λαοῦ ἀπέσταλτο ἐκεῖνος ὑπὸ ἀγγέλου;

e. Associate the following words with new Greek words presented in this lesson.

1) lay: related to the people as distinguished from the clergy.
2) prologue: a statement made before the main part of a play or poem.
3) hypodermic: related to what is under the skin.

95

223. A PROPHETIC MEMORIAL.

ὁ Μωυσῆς ἐπέμφθη ὑπὸ τοῦ θεοῦ ἐντέλλεσθαι τῷ Φαραώ, "οἱ υἱοὶ τοῦ Ἰσραὴλ ἐκ τῆς γῆς Αἰγύπτου ὑπὸ σοῦ ἀποσταλήσονται."

ἀλλὰ οὗτοι οὐκ ἀπεστάλησαν. ὁ γὰρ βασιλεὺς εἶχεν αὐτοὺς καὶ οὐκ ἀπελθόθησαν. διὰ τοῦτο ἐγενήθησαν πληγαὶ ἐπὶ τοὺς Αἰγυπτίους καὶ ἐπὶ
5 τὴν γῆν αὐτῶν καὶ ἐπὶ τὸν Φαραὼ αὐτόν.

πρὸ τῆς ἐσχάτης πληγῆς ὁ Φαραὼ ἐρρέθη ὑπὸ τοῦ Μωυσέως, "ἐν ταύτῃ τῇ ἐσχάτῃ πληγῇ ὁ πρῶτος υἱὸς σοῦ ἀποκτανθήσεται." ὁ δὲ Φαραὼ τῷ θεῷ οὐκ ἐπείσθη καὶ ὁ πρῶτος υἱὸς αὐτοῦ ἀπεκτάνθη ἐν τῇ ἐσχάτῃ πληγῇ καὶ οἱ ἄλλοι υἱοὶ οἱ πρῶτοι καὶ ἀπεκτάνθησαν ὑπό τινος ἀγγέλου τοῦ κυρίου.
10 μετὰ ταῦτα ὁ Ἰσραὴλ ἐβλήθη ἐκ τῆς Αἰγύπτου ὑπὸ τῶν Αἰγυπτίων.

πρὸ δὲ ταύτης τῆς ἐσχάτης πληγῆς ὁ λαὸς τοῦ Ἰσραὴλ ἐδιδάχθη τὴν ἑορτὴν τοῦ πάσχα. ἐν τῇ ἑορτῇ ταύτῃ ἀρνίον καλὸν ἐτύθη καὶ τὸ αἷμα τοῦ ἀρνίου ἐβλήθη ἐπὶ τὴν θύραν τοῦ οἴκου. διὰ τὸ αἷμα ἐπὶ ταῖς θύραις ὁ ἄγγελος τοῦ κυρίου οὐκ ἀπέκτεινε τοὺς πρώτους υἱοὺς ἐν τῷ λαῷ
15 τοῦ Ἰσραήλ. ἀλλὰ οὐκ ἦν αἷμα ἐπὶ ταῖς θύραις τῶν Αἰγυπτίων. τὸ ἀρνίον τοῦ πάσχα οὐκ ἐτύθη ὑπὸ αὐτῶν καὶ οὐκ ἴσχυον χαρῆναι. ἀλλ' ὅτι οἱ πρῶτοι υἱοὶ τοῦ λαοῦ Ἰσραὴλ οὐκ ἀπεκτάνθησαν, ὁ λαὸς ἐχάρη.

αὕτη ἦν ἡ πρώτη ἑορτὴ τοῦ πάσχα. ὁ δὲ κύριος τῷ λαῷ ἐνετείλατο μνημονεύειν ταύτης τῆς ἑορτῆς καὶ τοῦ καλοῦ ἀρνίου. διὰ τῆς ἑορτῆς
20 τοῦ πάσχα καὶ διὰ τοῦ ἀρνίου ὁ λαὸς ἐδιδάχθη περὶ τοῦ ἀρνίου τοῦ θεοῦ, τοῦ κυρίου ἡμῶν Ἰησοῦ. μετὰ δὲ χρόνον λίαν μακρὸν οὗτος ἐτύθη καὶ διὰ τὸ αἷμα αὐτοῦ ἡμεῖς, οἱ δοῦλοι αὐτοῦ, χαίρομεν. οὐκέτι θύομεν τὰ ἀρνία ἐν τῇ ἑορτῇ πάσχα. οὐκέτι βάλλομεν τὸ αἷμα ἐπὶ τὰς θύρας τῶν οἴκων ἡμῶν. χαίρομεν καὶ χαρησόμεθα ὅτι Ἰησοῦς, τὸ ἀρνίον ἡμῶν,
25 ἐτύθη καὶ ὅτι ὁ θεὸς βλέπει τὸ αἷμα τούτου τοῦ ἐσχάτου πάσχα οὐκ ἐπὶ ταῖς θύραις τῶν οἴκων ἡμῶν ἀλλ' ἐπὶ ταῖς καρδίαις ἡμῶν.

224. VOCABULARY.

αἷμα (nom. and acc. sing.), τό: blood

ἑορτή, -ῆς, ἡ: festival, feast

ἐπί: (with gen.) on, over, upon; (with loc.) on, at, upon, concerning; (with acc.) on, over, to, against

ἔσχατος, -η, -ον: last

θύρᾱ, -ᾱς, ἡ: door

θύω, --- , ἔθυσα, --- , τέθυμαι, ἐτύθην: I sacrifice, kill, slay, offer

'Ιησοῦς, -οῦ (gen., abl., loc., instr., dat.), -οῦν, -οῦ, ὁ: Jesus, Joshua

πάσχα (indecl.), τό: Passover, paschal lamb

πληγή, -ῆς, ἡ: plague, calamity, blow

πρῶτος, -η, -ον: first, chief, principal

χαίρω, --- , --- , --- , --- , ἐχάρην: I rejoice, am glad

225. LIST OF AORIST AND FUTURE PASSIVES USED IN #223.

ἀπεκτάνθη (ἀποκτείνω): he was killed

ἀπεκτάνθησαν (ἀποκτείνω): they were killed

ἀπελύθησαν (ἀπολύω): they were released

ἀπεστάλησαν (ἀποστέλλω): they were sent away

ἀποκτανθήσεται (ἀποκτείνω): he will be killed

ἀποσταλήσονται (ἀποστέλλω): they shall be sent forth

ἐβλήθη (βάλλω): it was put

ἐγενήθησαν (γίνομαι): they were brought (upon)

ἐδιδάχθη (διδάσκω): it was taught

ἐπείσθη (πείθω): he obeyed

ἐπέμφθη (πέμπω): he was sent

ἐρρέθη (λέγω): he was told

ἐτύθη (θύω): it was slain

ἐχάρη (χαίρω): it rejoiced

χαρῆναι (χαίρω): to rejoice

χαρησόμεθα (χαίρω): we shall rejoice

226. TENSES WITH DISTINCT PASSIVE FORMS. Unlike the present, imperfect, perfect, and pluperfect (see #213), whose middle and passive forms have the same spelling, the aorist and future tenses have passives that differ from their middle forms.

227. FIRST PASSIVE SYSTEM: AORIST.

Indicative

ἐθεραπεύθην	ἐθεραπεύθημεν
ἐθεραπεύθης	ἐθεραπεύθητε
ἐθεραπεύθη	ἐθεραπεύθησαν

Imperative

θεραπεύθητι	θεραπεύθητε
θεραπευθήτω	θεραπευθήτωσαν

Infinitive

θεραπευθῆναι

To the unreduplicated perfect middle and passive stem is added -θη-
and the personal or infinitive endings. The indicative forms have
augment.

228. SECOND PASSIVE SYSTEM: AORIST

Indicative

ἀπεστάλην	ἀπεστάλημεν
ἀπεστάλης	ἀπεστάλητε
ἀπεστάλη	ἀπεστάλησαν

Imperative

ἀποστάληθι	ἀποστάλητε
ἀποσταλήτω	ἀποσταλήτωσαν

Infinitive

ἀποσταλῆναι

To the unreduplicated perfect middle and passive stem is added   -η-
and the personal or infinitive endings. The indicative forms have
augment. Notice that the second singular imperative has the personal
ending -θι instead of the -τι in the first aorist passive.

229. FIRST PASSIVE SYSTEM: FUTURE.

Indicative

		Infinitive
θεραπευθήσομαι	θεραπευθησόμεθα	θεραπευθήσεσθαι
θεραπευθήσῃ	θεραπευθήσεσθε	
θεραπευθήσεται	θεραπευθήσονται	

To the unreduplicated perfect middle and passive stem is added -θη-,
then -σο/ε- and finally the primary middle personal endings. The
ending -σῃ is a shortened form of -σεσαι.

230. SECOND PASSIVE SYSTEM: FUTURE.

Indicative

		Infinitive
ἀποσταλήσομαι	ἀποσταλησόμεθα	ἀποσταλήσεσθαι
ἀποσταλήσῃ	ἀποσταλήσεσθε	
ἀποσταλήσεται	ἀποσταλήσονται	

Instead of -θη- the second future passive uses -η-. Otherwise, this
formation is the same as the first future passive.

231. AORIST AND FUTURE PASSIVES IN VERBS WHOSE STEMS END WITH A MUTE.

a. Verbs whose stems end with π, β, or φ use φ before -θη.

ἐπέμφθην	(πεμπ-)
ἐλήμφθην	(λημβ-)

(γράφω has second aorist and future passives: ἐγράφην & γραφήσεται.)

b. Verbs whose stems end with κ, γ, or χ use χ before -θη-.

ἐδιώχθην	(διωκ-)
ἤχθην	(ἀγ-)

c. Verbs whose stems end with τ, δ, or θ use σ before -θη-.

ἐπείσθην	(πειθ-)

232. REFERENCE LIST FOR AORIST AND FUTURE PASSIVES.

Present Active	Aorist Passive	Future Passive
ἄγω	ἤχθην	ἀχθήσομαι
ἀκούω	ἠκούσθην	ἀκουσθήσομαι
ἀποκτείνω	ἀπεκτάνθην	ἀποκτανθήσομαι
ἀπολύω	ἀπελύθην	ἀπολυθήσομαι
ἀποστέλλω	ἀπεστάλην	ἀποσταλήσομαι
βάλλω	ἐβλήθην	βληθήσομαι
γίνομαι	ἐγενήθην	γενηθήσομαι
γράφω	ἐγράφην	γραφήσομαι
διδάσκω	ἐδιδάχθην	διδαχθήσομαι
διώκω	ἐδιώχθην	διωχθήσομαι
ἐπιγινώσκω	ἐπεγνώσθην	ἐπιγνωσθήσομαι
θεραπεύω	ἐθεραπεύθην	θεραπευθήσομαι
θύω	ἐτύθην	τυθήσομαι
λαμβάνω	ἐλήμφθην	λημφθήσομαι
λέγω	ἐρρέθην	ῥεθήσομαι
πείθω	ἐπείσθην	πεισθήσομαι
πέμπω	ἐπέμφθην	πεμφθήσομαι
φέρω	ἠνέχθην	ἐνεχθήσομαι
χαίρω	ἐχάρην	χαρήσομαι

233. EXERCISES.

a. Translate #223.

b. Locate.

1) ἐνεχθῆναι
2) λημφθήσεσθε
3) ῥεθήσεται
4) ἀποστάληθι
5) ἐδιώχθησαν

6) διδαχθησόμεθα
7) ἀκουσθήτωσαν
8) ἀχθήσονται
9) ἐπέμφθης
10) χάρηθι

c. Translate into Greek.

1) We shall be healed because of the paschal lamb.
2) You (pl.) will be persuaded.
3) Joshua was recognized.
4) It will be made.
5) They were written upon the door.
6) You (sing.) will be thrown out of the doors.
7) I was released from the door.

8) We shall be killed.
9) Joshua will be glad because of the paschal lamb.
10) It was said at the festival.

d. Associate the following English words with new Greek words used in this lesson.

1) <u>anem</u>ia: a deficiency in the <u>blood</u>.
2) <u>eschatology</u>: teachings concerning the <u>last</u> events in Biblical revelation.
3) hemi<u>plegia</u>: a <u>stroke</u> that causes paralysis in half the body.

LESSON 30

234. VOCABULARY. Review thoroughly the vocabulary introduced since Lesson 24.

NOUNS	VERBS	ADJECTIVES
αἷμα	βάλλω	ἕκαστος
ἀργύριον	γράφω	ἔσχατος
Βηθλεέμ	δέχομαι	πρεσβύτερος
ἑορτή	ἐντέλλομαι	πρῶτος
θύρα	θύω	
Ἱεροσόλυμα	πείθω	
Ἰησοῦς	χαίρω	
Ἰσραήλ		
λαός		
μήτηρ		PREPOSITIONS
Μωυσῆς		
πάσχα		
πατέρα	PRONOUNS	ἀντί
πατήρ		διά
πληγή		ἐπί
		μεθ'
ADVERB	ἑαυτοῦ	μετ'
	ἐμαυτοῦ	πρό
οὕτως	σεαυτοῦ	ὑπό

235. CLASSIFICATION DRILL. Classify each of the following forms as
(1) a primary tense (present, future, or perfect),
(2) a secondary tense (imperfect, aorist, or pluperfect), or
(3) an ambiguous form if out of context.

a. ἀπεστάλμεθα

b. εἴρητο

c. ἀπολέλυνται

d. ἀπελύσω

e. πέπεισθε

f. συνήγμεθα

g. εἰχόμην

h. διώξονται

i. ἠρχόμην

j. ἀπεληλύθει

236. **VERB DRILL.** Change each underlined verb to the perfect or future tense as the sense requires.

ἐπεὶ ἐδεδέγμεθα ὑπὸ τούτου ἐν ʽΙεροσολύμοις, ἐπεπείσμεθα τοῖς

διδασκάλοις αὐτοῦ καὶ ἀπηληλύθειμεν ἀπὸ τῶν ʽΙεροσολύμων ἐπὶ τὴν

Βηθλεέμ. ἐκεῖ τὸ τέκνον ᾽Ιησοῦν ἐβλέψαμεν, ἀλλ᾽ ὅτι εἰρήκει ἡμῖν ὁ

θεὸς μὴ ἐλθεῖν πάλιν ἐπὶ ʽΙεροσόλυμα, ἀπήλθομεν πρὸς τὴν ἑαυτῶν γῆν

διὰ τόπου ἄλλου.

237. A REFERENCE LIST OF THE PRINCIPAL PARTS OF THE VERBS PRESENTED THUS FAR.

(The forms in parentheses, although not in the N. T., are given to
help students become familiar with complete verb systems. A form
with a hyphen is represented by compound verbs occurring in the N. T.
or in the early Christian literature surveyed by Arndt and Gingrich.)

Pres. Act. or Mid.	Fut. Act. or Mid.	Aor. Act. or Mid.	Perf. Act.	Perf. Mid. and Pass.	Aor. Pass.
ἄγω	ἄξω	ἤγαγον	(ἦχα)	(-ἦγμαι)	ἤχθην
ἀκούω	ἀκούσω	ἤκουσα	ἀκήκοα	(ἤκουσμαι)	ἠκούσθην
ἀπέρχομαι	ἀπελεύσομαι	ἀπῆλθον	ἀπελήλυθα	----	---
ἀποθνῄσκω	ἀποθανοῦμαι	ἀπέθανον	---	----	---
ἀποκτείνω	ἀποκτενῶ	ἀπέκτεινα	---	----	ἀπεκτάνθην
ἀπολύω	ἀπολύσω	ἀπέλυσα	---	ἀπολέλυμαι	ἀπελύθην
ἀποστέλλω	ἀποστελῶ	ἀπέστειλα	ἀπέσταλκα	ἀπέσταλμαι	ἀπεστάλην
βάλλω	βαλῶ	ἔβαλον	βέβληκα	βέβλημαι	ἐβλήθην
βλέπω	βλέψω	ἔβλεψα	----	----	---
γίνομαι	γενήσομαι	ἐγενόμην	γέγονα	γεγένημαι	ἐγενήθην
γράφω	(-γράψω)	ἔγραψα	γέγραφα	γέγραμμαι	ἐγράφην
δέχομαι	(-δέξομαι)	ἐδεξάμην	---	δέδεγμαι	ἐδέχθην
διδάσκω	διδάξω	ἐδίδαξα	---	----	ἐδιδάχθην
διώκω	διώξω	ἐδίωξα	(δεδίωχα)	δεδίωγμαι	ἐδιώχθην
δουλεύω	δουλεύσω	ἐδούλευσα	δεδούλευκα	(δεδούλευμαι)	(ἐδουλεύθην)
εἰμί	ἔσομαι	---	---	----	----
ἐλπίζω	ἐλπιῶ	ἤλπισα	ἤλπικα	----	----
ἐντέλλομαι	ἐντελοῦμαι	ἐνετειλάμην	---	ἐντέταλμαι	----
ἐπιγινώσκω	ἐπιγνώσομαι	ἐπέγνων (Cf.#262)	ἐπέγνωκα	(ἐπέγνωσμαι)	ἐπεγνώσθην
ἔρχομαι	ἐλεύσομαι	ἦλθον	ἐλήλυθα	----	----
ἐσθίω	φάγομαι	ἔφαγον	---	----	----
ἔχω	ἕξω	ἔσχον	ἔσχηκα	(ἔσχημαι)	(ἐσχέθην)

Pres. Act. or Mid.	Fut. Act. or Mid.	Aor. Act. or Mid.	Perf. Act.	Perf. Mid. and Pass.	Aor. Pass.
θέλω	θελήσω	ἠθέλησα	---	---	---
θεραπεύω	θεραπεύσω	ἐθεράπευσα	---	τεθεράπευμαι	ἐθεραπεύθην
θύω	(θύσω)	ἔθυσα	(τέθυκα)	τέθυμαι	ἐτύθην
ἰσχύω	ἰσχύσω	ἴσχυσα	(ἴσχυκα)	---	(ἰσχύθην)
λαμβάνω	λήμψομαι	ἔλαβον	εἴληφα	εἴλημμαι	(-ελήμφθην)
λέγω	ἐρῶ	εἶπον	εἴρηκα	εἴρημαι	ἐρρέθην
μανθάνω	(μαθήσω)	ἔμαθον	μεμάθηκα	---	---
μένω	μενῶ	ἔμεινα	μεμένηκα	---	---
μνημονεύω	---	ἐμνημόνευσα	(ἐμνημόνευκα)	(ἐμνημόνευμαι)	(ἐμνημονεύθην)
πείθω	πείσω	ἔπεισα	πέποιθα	πέπεισμαι	ἐπείσθην
πέμπω	πέμψω	ἔπεμψα	πέπομφα	(πέπεμμαι)	ἐπέμφθην
πίνω	πίομαι	ἔπιον	πέπωκα	---	(-επόθην)
πιστεύω	πιστεύσω	ἐπίστευσα	πεπίστευκα	πεπίστευμαι	ἐπιστεύθην
συνάγω	συνάξω	συνήγαγον	(συνῆχα)	συνῆγμαι	συνήχθην
φέρω	οἴσω	ἤνεγκα	(-ενήνοχα)	(-ενήνεγμαι)	ἠνέχθην
φονεύω	φονεύσω	ἐφόνευσα	---	---	ἐφονεύθην
χαίρω	---	---	---	---	ἐχάρην

LESSON 31

238. PHARAOH'S FIASCO.

ἐπεὶ ἀπέστειλε Φαραὼ τὸν λαὸν ἐκ τῆς γῆς Αἰγύπτου, ὁ θεὸς ἦγε αὐτοὺς τὴν ἡμέραν ἐν στύλῳ νεφέλης, τὴν δὲ νύκτα ἐν στύλῳ πυρός. ἔμενε δὲ ὁ στύλος τῆς νεφέλης ἡμέρας, καὶ ὁ στύλος τοῦ πυρὸς νυκτὸς πρὸ τοῦ λαοῦ παντός.

5   εἶπε κύριος πρὸς Μωυσῆν, "ἐρεῖ Φαραὼ τῷ λαῷ αὐτοῦ, 'ἄγειν πάλιν τοὺς υἱοὺς Ἰσραὴλ δυνατοί ἐσμεν.' ἐγὼ δὲ σκληρυνῶ τὴν καρδίαν Φαραὼ κατὰ αὐτῶν, καὶ διώξει αὐτούς. ἐπιγνώσονται δὲ πάντες οἱ Αἰγύπτιοι

ὅτι ἐγώ εἰμι κύριος."

ἐσκλήρυνε οὖν κύριος τὴν καρδίαν τοῦ Φαραώ, καὶ ἐδίωξεν τοὺς
10 υἱοὺς 'Ισραήλ. ἐπεὶ οἱ υἱοὶ 'Ισραηλ ἤρχοντο ἐκ τῆς Αἰγύπτου ἐν χειρὶ
ὑψηλῇ, ἐδίωξαν οἱ Αἰγύπτιοι αὐτοὺς κατὰ τὴν θάλασσαν.

ἐγένετο δὲ ὁ φόβος ἐπὶ τοὺς υἱοὺς 'Ισραηλ ὅτε ἔβλεψαν τοὺς Αἰγυπτίους. τότε εἶπε κύριος πρὸς Μωυσῆν, "ἐλθέτωσαν οἱ υἱοὶ 'Ισραηλ εἰς
μέσον τῆς θαλάσσης κατὰ τὸ ξηρόν. καὶ ἐγὼ σκληρυνῶ τὴν καρδίαν τοῦ
15 Φαραὼ καὶ τῶν Αἰγυπτίων πάντων, καὶ διώξουσιν ὑμᾶς. τότε ἐπιγνώσονται
πάντες οἱ Αἰγύπτιοι ὅτι ἐγώ εἰμι κύριος."

πᾶσαν τὴν νύκτα ἡ θάλασσα ἐγίνετο ξηρά. ὅτε ἦλθον οἱ υἱοὶ 'Ισραηλ
εἰς μέσον τῆς θαλάσσης κατὰ τὸ ξηρόν, ἐδίωξαν αὐτοὺς οἱ Αἰγύπτιοι εἰς
τὴν θάλασσαν κατὰ τὸ ξηρόν.

20 εἶπε δὲ κύριος, "ἐλθέτω τὸ ὕδωρ πάλιν εἰς τὸν ἑαυτοῦ τόπον, καὶ
ἀποκτεινάτω τοὺς Αἰγυπτίους."

ἀπέκτεινε οὖν τὸ ὕδωρ τοὺς Αἰγυπτίους πάντας, καὶ ἀπέθανον ἐν τῇ
θαλάσσῃ. διὰ τοῦτο ἐχάρησαν λίαν οἱ υἱοὶ 'Ισραηλ ὅτι ἡληλύθεισαν διὰ
τῆς θαλάσσης κατὰ τὸ ξηρὸν ἐν μέσῳ τῶν ὑδάτων.

239. VOCABULARY.

εἰς μέσον: into the middle

ἐν χειρὶ ὑψηλῇ: with a high hand

ἡμέρᾱ, -ᾱς, ἡ: day

θάλασσα, -ης, ἡ: sea

κατά: (with gen.) down upon, against; (with abl.) down from;
(with acc.) down along, through, by, according to

κατὰ τὸ ξηρόν: by dry land

μέσος, -η, -ον: middle, in the middle of

νεφέλη, -ης, ἡ: cloud

νύξ, νυκτός, ἡ: night

ξηρός, -ά, -όν: dry

πᾶς, πᾶσα, πᾶν: all, every

πῦρ, πυρός, τό: fire

σκληρύνω, σκληρυνῶ, ἐσκλήρυνα, ---, --- , ἐσκληρύνθην: I harden,
make stubborn

στύλος, -ου, ὁ: pillar

ὕδωρ, ὕδατος, τό: water

ὑψηλός, -ή, -όν: high, lofty

χείρ, χειρός, ἡ: hand

240. THIRD DECLENSION NOUNS. The nouns νύξ, πῦρ, ὕδωρ, and χείρ belong to
the third declension. Their stems end in consonants and may nearly
always be discovered by omitting the -ος from the second inflectional
form in the singular. A fifth inflectional form (vocative) will be
given in the declensions only when this form is distinct from the first.
(See #383 and #384 for 1st and 2nd declensions.)

(ἡ)	νύξ		νύκτες
	νυκτός		νυκτῶν
	νυκτί		νυξί
	νύκτα		νύκτας

(ἡ)	χείρ		χεῖρες
	χειρός		χειρῶν
	χειρί		χερσί
	χεῖρα		χεῖρας

(τό)	πῦρ		
	πυρός		No plural in N. T.
	πυρί		
	πῦρ		

(τό)	ὕδωρ		ὕδατα
	ὕδατος		ὑδάτων
	ὕδατι		ὕδασι
	ὕδωρ		ὕδατα

πῦρ and ὕδωρ are neuter and have the same form for both first and
fourth inflectional forms.

Stems of one syllable accent the ultima in the second and third inflectional forms, e. g., νυκτός, χερσί, and πυρί, but ὕδατος.

241. THIRD DECLENSION ADJECTIVES. All the adjectives used before this
lesson have belonged to the first and second declensions. In #238 forms
of πᾶς, πᾶσα, πᾶν have been introduced. This adjective has its feminine
forms in the first declension, but its masculine and neuter forms in
the third declension. (See #397 for 1st and 2nd declension adjectives.)

Masculine	Feminine	Neuter
πᾶς	πᾶσα	πᾶν
παντός	πάσης	παντός
παντί	πάσῃ	παντί
πάντα	πᾶσαν	πᾶν
πάντες	πᾶσαι	πάντα
πάντων	πασῶν	πάντων
πᾶσι	πάσαις	πᾶσι
πάντας	πάσᾱς	πάντα

242. ACCUSATIVE OF EXTENT OF TIME. The accusative may in a fitting context
indicate a period of time throughout which some action occurs or some
situation continues.

ὁ θεὸς ἦγε αὐτοὺς τὴν ἡμέραν.
God was leading them throughout the day (all day long).

243. GENITIVE OF TIME. The genitive may in a fitting context indicate a
period of time within the limits of which some action occurs or some
situation exists. This construction does not, however, carry the idea
of duration as the accusative does.

νυκτὸς οὐκ ἀπῆλθεν ὁ στύλος τοῦ πυρός.
The pillar of fire did not go away <u>at</u> <u>night</u> (<u>within</u> <u>the</u> <u>limits</u> <u>of</u> <u>the</u>
<u>night</u>).

244. GENITIVE OF MATERIAL OR CONTENT. In the phrase ἐν στύλῳ <u>νεφέλης</u> and
ἐν στύλῳ <u>πυρός</u> the underlined words tell us the materials from which
the pillars were made. For that reason this construction is known as
the genitive of material or content.

245. EXERCISES.

    a. Translate #238.

    b. Select an adjective in Column II to agree with every noun in Column I.

Column I	Column II
___ νυκτί	1) ὑψηλούς
___ ἡμέραι	2) μέσου
___ νεφέλᾱς	3) κακῆς
___ χεῖρας	4) ὑψηλήν
___ λαός	5) πάσῃ
___ πυρός	6) πρεσβύτεροι
___ ὑδάτων	7) ὑψηλαῖς
___ νεφέλαις	8) ἰδίᾱς
___ καρδίαις	9) πρῶτος
___ νεφελῶν	10) ὑψηλαί
___ στύλῳ	11) τούτων
___ νεφέλῃ	12) μέσαις
	13) ὑψηλῷ
	14) πάντας
	15) ξηρᾷ

    c. Translate the sentences and give the case usage of the underlined
       words.

       1) μὴ σκληρύνου τὴν κακὴν καρδίᾱν τὴν <u>νύκτα</u> πᾶσαν.

       2) σκληρυνεῖ ὁ κύριος τὰς ὑψηλὰς καρδίας τῶν κακῶν <u>νυκτί</u>.

       3) ὁ Ἰωσὴφ ἔμενεν ἐν τῇ Αἰγύπτῳ ἑπτὰ <u>ἔτη</u>.

       4) ταύτης τῆς <u>ἡμέρᾱς</u> φάγεται ἄρτον καὶ πίεται ὕδωρ.

       5) οὐκ ἔβλεψας ἡμᾶς ἐκείνης τῆς <u>νυκτός</u>.

       6) <u>νυκτὸς</u> ἡμᾶς ἐπιγνώσονται;

       7) ἐπεγνώσθητε τῆς <u>νυκτός</u>;

       8) ἐλθέ, Αἰγύπτιε, εἰς τὴν θάλασσαν, εἰς μέσον τῶν ὑδάτων, καὶ
          ἀπόθανε ταύτῃ τῇ <u>νυκτί</u>.

    d. Associate each of the following English words with Greek words
       introduced in this lesson.

       1) nephelometer: a device for measuring the <u>cloudiness</u> of a liquid.
       2) <u>nyctalopia</u>: <u>night</u> blindness, an inability to see well except
              in strong light.
       3) Pandemonium: where <u>all</u> demons dwell, John Milton's capital of
              Hell.
       4) scleroderma: a disease in which the skin is <u>hardened</u>.
       5) <u>Simeon Stylites</u>: Simeon who lived at the top of a <u>pillar</u>.
       6) <u>hydroelectric</u>: related to the production of electricity by
              the use of <u>water</u>.
       7) <u>chirography</u>: <u>handwriting</u>.

246. EAT A MAN!

ἡμέρᾳ τινὶ πάλαι διὰ τὸν Ἰησοῦν ἔφαγον ἄρτους καὶ ὀψάρια
πεντακισχίλιοι. μετὰ τὸ δεῖπνον ἐκεῖνο πάντας ἀπέστειλεν ὁ
διδάσκαλος. ἤθελε γὰρ προσεύχεσθαι τῷ θεῷ μόνος ἐκείνῃ τῇ νυκτί.
μακρὸν χρόνον προσηύξατο καὶ τότε πέραν τῆς θαλάσσης ἦλθεν. αὔριον
5 δὲ ὁ ὄχλος ἔβλεψεν Ἰησοῦν διδάσκοντα ἐν συναγωγῇ ἐν Καφαρναούμ.
"πῶς ἦλθες ὧδε;" εἶπέν τις τοῦ ὄχλου.

ἀπεκρίθη δὲ ὁ Ἰησοῦς, "ὅτι ἐφάγετε τὸν ἄρτον τὸν μένοντα χρόνον
μικρόν, ἐληλύθατε πρὸς ἐμὲ σήμερον. θέλετε τὸν ἄρτον τὸν αἰώνιον;"

τότε οὖν ἀπεκρίθη τις ἄλλος τοῦ ὄχλου, "θέλομεν σχεῖν τοῦτον τὸν
10 αἰώνιον ἄρτον."

ἀπεκρίθη οὖν ὁ Ἰησοῦς, "ὁ αἰώνιος ἄρτος ἐστὶν ὁ καταβαίνων ἐκ
τοῦ οὐρανοῦ. οὗτός ἐστιν ὁ ἄρτος ὁ ἀληθινός. οὗτος ὁ ἄρτος οἴσει τὴν
ζωὴν τὴν αἰώνιον τῷ ἐσθίοντι αὐτόν. καὶ ἐγώ εἰμι ὁ ἄρτος ὁ καταβαίνων
ἐκ τοῦ οὐρανοῦ. ὁ δὲ ἐσθίων ἐμὲ ἔχει τὴν ζωὴν τὴν μένουσαν."

15 ἀπεκρίθη δὲ ὁ ὄχλος, "πῶς ἰσχύσομεν ἐσθίειν σέ;"

ἀπεκρίθη οὖν ὁ Ἰησοῦς, "ὁ πιστεύων εἰς ἐμὲ ἐσθίει τοῦτον τὸν ἄρτον τὸν ἀληθινόν, καὶ ὁ πιστεύων εἰς ἐμὲ ἕξει τὴν ζωὴν τὴν ἀληθινήν."

οὕτως εἶπεν ὁ Ἰησοῦς πρὸς τὸν ὄχλον ἐν συναγωγῇ ἐν Καφαρναούμ.
τότε οὖν ἐπίστευσάν τινες αὐτῶν, ἄλλοι δὲ ἀπῆλθον ὅτι αἱ καρδίαι
20 ἐσκληρύνθησαν.

247. VOCABULARY.

αἰώνιος, -ᾱ (but distinct fem. endings are rarely used, -ος, -ου, etc.
        being usually found in forms agreeing with fem. nouns),
        -ον: eternal, everlasting

ἀληθινός, -ή, -όν: true, genuine (as opposed to spurious), real

ἀποκρίνομαι, --- , ἀπεκρινάμην (rare), --- , ἀπεκρίθην (frequent):
        I answer

ζωή, -ῆς, ἡ: life

καταβαίνω, καταβήσομαι, κατέβην (conjugation to be given in #262),
        καταβέβηκα, --- , --- : I go down, come down, descend

Καφαρναούμ (indecl.), ἡ: Capernaum

μόνος, -η, -ον: alone, only

οὐρανός, -οῦ, ὁ: heaven

ὄχλος, -ου, ὁ: crowd, multitude, throng

πεντακισχίλιοι, -αι, -α: five thousand

πέραν: (with abl. or gen.) beyond, across, on the other side of

προσεύχομαι, προσεύξομαι, προσηυξάμην, --- , --- :   I pray

248.   THE PARTICIPLE: ITS FUNCTION.   In #246 participles have been used several times.

ὁ ὄχλος ἔβλεψεν ᾿Ιησοῦν διδάσκοντα ἐν συναγωγῇ ἐν Καφαρναούμ.
The crowd saw Jesus teaching in a synagogue in Capernaum.

ἐφάγετε τὸν ἄρτον τὸν μένοντα χρόνον μικρόν.
You ate the bread which was lasting a little time,(literally) the lasting a little time.

ὁ αἰώνιος ἄρτος ἐστὶν ὁ καταβαίνων ἐκ τοῦ οὐρανοῦ.
The everlasting bread is that which comes down out of heaven, (literally) the /bread/ coming down out of heaven.

οὗτος ὁ ἄρτος οἴσει τὴν ζωὴν τῷ ἐσθίοντι αὐτόν.
This bread will bring life to the one who eats it, (literally) to the /man/ eating it.

A participle functions both as an adjective and as a verb. As an adjective, it modifies a noun or pronoun. In the following example μενῶν stands in restrictive attributive position. (#108)

ὁ ἄρτος ὁ μενῶν...
The bread which will last..., (literally) the bread the lasting.

As a verb, a participle of a transitive verb, for example, can have a direct object, an indirect object, and adverbial modifiers.

... τῷ ἐσθίοντι τοῦτον τὸν ἄρτον.
... to the one who eats this bread.   (direct object)

ὁ καταβαίνων ἐκ τοῦ οὐρανοῦ...
He who comes down out of heaven...   (adverbial phrase)

Like other adjectives (See #110) a participle may serve as a noun.

ὁ πιστεύων εἰς ἐμὲ ἕξει τὴν ζωὴν τὴν αἰώνιον.
He who believes, (literally) the believing /man/, in me will have everlasting life.

Other functions of the participle will be explained later.

249.   PRESENT ACTIVE PARTICIPLE.

Masculine	Feminine	Neuter
πιστεύων	πιστεύουσα	πιστεῦον
πιστεύοντος	πιστευούσης	πιστεύοντος
πιστεύοντι	πιστευούσῃ	πιστεύοντι
πιστεύοντα	πιστεύουσαν	πιστεῦον
πιστεύοντες	πιστεύουσαι	πιστεύοντα
πιστευόντων	πιστευουσῶν	πιστευόντων
πιστεύουσι	πιστευούσαις	πιστεύουσι
πιστεύοντας	πιστευούσᾱς	πιστεύοντα

The masculine and neuter forms belong to the third declension while the feminine forms belong to the first. The forms πιστεύουσι (masc. and neut.) represent a change from πιστεύοντσι. (Cf. ὧν p. 136 #305.)

250. FUTURE ACTIVE PARTICIPLE. The future active participle of most verbs studied thus far differs from the present active participle as the future active indicative differs from the present active indicative.

πιστεύω	πιστεύσω	πιστεύων	πιστεύσων
I believe	I shall believe	believing	being about to believe

μένω	μενῶ	μένων	μενῶν
I remain	I shall remain	remaining	being about to remain

διδάσκω	διδάξω	διδάσκων	διδάξων
I teach	I shall teach	teaching	being about to teach

Future Active Participle of πιστεύω

πιστεύσων	πιστεύσουσα	πιστεῦσον
πιστεύσοντος	πιστευσούσης	πιστεύσοντος
πιστεύσοντι	πιστευσούσῃ	πιστεύσοντι
πιστεύσοντα	πιστεύσουσαν	πιστεῦσον
πιστεύσοντες	πιστεύσουσαι	πιστεύσοντα
πιστευσόντων	πιστευσουσῶν	πιστευσόντων
πιστεύσουσι	πιστευσούσαις	πιστεύσουσι
πιστεύσοντας	πιστευσούσᾱς	πιστεύσοντα

Future Active Participle of μένω

μενῶν	μενοῦσα	μενοῦν
μενοῦντος	μενούσης	μενοῦντος
μενοῦντι	μενούσῃ	μενοῦντι
μενοῦντα	μενοῦσαν	μενοῦν
μενοῦντες	μενοῦσαι	μενοῦντα
μενούντων	μενουσῶν	μενούντων
μενοῦσι	μενούσαις	μενοῦσι
μενοῦντας	μενούσᾱς	μενοῦντα

Liquid verbs and other nasal verbs besides μένω have future active participles like μενῶν.

251. EXERCISES.

a. Translate #246.

b. After studying the examples in #248, translate the following expressions.

1) ὁ διδάσκαλος ὁ διδάσκων τὴν σχολὴν ἔσται μόνος ἐν Καφαρναοὺμ.

2) ὁ ἀδελφὸς τοῦ ἀληθινοῦ ἀγγέλου τοῦ σκληροῦντος τὴν καρδίᾱν αὐτοῦ....

3) ἐροῦμεν ταῖς ἀδελφαῖς ταῖς ἐπιγινωσκούσαις τὴν ἀλήθειαν.

4) συνηγάγετε τοὺς γεωργοὺς τοὺς θύοντας τὰ ἀρνία.

5) ὁ καταβαίνων ἐκ τῶν νεφελῶν ἦν ὁ μόνος βασιλεύς.

6) ἐν τῷ ἄρτῳ τῷ καταβαίνοντι ἐκ τοῦ οὐρανοῦ ζωή ἐστιν.

7) ἡ ζωὴ ἡ μενοῦσα ἔσται τοῖς ἐσθίουσι τὸν ἀληθινὸν ἄρτον.

8) ὁ μόνος ἐν Καφαρναοὺμ ἦν ὁ διδάξων πέραν τῆς θαλάσσης.

9) οἱ ἐσθίοντες ἦσαν πεντακισχίλιοι, αὐτῶν δὲ μόνοι οἱ πιστεύοντες προσηύξαντο.

10) ἡ μενοῦσα πέραν τῆς κώμης ἐν Καφαρναούμ προσεύξεται τῷ θεῷ ἐν τῷ οὐρανῷ περὶ τῶν πεντακισχιλίων.

11) πέραν τῆς θαλάσσης ἤγαγεν ὁ ὄχλος τῶν πεντακισχιλίων τὸν διδάσκαλον τὸν μένοντα ἐν τῇ ουναγωγῇ ἐν Καφαρναούμ.

c. Translate the English in parentheses so as to fit the Greek that is given. Use participles for all the verbal ideas.

1) (A hardening) θεός.

2) θεός (hardening hearts).

3) ὁ θεός (who hardens hearts).

4) μήτηρ (who is about to teach).

5) μήτηρ (who will teach).

6) τέχνου (remaining).

7) τέχνου (who remains).

8) τέχνῳ (who will remain in heaven).

9) τέχνοις (who will remain in heaven).

10) ἀπὸ πεντακισχιλίων μητρῶν (who eat).

11) πεντακισχιλίοις τέχνοις (who will believe).

12) ἐν πεντακισχιλίοις ἀνθρώποις (who will teach).

LESSON 33

252. CALEB AND JOSHUA.

        μακρὸν χρόνον ἐν τῇ ἐρήμῳ Μωυσῆς ἦγε τοὺς υἱοὺς Ἰσραήλ.
οὗτοι γὰρ οἱ ἐλθόντες διὰ τῆς θαλάσσης κατὰ τὸ ξηρὸν ἔμειναν
ἐν τῇ ἐρήμῳ ἔτη καὶ ἐκεῖ τὸν νόμον ἔλαβον.

        ὁ θεὸς ὁ γράψας τοῦτον τὸν νόμον ἐπὶ δύσι λίθοις εἶπε
5   τῷ Μωυσεῖ διδάσκειν τὸν λαὸν τὸν νόμον. ἀλλ’ οὗτος ὁ λαὸς ὁ
εἰπὼν ὅτι πείσονται τῷ νόμῳ τοῦ θεοῦ οὐκ ἴσχυον. διὰ τοῦτο
ἀπέθανον ἐκεῖ ἐν τῇ ἐρήμῳ. μόνοι οὖν δύο τῶν ἐλθόντων ἐκ τῆς
Αἰγύπτου, Ἰησοῦς καὶ Χαλέβ, εἰς τὴν γῆν τῆς Χαναὰν ἦλθον.
ἐπιγινώσκομεν οὖν τὰ ὀνόματα τῶν δύο εἰπόντων καλὰ περὶ τοῦ

10 θεοῦ καὶ περὶ τῆς Χαναάν. Χαλὲβ καὶ Ἰησοῦς, ταῦτά ἐστι τὰ

δύο ὀνόματα τῶν ἐλθόντων εἰς τὴν Χαναὰν καὶ μεινάντων ἐκεῖ κατὰ

τὴν ἐπαγγελίαν τοῦ θεοῦ. τόπους ἑαυτοῖς ἐν τῇ γῇ Χαναὰν ἔλαβον

Χαλὲβ καὶ Ἰησοῦς δύο οἱ πιστεύσαντες τῷ κυρίῳ τῷ σωτῆρι ἑαυτῶν.

τὰ οὖν ὀνόματα τούτων δύο μεμένηκεν. ἐπιγνώσῃ δὲ σὺ ὅτι

15 Ἰησοῦς ἐστι τὸ ὄνομα τοῦ κυρίου ἡμῶν ἐν τῇ γλώσσῃ τῇ Ἑλληνικῇ.

τοῦτο τὸ ὄνομα ἡμῖν λέγει ὅτι σωτήρ ἐστιν ὁ κύριος.

253. VOCABULARY.

δύο (nom., abl., gen., acc.), δυσί (loc., instr., dat.): two

ἔρημος, -ου, ἡ: desert, wilderness

λίθος, -ου, ὁ: stone

νόμος, -ου, ὁ: law

ὄνομα, -ατος, τό: name

σωτήρ, -τῆρος, ὁ: savior, deliverer, preserver

Χαλέβ (indecl.), ὁ: Caleb

Χαναάν (indecl.), ἡ: Canaan

254. MORE THIRD DECLENSION NOUNS: ὁ σωτήρ & τὸ ὄνομα.

σωτήρ	σωτῆρες	ὄνομα	ὀνόματα
σωτῆρος	σωτήρων	ὀνόματος	ὀνομάτων
σωτῆρι	σωτῆρσι	ὀνόματι	ὀνόμασι
σωτῆρα	σωτῆρας	ὄνομα	ὀνόματα

αἷμα, given in #224, is declined like ὄνομα.

255. AORIST ACTIVE PARTICIPLE. (Notice that no augment is used.)

First Aorist

πιστεύσᾱς	πιστεύσᾱσα	πιστεῦσαν
πιστεύσαντος	πιστευσάσης	πιστεύσαντος
πιστεύσαντι	πιστευσάσῃ	πιστεύσαντι
πιστεύσαντα	πιστεύσᾱσαν	πιστεῦσαν
πιστεύσαντες	πιστεύσᾱσαι	πιστεύσαντα
πιστευσάντων	πιστευσᾱσῶν	πιστευσάντων
πιστεύσᾱσι	πιστευσάσαις	πιστεύσᾱσι
πιστεύσαντας	πιστευσάσᾱς	πιστεύσαντα

Second Aorist

ἐλθών	ἐλθοῦσα	ἐλθόν
ἐλθόντος	ἐλθούσης	ἐλθόντος
ἐλθόντι	ἐλθούσῃ	ἐλθόντι
ἐλθόντα	ἐλθοῦσαν	ἐλθόν
ἐλθόντες	ἐλθοῦσαι	ἐλθόντα
ἐλθόντων	ἐλθουσῶν	ἐλθόντων
ἐλθοῦσι	ἐλθούσαις	ἐλθοῦσι
ἐλθόντας	ἐλθούσᾱς	ἐλθόντα

Notice the accent in the second aorist active participle.

μείνᾱς	μείνᾱσα	μεῖναν
μείναντος	μεινᾱσης	μείναντος
μείναντι	μεινᾱσῃ	μείναντι
μείναντα	μείνᾱσαν	μεῖναν
μείναντες	μείνᾱσαι	μείναντα
μεινάντων	μεινᾱσῶν	μεινάντων
μείνᾱσι	μεινᾱσαις	μείνᾱσι
μείναντας	μεινᾱσᾱς	μείναντα

The endings for liquid and nasal aorist active participles are the same as those for the first aorist minus the -σ-.

256. SIGNIFICANCE OF TENSE IN PARTICIPLES.

a. Kind of action. Tense implies kind of action in participles as in finite forms of verbs.

The present participle indicates linear action.

ὁ λέγων ἐσθίει.
The man who is speaking is eating.

The aorist participle indicates punctiliar action.

ὁ εἰπών ἐσθίει.
The man who spoke is eating.

The perfect participle, which will be introduced later, indicates completed action.

b. Relative time. Besides kind of action the tense of a participle indicates time relative to that of the context.

1) Time previous to that of the context, when expressed by a participle, is usually indicated by the aorist or perfect.

ὁ εἰπών ἐσθίει.
The man who has spoken is eating.

ὁ εἰπών φάγεται.
The man who will have spoken will eat.

ὁ εἰπών ἔφαγε.
The man who had spoken ate.

2) Time coincident with that of the context, when expressed by a participle, is usually indicated by the present but frequently also by the aorist accompanying an aorist indicative.

ὁ λέγων ἐσθίει.
The man who is speaking is eating.

ὁ λέγων ἤσθιε.
The man who was speaking was eating.

ὁ λέγων φάγεται.
The man who will be speaking will be eating.

ὁ εἰπών ἔφαγεν.
The man who spoke ate.

This last example by itself is ambiguous and may be translated, "The man who had spoken ate." A wider context than we have here is needed to establish εἰπών as expressing either previous or coincident time.

3) Time subsequent to that of the context, when expressed by a participle, is usually indicated by the future.

ὁ ἐρῶν ἐσθίει.
The man who will speak is eating.

ὁ ἐρῶν αὔριον φάγεται σήμερον.
The man who will speak tomorrow will eat today.

ὁ ἐρῶν σήμερον ἔφαγεν ἐχθές.
The man who was to speak today ate yesterday.

257. COLLECTIVE NOUN IN SINGULAR AS SUBJECT OF A PLURAL VERB. In the sentence ὁ λαὸς πείθεσθαι τῷ νόμῳ οὐκ ἴσχυον, the people were not able to obey the law, the subject λαός is singular in form while the verb ἴσχυον with which it is used is plural. The reason for this plural verb lies in the fact that the subject λαός is a collective noun comprehending in its meaning many individuals. The plural verb shows that the individuals in the group were unable to obey the law. The construction is not infrequently used.

258. NEUTER NOUN IN PLURAL AS SUBJECT OF A SINGULAR VERB. In the sentence τὰ οὖν ὀνόματα τούτων δύο μεμένηκεν, the names, therefore, of these two have remained, we have an illustration of a frequent occurrence in the New Testament. Often a neuter plural subject is followed by a singular verb.

259. EXERCISES.

a. Translate #252.

b. Give the appropriate form of μείνᾱς, ἐλθών, ἐρῶν, and ἀκούσᾱς to agree with each of the following nouns.

1) λίθῳ		9) λίθους	
2) τὴν Χαναάν		10) προβάτοις	
3) σωτῆρα		11) ἡ γυνή	
4) τοῦ Χαλέβ		12) προβάτου	
5) νόμων		13) Μαρίᾳ	
6) λίθου		14) νεφέλᾱς	
7) ὑπηρέται		15) ἐρήμῳ	
8) τέκνα		16) λίθοις	

c. Translate.

1) ἐγὼ Χαλέβ ὁ βλέπων σε ὧδέ εἰμι ἐν τῇ ἐρήμῳ.

2) σὺ ὁ βλέψων ἐμὲ μενεῖς ἐν τῷ οἴκῳ.

3) ἡμεῖς οἱ βλέψαντες Χαλέβ ἦμεν μακάριοι.

d. Translate.

1) The thing that persuaded me was a stone.
2) The woman who taught the children. . .
3) The man who will want to throw stones is Caleb.

112

e. By combining each item in Column I with each item in Column II, form nine sentences and translate them.

Column I	Column II
1) ὁ λαμβάνων τὸν σωτῆρα	1) βλέπει τὴν ἀλήθειαν ἐν αὐτῷ.
2) ὁ ἕξων τὸν σωτῆρα	2) βλέψει τὴν ἀλήθειαν ἐν αὐτῷ.
3) ὁ σχὼν τὸν σωτῆρα	3) ἔβλεψε τὴν ἀλήθειαν ἐν αὐτῷ.

f. Associate the following English words with the new Greek words in this lesson.

1) lithography: printing by the use of stone.
2) astronomy: the laws of the stars, the body of knowledge about the stars.
3) onomatopoeia: making a name to imitate a sound.
4) soteriology: that division of theology which deals with Jesus Christ as Savior.

LESSON 34

260. STIRRING WORDS FROM AN OLD SOLDIER.

ἀγαγὼν τοὺς υἱοὺς Ἰσραὴλ πέραν τοῦ Ἰορδάνου εἰς τὴν Χαναὰν καὶ σχὼν τὴν γῆν Χαναάν, ὁ Ἰησοῦς δοῦλος κυρίου συνήγαγε πάντας τοὺς υἱοὺς τοῦ Ἰσραήλ.

καὶ πρὸς τὸν λαὸν εἶπεν Ἰησοῦς, "ταῦτα λέγει κύριος ὁ θεὸς Ἰσ-
5   ραήλ, 'πάλαι ἐν γῇ μακρᾷ οἱ πατέρες ὑμῶν οὐκ ἐλάτρευσαν ἐμοί. καὶ εἰληφὼς τὸν πατέρα ὑμῶν τὸν Αβραμ ἐκ τῆς γῆς ἐκείνης, ἤγαγον αὐτὸν εἰς ταύτην τὴν γῆν. ἀλλὰ τότε ταύτην τὴν γῆν αὐτῷ οὐκ ἔδωκα. καὶ ἔδωκα αὐτῷ υἱόν, καὶ ἔδωκα τῷ υἱῷ τούτῳ τὸν Ἰακὼβ καὶ τὸν ἀδελφόν. καὶ Ἰακὼβ καὶ οἱ υἱοὶ αὐτοῦ κατέβησαν εἰς Αἴγυπτον, καὶ ἐγένοντο ἐκεῖ
10 ἔθνος. ἀλλ' ἐγένοντο δοῦλοι τῶν Αἰγυπτίων. καὶ ἐπεὶ ἐγένοντο αἱ πληγαὶ ἐν τῇ Αἰγύπτῳ, ἤγαγον τοὺς πατέρας ὑμῶν ἐκ τῆς γῆς. καὶ ὑμεῖς ἐβλέψατε τὰς τοῦ κυρίου πληγὰς ἐν τῇ γῇ Αἰγύπτῳ, καὶ ἦτε ἐν τῇ ἐρήμῳ χρόνον μακρόν.'

"ἐγὼ ἤγαγον ὑμᾶς διὰ τοῦ Ἰορδάνου, καὶ ἔδωκε ταύτην τὴν γῆν

15 κύριος ὑμῖν. καὶ νῦν λατρεύσατε τῷ κυρίῳ. μὴ δὲ θέλοντες λατρεύειν

κυρίῳ, τίνι λατρεύσετε; τοῖς θεοῖς τῶν πατέρων ὑμῶν, τοῖς ἐν τῇ μακρᾷ

γῇ ἐκείνῃ λατρεύσετε; ἢ τοῖς θεοῖς τῶν ἐχθρῶν ἐν ταύτῃ τῇ γῇ λατρεύ-

σετε; ἐγὼ δὲ καὶ ὁ οἶκός μου λατρεύσομεν κυρίῳ."

καὶ ὁ λαὸς εἶπε, "κύριος ὁ θεὸς ἡμῶν αὐτὸς θεός ἐστιν. αὐτὸς

20 ἤγαγεν ἡμᾶς καὶ τοὺς πατέρας ἡμῶν ἐξ Αἰγύπτου, ἔβαλεν ἐκ τῆς γῆς ἡμῶν

κύριος πάντα τὰ ἔθνη τὰ μεμενηκότα ὧδε, καὶ ἔδωκεν ἡμῖν τὴν γῆν. ἡμεῖς

καὶ λατρεύσομεν κυρίῳ, οὗτος γὰρ θεὸς ἡμῶν ἐστι."

261. VOCABULARY.

ἔδωκα (aor. indic. act. 1st sing. δίδωμι: I give): I gave, have given

ἔδωκε (3rd sing. of ἔδωκα): he gave, has given

ἔθνος, -ους, τό: nation, people; (pl.) nations, Gentiles

λατρεύω, λατρεύσω, ἐλάτρευσα, --- , --- , --- : I serve, worship (with
                                                            (dat. dir. obj.)

262. MI AORIST: καταβαίνω AND ἐπιγινώσκω. The aorist actives of καταβαίνω
and ἐπιγινώσκω are classified with those of verbs whose first principal
part ends in -μι. These verbs will be studied later.

καταβαίνω

Indicative

κατέβην	κατέβημεν
κατέβης	κατέβητε
κατέβη	κατέβησαν

Imperative

κατάβηθι	κατάβατε
καταβάτω	καταβάτωσαν

Infinitive

καταβῆναι

Participle

καταβάς	καταβᾶσα	καταβάν
καταβάντος	καταβάσης	καταβάντος
καταβάντι	καταβάσῃ	καταβάντι
etc.	etc.	etc.

ἐπιγινώσκω

Indicative

ἐπέγνων	ἐπέγνωμεν
ἐπέγνως	ἐπέγνωτε
ἐπέγνω	ἐπέγνωσαν

Imperative

ἐπίγνωθι	ἐπιγνῶτε
ἐπιγνώτω	ἐπιγνώτωσαν

Infinitive

ἐπιγνῶναι

Participle

ἐπιγνούς	ἐπιγνοῦσα	ἐπιγνόν
ἐπιγνόντος	ἐπιγνούσης	ἐπιγνόντος
ἐπιγνόντι	ἐπιγνούσῃ	ἐπιγνόντι
etc.	etc.	etc.

263. OTHER THIRD DECLENSION NOUNS: ὁ πατήρ & τὸ ἔθνος.

πατήρ	πατέρες	ἔθνος	ἔθνη
πατρός	πατέρων	ἔθνους	ἐθνῶν
πατρί	πατράσι	ἔθνει	ἔθνεσι
πατέρα	πατέρας	ἔθνος	ἔθνη
πάτερ			

ἔτος introduced in #173 by the form ἔτη is declined like ἔθνος.

Notice the three grades of the last stem vowel in πατήρ, πατέρα, and πατρός: -η-, -ε-, and no vowel at all. We have a distinct vocative in the singular of this noun.

264. PERFECT ACTIVE PARTICIPLE.

First Perfect: θεραπεύω.

τεθεραπευκώς	τεθεραπευκυῖα	τεθεραπευκός
τεθεραπευκότος	τεθεραπευκυίᾱς	τεθεραπευκότος
τεθεραπευκότι	τεθεραπευκυίᾳ	τεθεραπευκότι
τεθεραπευκότα	τεθεραπευκυῖαν	τεθεραπευκός
τεθεραπευκότες	τεθεραπευκυῖαι	τεθεραπευκότα
τεθεραπευκότων	τεθεραπευκυιῶν	τεθεραπευκότων
τεθεραπευκόσι	τεθεραπευκυίαις	τεθεραπευκόσι
τεθεραπευκότας	τεθεραπευκυίᾱς	τεθεραπευκότα

Second Perfect: λαμβάνω.

εἰληφώς	εἰληφυῖα	εἰληφός
εἰληφότος	εἰληφυίᾱς	εἰληφότος
εἰληφότι	εἰληφυίᾳ	εἰληφότι
εἰληφότα	εἰληφυῖαν	εἰληφός
εἰληφότες	εἰληφυῖαι	εἰληφότα
εἰληφότων	εἰληφυιῶν	εἰληφότων
εἰληφόσι	εἰληφυίαις	εἰληφόσι
εἰληφότας	εἰληφυίᾱς	εἰληφότα

265. RÉSUMÉ OF ADJECTIVAL AND SUBSTANTIVAL EMPHASES OF PARTICIPLES. We have met in the last lesson participles used with an emphasis on the adjectival or substantival function.

ὁ λέγων ἄνθρωπος ἐσθίει.
The speaking man is eating.

ὁ εἰρηκὼς ἄνθρωπος ἐσθίει.
The having-spoken man is eating.

ὁ λέγων ἐσθίει.
The one who speaks is eating.

ὁ εἰρηκώς ἐσθίει.
The one who has spoken is eating.

In the first two sentences λέγων and εἰρηκώς are used as adjectives modifying ἄνθρωπος; in the second two sentences λέγων and εἰρηκώς are used as substantives or nouns. In ὁ λέγων ἄνθρωπος the participle is in ascriptive attributive position. In ὁ ἄνθρωπος ὁ λέγων the participle is in restrictive attributive position.

266. ADVERBIAL EMPHASIS. Participles may be used in predicate position as well as in attributive position. Since no article is used with ἄνθρωπος in the following example, εἰρηκώς may be considered either attributive or predicate.

εἰρηκὼς ἄνθρωπος ἐσθίει. (attributive use assumed)
A having-spoken man is eating, (or) a man who has spoken is eating.

Understood this way, εἰρηκώς has an adjectival emphasis, but another interpretation is possible when an adverbial emphasis is understood.

εἰρηκὼς ἄνθρωπος ἐσθίει. (predicate use assumed)
Having spoken, a man eats.

But this ambiguity of interpretation immediately disappears when a definite article is used with ἄνθρωπος. Now εἰρηκώς is inevitably in predicate position.

εἰρηκὼς ὁ ἄνθρωπος ἐσθίει.
Having spoken, the man eats.

This may mean any one of several things, but in all of them the participle has an adverbial emphasis.

After he has spoken, the man eats. (He performs one action after the other.)

Although he has spoken, the man eats. (In spite of his having threatened not to eat, he eats anyway.)

Because he has spoken, the man eats. (He earns his living by public speaking.)

If he has spoken, the man eats. (His livelihood is dependent on his speaking.)

All of these various interpretations are merely deductions from imagined contexts, which are not given here. Still εἰρηκώς by itself means having spoken, and this is all the Greek says. The rest of the ideas suggested are legitimately expressed in a translation when the contexts justify them, not otherwise.

A participle with adverbial emphasis may be used in a context implying the following ideas listed in the probable order of the frequency of their occurrence: time, cause, attendant circumstance, condition, concession, manner, means, and purpose. These ideas applied to λέγων ὁ ἄνθρωπος ἐσθίει yield the following phrasings for λέγων.

a. Time: While he speaks . . .
          (εἰπών would mean "After he has spoken . . ."

b. Cause: Because he speaks . . .

c. Attendant circumstance: The man speaks and (eats).

d. Condition: If he speaks . . .

e. Concession: Although he speaks . . .

f. Manner: In speaking . . .
            By way of speaking . . .
            (Such an interpretation is nonsense here.)

g. Means: By means of speaking . . .

h. Purpose: In order to speak . . .(a rather infrequent use)

267. EXERCISES.

a. Translate #260.

b. Translate literally and then more freely, using devices listed in #266 for each indicated emphasis.

1) (Time) δουλεύουσα ἐν τῷ οἴκῳ ἤκουσε τοῦ πρεσβυτέρου.

2) (Time) δουλεύσασα ἐν τῷ οἴκῳ ἤκουσε τοῦ πρεσβυτέρου.

3) (Cause) τεθεραπευκότες ἐλάβετε δωρεὰς ἐκ τῶν ἐθνῶν.

4) (Attendant circumstance) ἐλθὼν εἰς τὸν οἶκον ὁ δοῦλος ἤνεγκε τὸ δεῖπνον τῷ κυρίῳ.

5) (Condition) μεμενηκυῖαι ἐν τῇ ἀληθείᾳ ἐπιγνώσονται τὸν θεόν.

6) (Manner) ἐλπίζων, μνημονεύει τῆς ἐπαγγελίας.

7) (Means) διδάσκοντες τὴν ἀλήθειαν ἐλπίζομεν πείθειν τὰ ἔθνη.

8) (Purpose) ὁ ὄχλος ἀπῆλθε πέραν τῆς θαλάσσης βλέψων τὸν διδάσκαλον.

c. Translate the following sentences. Notice that the sentence patterns are simple and that the Greek participles are usually more compact than the English needed to convey the meaning of the participles.

1) τίσι δωρεὰς οἴσετε πέραν τῆς θαλάσσης;

2) τίσι δύο δωρεὰς μενούσας (pres.) οἴσετε;

3) τίσι τὰς δωρεὰς τὰς μενούσας (fut.) πάντοτε οἴσετε;

4) τίσι τὰς δωρεὰς τὰς μεμενηκυίας ὧδε χρόνον μακρὸν οἴσετε;

5) τίσι ἔχουσι τὸ ἀργύριον οἴσετε δωρεάς;

6) τίσι σχοῦσι τὸ ἀργύριον οἴσεις δωρεάς;

7) τίσι ἐσχηκυίαις τὸ ἀργύριον οἴσεις τὰς δωρεὰς τὰς μεινάσας ἐν τούτῳ τῷ οἴκῳ;

8) τινῶν τὰ τέκνα βλέπομεν;

9) τὰ τέκνα τινῶν ἀνθρώπων ἐπιγνόντων τὴν ἀλήθειαν βλέπομεν;

10) τινῶν τὰ τέκνα τὰ σκληρύνοντα τὰς καρδίας βλέπομεν;

11) τινῶν τὰ τέκνα βλέπομεν καταβαίνοντες ἐκ τῶν ‘Ιεροσολύμων;

12) τινῶν ἀνθρώπων ἐπιγνόντων τὴν ἀλήθειαν βλέπομεν τὰ σκληρύνοντα τὰς καρδίας τέκνα καταβαίνοντες ἐκ τῶν ‘Ιεροσολύμων;

d. Make the perfect active participle of each of the verbs in Column II agree with each of the nouns in Column I.

Column I	Column II
1) τοῦ ἔθνους	λέγω
2) ἡ ἡμέρᾳ	πείθω
3) τῷ ὀνόματι	μένω
4) τὴν θάλασσαν	ἔρχομαι
5) τὸν σωτῆρα	λαμβάνω
6) τὰς νεφέλᾱς	θεραπεύω

7) τῇ ζωῇ
8) αἱ νύκτες
9) ταῖς χερσί
10) τῷ πυρί
11) τὰ ὕδατα
12) τῶν στύλων
13) τῇ πληγῇ
14) τῷ ξηρῷ

e. Associate the following English words with new Greek words in this lesson.

1) ethnology: study of racial divisions of mankind.
2) idolatry: worship of an image.

LESSON 35

268. A NEW GENERATION THAT KNEW NOT THE LORD.

καὶ ἐδούλευσεν ὁ λαὸς τῷ κυρίῳ πάσᾱς τὰς ἡμέρᾱς 'Ιησοῦ τοῦ δούλου κυρίου καὶ πάσᾱς τὰς ἡμέρᾱς τῶν πρεσβυτέρων τῶν ἐπιγνόντων πᾶν
τὸ ἔργον κυρίου καὶ πῶς ἐσεσώκει τὸν 'Ισραήλ.

ἐπεὶ ἀπέθανεν 'Ιησοῦς ὁ δοῦλος κυρίου καὶ ἀπέθανε πᾶσα ἡ γενεὰ
5   ἐκείνη, οὐκέτι ἐμνημόνευεν ὁ λαὸς τῶν ἔργων τοῦ κυρίου. καὶ ἐγένοντο
οἱ υἱοὶ 'Ισραηλ κακοί, καὶ ἐλάτρευσαν τοῖς θεοῖς τῶν ἐθνῶν. καὶ ἐγκατέλιπον τὸν κύριον τὸν θεὸν τῶν πατέρων αὐτῶν τὸν ἀγαγόντα αὐτοὺς
ἐκ γῆς Αἰγύπτου, καὶ ἐδίωξαν τοὺς θεοὺς τῶν ἐθνῶν.

ὀργιζόμενος τοῖς ἔργοις τοῦ 'Ισραηλ, οὐκ ἔσωσεν ὁ θεὸς αὐτοὺς ἐκ
10 τῶν ἐχθρῶν αὐτῶν. προσευξαμένοις δὲ τῷ θεῷ διὰ τοὺς ἐχθροὺς αὐτῶν,
τοῖς υἱοῖς 'Ισραηλ οὐκ ὠργίζετο ἀλλ' ἔδωκεν ὁ θεὸς σωτῆρα κριτὴν σώ-
σοντα 'Ισραηλ ἐκ τῶν χειρῶν τῶν ἐχθρῶν αὐτῶν. καὶ ἦν κύριος μετὰ τοῦ
κριτοῦ. σωζόμενοι οὖν ἦσαν πάσᾱς τὰς ἡμέρᾱς τοῦ κριτοῦ.

ὅτε δὲ ἀπέθνησκε ὁ κριτής, πάλιν ἐγκατέλειπον τὸν κύριον τὸν θεὸν
15 τῶν πατέρων αὐτῶν διώξοντες τοὺς θεοὺς τῶν ἐθνῶν καὶ λατρεύσοντες αὐτοῖς. πάλιν ὀργιζόμενος τοῖς κακοῖς ἔργοις οὐκ ἔσωσεν ὁ θεὸς ἐκ τῶν
ἐχθρῶν αὐτῶν.

269. VOCABULARY.

γενεά, -ᾶς, ἡ: generation

ἐγκαταλείπω, ἐγκαταλείψω, ἐγκατέλιπον, ---- , ---- , ἐγκατελείφθην:
I abandon, forsake, desert, leave behind

ἔργον, -ου, τό: work, task, deed, action

κριτής, -οῦ, ὁ: judge

(with dat. of person)

ὀργίζομαι, ---- , ---- , ---- , ὠργίσθην: I am provoked to anger, am angry

σῴζω, σώσω, ἔσωσα, σέσωκα, σέσωσμαι, ἐσώθην: I save, preserve, rescue,
keep safe

270. MIDDLE PARTICIPLES. (Forms ending in -μενος, -μένη, -μενον.)

  a. Tenses having middle participles distinct in form from the corresponding passive.

    1) Future.

λατρευσόμενος	λατρευσομένη	λατρευσόμενον
λατρευσομένου	λατρευσομένης	λατρευσομένου
etc.	etc.	etc.

    The endings of all middle participles are like those of καλός,
καλή, καλόν given in #107, but the accent is like that of
ἕκαστος, except for the perfect in b.2 below.

ἀποστελούμενος	ἀποστελουμένη	ἀποστελούμενον

    Liquid and nasal stems differ from λατρεύω only in having -ου-
instead of -σο-.

    2) Aorist.

λατρευσάμενος	λατρευσαμένη	λατρευσάμενον
λατρευσαμένου	λατρευσαμένης	λατρευσαμένου
etc.	etc.	etc.

    Notice again that the aorist participle has <u>no augment</u>.

ἐντειλάμενος	ἐντειλαμένη	ἐντειλάμενον

    Liquid and nasal stems differ from λατρεύω only in having -α-
instead of -σα-.

γενόμενος	γενομένη	γενόμενον

    The second aorist middle participle differs from the present
(γινόμενος) only in the stem.

  b. Tenses having middle participles identical in form with the corresponding passive.

    1) Present.

λατρευόμενος	λατρευομένη	λατρευόμενον
λατρευομένου	λατρευομένης	λατρευομένου
etc.	etc.	etc.

    2) Perfect.

τεθεραπευμένος	τεθεραπευμένη	τεθεραπευμένον
τεθεραπευμένου	τεθεραπευμένης	τεθεραπευμένου
etc.	etc.	etc.

The accent <u>always falls</u> <u>on</u> <u>the penult</u> in the perfect middle and passive participle.

271. A COMPARISON OF THE INDICATIVE AND THE PARTICIPLE IN THE MIDDLE.

Present	θεραπεύομαι	I heal myself I am healed
	θεραπευόμενος	healing oneself being healed
Future	θεραπεύσομαι θεραπευσόμενος	I shall heal myself being about to heal oneself
Aorist	ἐθεραπευσάμην θεραπευσάμενος	I healed myself having healed oneself
Perfect	τεθεράπευμαι	I have healed myself I have been healed
	τεθεραπευμένος	having healed oneself having been healed

272. THE SUPPLEMENTARY PARTICIPLE.

a. In periphrastic verbs. In addition to the uses of the participle summarized or explained in Lesson 34 we have in #268 an example of a supplementary use.

ἦσαν σωζόμενοι πάσας τὰς ἡμέρας τοῦ κριτοῦ.
<u>They</u> <u>were</u> <u>being</u> <u>preserved</u> all the days of the judge.

The thought could have been expressed by an imperfect passive thus: ἐσώζοντο. This single word and the longer form, which is called a periphrastic imperfect passive, were both in use at the time the New Testament was written.

The term <u>supplementary</u> carries the idea that the participle furnishes what is otherwise lacking in the meaning expressed by the verb.

b. With some verbs indicating sense perception, often equivalent to indirect discourse.

ὁ λαὸς ἤκουσε τοῦ διδασκάλου λέγοντος περὶ τῶν ἑαυτοῦ ἔργων.
The people heard the prophet <u>speaking</u> about his own deeds.

ὁ μαθητὴς ἀκούει τοὺς ἀνθρώπους πιστεύσαντας εἰς Ἰησοῦν.
The disciple hears that the men <u>believed</u> on Jesus, (literally) the men <u>having</u> <u>believed</u> on Jesus.

It will be observed that ἀκούω is both a verb of sense perception and one capable of introducing indirect discourse.

273. EXERCISES.

a. Translate #268.

b. Translate.

1) αὕτη ἡ γενεὰ τῶν υἱῶν τοῦ Ἰσραὴλ ὑπὸ τοῦ διδασκάλου πειθομένη ἦν ἐγκαταλιπεῖν τὸν ἀληθινὸν θεόν.

2) οὗτος εἴληπται λέγων ταύτῃ τῇ γενεᾷ ὅτι οἱ θεοὶ τῶν ἐθνῶν εἰσι καλοί.

3) ὁ λέγων ταῦτα πείθεται τῷ ἀληθινῷ θεῷ.

4) οὐχί. τῷ ἑαυτῶν κριτῇ τῷ κακῷ ἐπίστευσαν ἐκεῖναι αἱ γενεαί.

5) ἀποκτείνων τὸν ἐχθρὸν ὁ λαὸς χαρήσεται.

c. Locate the following participles by giving (1) tense, (2) voice, (3) gender, (4) number, (5) inflectional form, and (6) first principal part.

1) ἀπερχόμενοι

6) γενομένᾱς

2) ἐγκαταλιποῦσι

7) καταβησομένῃ

3) λατρεύουσι

8) ἄγον

4) ἐγκαταλειψόντων

9) προσευξαμένῳ

5) ὀργιζομένους

10) καταβάντα

d. Select the participles which correctly and most suitably complete the following sentences.

1) ἀκούσομεν ταύτης _____.

    a) διδάσκοντος
    b) διδάσκων
    c) διδαξομένῃ
    d) διδασκούσης
    e) διδασκομένων

2) ἡ _____ τὸ ἑαυτῆς ὄνομα ἀπῆλθεν ἐχθές.

    a) γραφομένης
    b) γράψᾱσα
    c) γράφουσαν
    d) γεγραμμένη
    e) γράψων

3) ἐβλέψατε τὰ τέκνα _____.

    a) φαγομένη
    b) φαγόν
    c) ἐσθίον
    d) ἐσθίουσα
    e) ἐσθίοντα

4) _____ οὐκ ἦν δυνατὸς θεραπεῦσαι τὸν πατέρα.

    a) ἐληλυθώς
    b) ἦλθον
    c) ἐλθόν
    d) ἐρχομένων
    e) ἐλευσομένου

e. Associate the following English words with new Greek words in this lesson.

1) genealogy: a record of generations, a family tree.
2) erg: a unit for measuring energy or work.
3) critic: one given to expressing judgment.

274. VOCABULARY. Review thoroughly the vocabulary introduced since Lesson 30.

NOUNS	VERBS	ADJECTIVES
γενεά	ἀποκρίνομαι	αἰώνιος
ἔθνος	ἐγκαταλείπω	ἀληθινός
ἔργον	ἔδωκα	δύο
ἔρημος	ἔδωκε	μέσος
ζωή	καταβαίνω	μόνος
ἡμέρα	λατρεύω	ξηρός
θάλασσα	ὀργίζομαι	πᾶς
Καφαρναούμ	προσεύχομαι	πεντακισχίλιοι
κριτής	σκληρύνω	ὑψηλός
λίθος	σώζω	
νεφέλη		
νόμος		
νύξ		
ὄνομα		
οὐρανός		
ὄχλος		
πῦρ		PHRASES
στῦλος	PREPOSITIONS	
σωτήρ		
ὕδωρ		
Χαλέβ		εἰς μέσον
Χαναάν	κατά	ἐν χειρὶ ὑψηλῇ
χείρ	πέραν	κατὰ τὸ ξηρόν

275. Notice carefully the following patterns for the position of participles (P) with relation to nouns (N) and definite articles (A).

Adjectival use: (APN
                    (ANAP

Substantival use: AP

Adverbial use: (PAN
                   (ANP

Ambiguous use: (PN
                   (NP

276. Select the translation most appropriate for each Greek sentence.

a. πιόντες ὕδωρ οὐκ ἐφάγομεν ἄρτον.

   1) By having drunk water, we do not eat bread.
   2) If we have drunk water, we do not eat bread.
   3) Although we had drunk water, we did not eat bread.
   4) Because we drank water, we shall not eat bread.
   5) In order that we have drunk water, we have not eaten bread.

b. μανθάνουσι τὴν ἀλήθειαν ὑμῖν δουλεύσω ἐν ταύτῃ τῇ σχολῇ.

   1) If you have learned the truth, I serve you in this school.
   2) While you are learning the truth, I will serve you in this school.
   3) Because you will learn the truth, I serve you in this school.
   4) I served you in this school in order to learn the truth.
   5) I serve although you have learned the truth in this school.

c. ἐλεύσεται εἰς τὴν σχολὴν διδάξων ὑμᾶς τὴν παρρησίαν.

1) He will proceed into the school in order that he may teach you boldness.
2) He will proceed into the school although he was teaching you boldness.
3) He will proceed into the school when it is about to teach you boldness.
4) He will proceed into the school if it is about to teach you boldness.
5) He will proceed into the school after he has taught you boldness.

277. Select the Greek most suitable for translating all the underlined English.

a. The elder brought fish into the village because he was wishing to eat them.

1) θελήσων
2) ἤθελων
3) θέλων
4) ἐθελήσᾱς
5) θέλει

b. After we have cast the slave out of the land, we shall rejoice.

1) βεβληκότες
2) βάλλοντες
3) βαλοῦντες
4) βεβλήκαμεν
5) βληθησόμεθα

c. We used to see him although he used to pursue his enemies only at night.

1) διώξοντα
2) διώξαντα
3) ἐδίωκεν
4) ἐδίωξεν
5) διώκοντα

d. You believed us at any particular time if we were speaking the truth.

1) λέγοντες
2) λεγόντων
3) λέγουσι
4) λέγοντας
5) εἰπόντες

e. Remember us at the moment when we shall be sending our sons across the sea.

1) πέμψαντας
2) πεμψάντων
3) πέμψοντας
4) πεμπόντων
5) πέμποντας

278. TERROR AT NIGHT.

καὶ πάλιν ἐγένετο ὁ λαὸς 'Ισραὴλ κακὸς καὶ ἔδωκεν αὐτοὺς κύριος
εἰς χεῖρα Μαδιὰμ ἑπτὰ ἔτη. καὶ προσεύξαντο οἱ υἱοὶ 'Ισραὴλ πρὸς
κύριον διὰ Μαδιάμ.

ἐκείνων ἀκουσθέντων, ἔδωκε κύριος κριτὴν Γεδεών. τριακοσίων ἀν-
5 δρῶν συναχθέντων κατὰ Μαδιάμ, εἶπε κύριος πρὸς Γεδεών, "ἐν τοῖς τρια-
κοσίοις ἀνδράσι τούτοις σώσω ὑμᾶς, καὶ δώσω τὴν Μαδιὰμ εἰς χεῖρα σοῦ."

καὶ εἶπε Γεδεών πρὸς τοὺς τριακοσίους ἄνδρας, "ἔδωκε κύριος εἰς
χεῖρα ἡμῶν τὴν παρεμβολὴν Μαδιάμ." καὶ ἔδωκε Γεδεών ἑκάστῳ τῶν τριακοσίων ἀνδρῶν κερατίνην καὶ λαμπάδα. καὶ εἶπε πρὸς αὐτούς, "ἐγὼ
10 ἐλεύσομαι πρὸς τῇ παρεμβολῇ. καὶ σαλπίσω ἐν τῇ κερατίνῃ ἐγώ, καὶ
πάντες ὑμεῖς μετ' ἐμοῦ σαλπίσετε ἐν ταῖς κερατίναις περὶ πᾶσαν τὴν
παρεμβολήν, καὶ ἐρεῖτε, 'τῷ κυρίῳ καὶ τῷ Γεδεών.'"

καὶ ἦλθον Γεδεών καὶ οἱ τριακόσιοι ἄνδρες περὶ τὴν παρεμβολὴν
νυκτός. Γεδεών δὲ ἐσάλπισεν ἐν τῇ κερατίνῃ, καὶ ἐσάλπισαν πάντες οἱ
15 τριακόσιοι ἄνδρες ἐν ταῖς κερατίναις καὶ ἔλαβον ἐν χερσὶν αὐτῶν τὰς
λαμπάδας, καὶ τὰς κερατίνας σαλπίσαντες εἶπον, "τῷ κυρίῳ καὶ τῷ
Γεδεών." καὶ πᾶσα ἡ παρεμβολὴ ἔφυγε. καὶ ἐδίωξαν οἱ υἱοὶ 'Ισραὴλ
Μαδιὰμ τὸν φεύγοντα. καὶ ἔφυγον οἱ ἐχθροί. ἠκηκόει δὲ 'Ισραὴλ
σωθησόμενος ἐν χειρὶ τοῦ Γεδεών, καὶ οὕτως ἐγένετο.

279. VOCABULARY.

ἀνήρ, ἀνδρός, ὁ: man, husband

Γεδεών (indecl.), ὁ: Gideon

δώσω (fut. indic. act. 1st sing. δίδωμι: I give): I shall give,
will give (See #337)

κερατίνη, -ης, ἡ: trumpet, horn

λαμπάς, λαμπάδος, ἡ: torch

Μαδιάμ (indecl.), ὁ: Midian

παρεμβολή, -ῆς, ἡ: camp, army

σαλπίζω, σαλπίσω, ἐσάλπισα, --- , --- , --- : I sound a trumpet, blow
a trumpet

τριακόσιοι, -αι, -α: three hundred

φεύγω, φεύξομαι, ἔφυγον, --- , --- , --- : I flee from, flee away,
take flight

280. DECLENSIONS OF ὁ ἀνήρ and ἡ λαμπάς.

ἀνήρ	ἄνδρες	λαμπάς	λαμπάδες
ἀνδρός	ἀνδρῶν	λαμπάδος	λαμπάδων
ἀνδρί	ἀνδράσι	λαμπάδι	λαμπάσι
ἄνδρα	ἄνδρας	λαμπάδα	λαμπάδας
ἄνερ			

The -δ- in ἀνδρός and similar forms seems to have been substituted
for an -ε- to facilitate pronunciation.

281. AORIST PASSIVE PARTICIPLE.

First Passive

ἀκουσθείς	ἀκουσθεῖσα	ἀκουσθέν
ἀκουσθέντος	ἀκουσθείσης	ἀκουσθέντος
ἀκουσθέντι	ἀκουσθείσῃ	ἀκουσθέντι
ἀκουσθέντα	ἀκουσθεῖσαν	ἀκουσθέν
ἀκουσθέντες	ἀκουσθεῖσαι	ἀκουσθέντα
ἀκουσθέντων	ἀκουσθεισῶν	ἀκουσθέντων
ἀκουσθεῖσι	ἀκουσθείσαις	ἀκουσθεῖσι
ἀκουσθέντας	ἀκουσθείσᾱς	ἀκουσθέντα

Second Passive

ἀποσταλείς	ἀποσταλεῖσα	ἀποσταλέν
ἀποσταλέντος	ἀποσταλείσης	ἀποσταλέντος
ἀποσταλέντι	ἀποσταλείσῃ	ἀποσταλέντι
ἀποσταλέντα	ἀποσταλεῖσαν	ἀποσταλέν
ἀποσταλέντες	ἀποσταλεῖσαι	ἀποσταλέντα
ἀποσταλέντων	ἀποσταλεισῶν	ἀποσταλέντων
ἀποσταλεῖσι	ἀποσταλείσαις	ἀποσταλεῖσι
ἀποσταλέντας	ἀποσταλείσᾱς	ἀποσταλέντα

It is evident that both first and second aorist passive participles
may be formed from the aorist passive indicative first singular by
dropping the augment and the ending -ην, and by adding the participial
endings -είς, -εῖσα, -όν.

282. FUTURE PASSIVE PARTICIPLE.

First Passive

ἀκουσθησόμενος	ἀκουσθησομένη	ἀκουσθησόμενον
etc.	etc.	etc.

Second Passive

ἀποσταλησόμενος	ἀποσταλησομένη	ἀποσταλησόμενον
etc.	etc.	etc.

283. GENITIVE ABSOLUTE. In #278 two phrases occur which cannot be explained
by any constructions given before this lesson.

ἐκείνων ἀκουσθέντων, ἔδωκε κύριος κριτὴν Γεδεών.
Those having been heard (or) because they were heard, the Lord
gave a judge Gideon.

τριακοσίων ἀνδρῶν συναχθέντων κατὰ Μαδιάμ, εἶπε κύριος πρὸς Γεδεών. . .
Three hundred men having been gathered together against Midian (or)
after three hundred men had been gathered together against Midian,
the Lord said to Gideon. . .

These groups of underlined words are called genitive absolutes.

The participles have adverbial emphasis, and the noun and the pronoun with which they agree have by themselves no grammatical construction in the rest of the sentence. Genitive absolutes are generally best translated as adverbial clauses since the group of words in absolute construction is the equivalent of a big adverb.

284. EXERCISES.

a. Translate #278.

b. Bearing in mind that the participle in a genitive absolute may be translated in as many different ways as any other adverbial participle (See #266), translate the following sentences as appropriately as possible.

1) τῆς παρεμβολῆς διωκομένης ὑπὸ τοῦ Γεδεών, ἔφευγον πάντες οἱ ἐχθροί.

2) πάντων φυγόντων διὰ τὰς κερατίνας, Γεδεὼν ἐχάρη.

3) τοῦ κριτοῦ ἀποθανόντος, ἐγκατέλιπεν 'Ισραὴλ τὸν ἀληθινὸν θεόν.

4) κυρίου ἐγκαταλειφθέντος ὑπὸ τοῦ λαοῦ, ἦλθεν Μαδιὰμ εἰς τὴν γῆν.

5) τούτων τῶν ἀνδρῶν λατρευσόντων κακοῖς ὀργισθήσεται ὁ θεὸς ἡμῶν.

c. Make the aorist passive participle of each of the verbs in Column II agree with each of the nouns in Column I.

Column I	Column II
1) τοῦ λίθου	γράφω
2) τὸν λίθον	ἐπιγινώσκω
3) οἱ ἄνδρες	ἀποστέλλω
4) τοὺς ἄνδρας	διδάσκω
5) τῇ λαμπάδι	
6) τὰς λαμπάδας	
7) ἡ παρεμβολή	
8) ταῖς παρεμβολαῖς	
9) τοῖς ἔργοις	
10) τὰ ἔργα	
11) τὸ ἔργον	
12) τῶν ἔργων	
13) τῇ γενεᾷ	
14) τὴν γενεάν	

285. A VOICE IN THE NIGHT.

καὶ τὸ τέκνον Σαμουὴλ ἦν ὑπηρέτης τοῦ κυρίου μετὰ Ἡλὶ τοῦ ἱερέως.
ἐν νυκτί τινι Ἡλὶ ἐκάθευδεν ἐν τῷ ἑαυτοῦ τόπῳ, καὶ Σαμουὴλ ἐκάθευδεν
ἐν ἄλλῳ τόπῳ. καὶ ἐκάλεσε κύριος, "Σαμουήλ, Σαμουήλ." καὶ εἶπεν,
"ἰδοὺ ἐγώ." καὶ ἔδραμε πρὸς Ἡλί, καὶ εἶπεν, "ἰδοὺ ἐγώ, ὅτι κέκληκάς."

5 καὶ εἶπεν, "οὐ κέκληκά σε, ἀνάστρεφε, κάθευδε." καὶ ἀνέστρεψε καὶ
ἐκάθευδε.

καὶ πάλιν ἐκάλεσε κύριος, "Σαμουήλ, Σαμουήλ." καὶ ἔδραμε πρὸς
Ἡλί, καὶ εἶπεν, "ἰδοὺ ἐγώ, ὅτι κέκληκάς με." καὶ εἶπεν, "οὐ κέκληκά
σε. ἀνάστρεφε. κάθευδε."

10 καὶ Σαμουὴλ οὔπω ἔγνω τὸν θεόν, καὶ οὔπω ἠκηκόει τὸ ῥῆμα τοῦ κυρίου. καὶ πάλιν ἐκάλεσε κύριος Σαμουήλ. καὶ πάλιν ἔδραμε πρὸς Ἡλί,
καὶ εἶπεν, "ἰδοὺ ἐγώ, ὅτι κέκληκάς με." καὶ ἐπέγνω Ἡλὶ ὅτι κύριος
κέκληκε Σαμουήλ. καὶ εἶπεν, "ἀνάστρεφε, κάθευδε, τέκνον. καὶ ὅτε
καλέσει σε, ἐρεῖς, 'λέγε, ὅτι ἀκούει ὁ δοῦλός σου.'"

15 καὶ ἀπῆλθε Σαμουήλ. καὶ ἐκάθευδεν ἐν τῷ ἑαυτοῦ τόπῳ. καὶ ἦλθε
κύριος καὶ ἐκάλεσε αὐτὸν πάλιν. καὶ εἶπε Σαμουήλ, "λέγε, ὅτι ἀκούει
ὁ δοῦλός σου." καὶ εἶπε κύριος πρὸς Σαμουήλ, "ἰδοὺ γενήσεται τὰ ῥή-
ματά μου ἐν Ἰσραήλ, τῷ γὰρ οἴκῳ Ἡλὶ κακὰ γενήσεται."

καὶ αὔριον διὰ τὸν φόβον Σαμουὴλ οὐκ ἤθελεν εἰπεῖν τῷ ἱερεῖ τὰ
20 κακὰ τὰ γενησόμενα τῷ οἴκῳ αὐτοῦ. ἀλλ' εἶπεν Ἡλὶ πρὸς Σαμουήλ, "τί
ἐστι τὸ ῥῆμα τὸ ῥηθὲν πρὸς σέ;" καὶ εἶπε Σαμουὴλ πάντα τὰ ῥήματα τοῦ
κυρίου. πᾶς οὖν ἔγνω ὅτι Σαμουὴλ ἔσται προφήτης.

286. VOCABULARY.

ἀναστρέφω, ---, ἀνέστρεψα, ---, ---, ἀνεστράφην: I overturn, re-
                                       turn, (pass.) sojourn, dwell

γινώσκω, γνώσομαι, ἔγνων, ἔγνωκα, ἔγνωσμαι, ἐγνώσθην: I come to know,
                                            perceive, understand

Ἡλί (indecl.), ὁ: Eli

ἰδού: behold, see, look

ἱερεύς, -έως, ὁ: priest

καθεύδω (only pres. and imperf. tenses in N. T.): I sleep

καλέω (the paradigm of the pres. to be given in #340), καλέσω, ἐκάλεσα,
    κέκληκα, κέκλημαι, ἐκλήθην: I call, invite

οὔπω: not yet

προφήτης, -ου, ὁ: prophet

ῥηθέν (aor. pass. part. neut. nom. sing. λέγω: I speak. See #237, 281. The part. has the stem ῥηθε- instead of ῥεθη- found in the indic.): spoken

ῥῆμα, -ατος, τό: word, statement, thing, matter

Σαμουήλ (indecl.), ὁ: Samuel

τρέχω, --- , ἔδραμον, --- , --- , --- : I run

287. DECLENSION OF ἱερεύς.

(ὁ)	ἱερεύς	ἱερεῖς
	ἱερέως	ἱερέων
	ἱερεῖ	ἱερεῦσι
	ἱερέα	ἱερεῖς
	ἱερεῦ	

βασιλεύς also follows this pattern.

At an earlier period of the language these stems ending in -ηυ- before consonants and -ηϝ- before vowels. ϝ is digamma, a letter lost from the Greek alphabet, equivalent to our "w." With the disappearance of ϝ a transfer of quantity occurred, e. g. βασιληϝος became βασιλέως.

288. INDIRECT DISCOURSE. The words of a speaker may be quoted exactly as they were first uttered. This kind of quotation is <u>direct</u> discourse.

εἶπε Πέτρος, "ἀναστρέψω."
Peter said, "I will return."

A speaker's words may also be quoted with appropriate alterations in person and tense to suit the introductory expression in such a way as to give the sense of what was said without presuming to furnish the accuracy of a verbatim quotation. This kind of quotation is <u>indirect discourse</u>.

Peter said that he would go away.

Greek has three ways of expressing indirect discourse: (1) with a participle, (2) with an infinitive, and (3) with a clause introduced by a conjunction like ὅτι. Very few verbs are followed by all three kinds of indirect discourse.

a. <u>With a participle</u>. The following verbs already used in these lessons may introduce participial indirect discourse: ἀκούω, βλέπω, γινώσκω. This type is infrequent in the New Testament.

ἤκουσε Πέτρος ἡμᾶς ἀναστρέφοντας.
Indirect: Peter heard that we were returning.
Direct: Peter heard (us say), "We are returning."

The tense of the participle in indirect discourse is that of the verb in the original quotation. The accusative ἡμᾶς is the direct object of ἤκουσε.

b. <u>With an infinitive</u>. The following verbs already used in these lessons may introduce the infinitive type of indirect discourse: ἀκούω, ἀποκρίνομαι, λέγω, πείθω, πιστεύω. This type is also infrequent in the New Testament.
ἤκουσε Πέτρος ἡμᾶς ἀναστρέφειν.
Indirect: Peter heard that we were returning.
Direct: Peter heard (us say), "We are returning."

Here again the tense of the original quotation is that of the indirect statement. NOTICE CAREFULLY that the agent performing the action of the infinitive is put in the accusative of general reference.

c. With a ὅτι clause. The following verbs already studied may introduce indirect discourse in a ὅτι clause: ἀκούω, βλέπω, γινώσκω, διδάσκω, ἐλπίζω, λέγω, πείθω, πιστεύω. This is the usual type in the New Testament.
ἤκουσε Πέτρος ὅτι ἀναστρέφομεν.
Indirect: Peter heard that we were returning.
Direct: Peter heard (us say), "We are returning."

Here as in the other two types the tense of the original statement is that of the indirect statement. Since a finite verb is used in the ὅτι clause no pronoun is necessary to express the subject of the dependent verb in this particular instance.

Let us study an instance of this type of indirect discourse in #285. καὶ ἐπέγνω Ἡλὶ ὅτι κύριος κέκληκε τὸ τέκνον, and Eli recognized that the Lord had called the child.

Although κέκληκε is a perfect, it is here translated as a pluperfect, ". . .the Lord had called. . ." This is due to English sequence of tenses. Suppose we change the Greek sentence thus, καὶ ἐπιγινώσκει Ἡλὶ ὅτι κύριος κέκληκε τὸ τέκνον. The ὅτι clause has not been changed, but notice the translation: And Eli recognizes that the Lord has called the child. This illustrates the fact that normal translations of tenses in indirect discourse are used after the tenses that are translated as English presents and futures. The changes necessary after tenses translated as English past tenses are shown in the tabulation below.

289. TRANSLATIONS OF GREEK TENSES IN INDIRECT DISCOURSE AFTER TENSES TRANSLATED AS ENGLISH PASTS.

Greek Tense in indirect discourse	English Translation
Present	
ἔγνω ὅτι ἔρχεσθε.	He understood that you were coming.
Future	
ἔγνω ὅτι ἐλεύσεσθε.	He understood that you would come.
Perfect	
ἔγνω ὅτι ἐληλύθατε.	He understood that you had come.
Imperfect	
ἔγνω ὅτι ἤρχεσθε.	He understood that you had been coming.
Aorist	
ἔγνω ὅτι ἤλθετε.	He understood that you had come.
Pluperfect.	
ἔγνω ὅτι ἐληλύθειτε.	He understood that you had come.

290. EXERCISES.

a. Translate #285.

b. In translating the following sentences, be careful to use the
    appropriate English in the subordinate clause.

1) ἔγνωμεν αὐτὸν ἐσόμενον προφήτην.

2) ὁ προφήτης οὐκ ἐπίστευσε τὸν θεὸν εἰπεῖν διὰ κερατίνης αὐτῷ
    τῆς νυκτός.

3) ἐλπίζει ὅτι οὗτος οὐκ ἐρεῖ πάλιν τῷ προφήτῃ.

4) ἤκουσεν Ἠλὶ ὁ ἱερεὺς τοῦ τέκνου δουλεύοντος τὴν νύκτα.

5) ἤκουσε Σαμουὴλ ὁ προφήτης τὸν κύριον ὀργισθῆναι τοῖς κακοῖς
    ἔργοις τῶν υἱῶν τοῦ ἱερέως.

6) οὔπω ἠκηκόει τὰ ῥήματα τοῦ ἱερέως.

7) γέγονε Σαμουὴλ ἀνήρ; οὔπω.

8) εἴπομεν ὅτι Σαμουὴλ τρέχει πρὸς τὸν ἱερέα.

9) δράματε νῦν, τέκνον.

10) ὠργίσθητε ἐμοί;

c. Change the indirect discourse in each of the sentences in b. into
    a direct form which could have been the original statement, for
    example:

    εἶπε Πέτρος τὸν δοῦλον ἀπελθεῖν.

    "ὁ δοῦλος ἀπῆλθε."

d. Associate the following English words with new Greek words in
    this lesson.

1) anastrophe: a rhetorical turning upside down of the usual
                 order of words in a sentence.
2) hieratic: related to priests.
3) rhematic: related to the formation of words.
4) dromedary: a running camel.

291.   ISRAEL ASKS FOR A KING.

πολλάκις εἶχεν 'Ισραὴλ κριτὰς οἳ ἔσωζον ἐν πολέμῳ τὸν λαὸν ἀπὸ
τῶν ἐχθρῶν. ἀποθανόντος δὲ ἑκάστου τῶν κριτῶν, πάλιν ἐγκατέλειπεν ὁ
λαὸς τὸν θεὸν οὗ ὁ κριτὴς αὐτοὺς σεσώκει. διὰ δὲ τὰ κακὰ ἔργα ὁ θεὸς
ἔδωκε τὸν ἴδιον λαὸν διὰ πολέμου εἰς τὰς χεῖρας τῶν ἐχθρῶν. ἀλλ' οἱ
5   υἱοὶ 'Ισραήλ, ὧν αἱ καρδίαι οὐκ ἐπείθοντο τῇ ἀληθείᾳ, ἔλεγον πολλάκις
ἀλλήλοις, "ὅτι οὐκ ἔχει ἡ γῆ ἡμῶν βασιλέα, διὰ τοῦτο ἀπέκτειναν ἡμᾶς
οἱ ἐχθροὶ ἡμῶν. δεῖ οὖν τὴν γῆν ἡμῶν σχεῖν βασιλέα. σὺν δὲ αὐτῷ δεῖ
ἔρχεσθαι εἰς πόλεμον ὑπὲρ ἀλλήλων."

ἀκούσᾱς οὖν ταῦτα τὰ ῥήματα Σαμουήλ, ὃς ἦν νῦν πρεσβύτερος,
10   προσηύξατο πρὸς κύριον. κακὰ γὰρ ἦν ταῦτα ἐν τοῖς ὠσὶ τοῦ προφήτου.
καὶ εἶπε κύριος πρὸς Σαμουήλ, "ἄκουε τῆς φωνῆς τοῦ λαοῦ. ἀπὸ τῆς
ἡμέρᾱς ἐν ᾗ ἐγὼ ἤγαγον τὸν λαὸν ἐμοῦ ἐξ Αἰγύπτου πολλάκις ἐγκατέλιπόν
με. οὕτως ἐγκαταλείπουσί σε. ἀλλὰ εἰπὲ αὐτοῖς ἃ γενήσεται ἐν πολέμῳ
ὅτε ἕξουσι βασιλέα. καὶ εἶπε Σαμουὴλ πᾶν τὸ ῥῆμα τοῦ κυρίου πρὸς τὸν
15   λαόν.

"ὁ βασιλεὺς λήμψεται ὑμῶν τοὺς υἱοὺς καὶ δουλεύσουσι αὐτῷ καὶ
λήμψεται ὑμῶν τὴν γῆν καὶ τὰ πρόβατα. καὶ οὐκ ἀκούσει κύριος ὑμῶν ἐν
ταῖς ἡμέραις ἐκείναις ὅτι ὑμεῖς ἐλάβεσθε ἑαυτοῖς βασιλέα."

τότε εἶπεν ὁ λαός, "οὐχί, ἀλλὰ δεῖ ἡμᾶς σχεῖν βασιλέα. πάντων
20   τῶν ἄλλων ἐθνῶν ἐχόντων βασιλεῖς, δεῖ καὶ ἡμᾶς σχεῖν βασιλέα."

καὶ ἤκουσε Σαμουὴλ πάντα τὰ ῥήματα τοῦ λαοῦ, καὶ εἶπεν αὐτὰ εἰς
τὰ ὦτα κυρίου.

καὶ εἶπε κύριος πρὸς Σαμουήλ, "ἄκουε τῆς φωνῆς αὐτῶν, ὅτι δεῖ
σχεῖν αὐτοῖς βασιλέα."

292.   VOCABULARY.

ἀλλήλων, ἀλλήλοις, ἀλλήλους: one another, each other (See #389)

δεῖ (pres. indic. act. 3rd sing. δέω): it is necessary (followed by
    an infinitive with an acc. of general reference), one must, one
    ought

ὅς, ἥ, ὅ: who, which, that, what

οὖς, ὠτός, τό: ear

πόλεμος, -ου, ὁ: war, battle

ὑπέρ: (with abl.) for, on behalf of, for the sake of, about;
       (with acc.) over, beyond (In N.T. always figurative. See Arndt
                          and Gingrich under ὑπέρ.)
φωνή, -ῆς, ἡ: voice, sound

293. ANOTHER THIRD DECLENSION NOUN.

(τὸ) οὖς   ὦτα
      ὠτός   ὤτων
      ὠτί   ὠσί
      οὖς   ὦτα

294. PARADIGM OF ὅς, ἥ, ὅ.

   ὅς   ἥ   ὅ   οἵ   αἵ   ἅ
   οὗ   ἧς   οὗ   ὧν   ὧν   ὧν
   ᾧ   ᾗ   ᾧ   οἷς   αἷς   οἷς
   ὅν   ἥν   ὅ   οὕς   ἅς   ἅ

295. RELATIVE PRONOUNS.

   a. Their function. Relative pronouns connect clauses. The relative
       clause is usually adjectival but may be substantival.

       1) Adjectival clause.

           . . . κριτὰς οἵ ἔσωζον. . . τὸν λαόν. . .
           . . . judges who used to save. . . the people. . .

       2) Substantival clause.

           εἶπε αὐτοῖς ἃ γενήσεται.
           Tell them what will happen.

   b. Their agreement. A relative pronoun usually agrees in gender and
       number with its antecedent but has a case conforming to the con-
       struction of its own clause. Not infrequently, however, the rela-
       tive pronoun is attracted into the case of its antecedent when this
       antecedent has a second or third inflectional form.
       1) Usual agreement.

           περὶ τοῦ λαοῦ ὃν ἔσωζον. . .
           Concerning the people whom they saved. . .

       2) Attraction of relative pronoun to the case of its antecedent.

           περὶ τοῦ λαοῦ οὗ ἔσωζον. . .
           Concerning the people whom they saved. . .

296. DEFINITE RELATIVE CLAUSES. Relative clauses which make specific ref-
      erence are called definite relative clauses. This kind only has been
      used in this lesson.

297. THE RECIPROCAL PRONOUN. ἀλλήλων, of one another, of each other, has
      no nominative function, and in the New Testament no feminine or neuter
      forms. The only forms occurring are masculine:

      ἤσθιον τοὺς ἄρτους ἀλλήλων.
      They used to eat one another's loaves.

      πιστεύομεν ἀλλήλοις.
      We believe one another.

298. EXERCISES.

    a. Translate #291.

    b. Translate the words in parentheses in each of the following
        sentences.

        1) οὔπω ἔδωκα βασιλέα ἐμοῦ τῷ λαῷ (who) ἐγκατέλιπέ με.

        2) ἤκουσε Σαμουὴλ πάντα τὰ ῥήματα (which) εἴρητο ὑπὸ τῶν υἱῶν
            Ἰσραήλ.

        3) οὗτός ἐστιν ὁ βασιλεὺς (to whom) οὔπω ἔδωκα τοῦτο τὸ ἔθνος.

        4) οὔπω ἐπιγινώσκεις τὸν Ἰσραὴλ (whose, of whom) οἱ υἱοί ἐσμεν;

        5) ἔβλεψας τὸν προφήτην (whom) βλέψομεν αὔριον.

        6) οὔπω δεῖ βλέπειν τὸν ἄνδρα εἰς τὰ ὦτα (of whom) εἰρήκαμεν.

        7) ὑπὲρ ἑαυτῶν ἀκούσομεν τῆς φωνῆς τοῦ βασιλέως (whose) ἐσμεν.

    c. Translate into Greek.

        1) On behalf of the Lord, Samuel spoke.
        2) Above the voices of the people the prophet heard the voice
            of God.
        3) Do stones speak with the voices of men?
        4) No, but some men who have voices throw stones.
        5) Stones which are very large cannot be thrown.
        6) Bread was not brought into being for the sake of our Lord.
        7) She carries a beautiful stone in her hand.

    d. Associate the following English words with new Greek words in
        this lesson.

        1) allelomorph: two distinctly different characteristics
                      observed in a family line as alternating with
                      one another.
        2) polemics: practice of controversy (war of words).
        3) phonology: description of sounds.
        4) otitis: inflammation of the ear.

299. SAMUEL FINDS THE HIDDEN KING.

τοῦ ἔθνους ἐκλεξαμένου βασιλέα ἀντὶ κριτοῦ, εἶπε Σαμουὴλ πρὸς
αὐτούς, "οὕτως εἶπε κύριος ὁ θεὸς Ἰσραήλ, λέγων, 'ἐγὼ ἤγαγον τοὺς
υἱοὺς Ἰσραὴλ ἐξ Αἰγύπτου. καὶ ὑμεῖς σήμερον θέλετε ἄνδρα βασιλέα
ὑμῶν ἀντὶ ἐμοῦ ὃς αὐτός εἰμι ὁ σωτὴρ ὑμῶν ἐκ πάντων τῶν κακῶν ὑμῶν καὶ
5 τῶν θλίψεων ὑμῶν. καὶ εἴπετε, "οὐχί, ἀλλὰ βασιλέα σχεῖν θέλομεν." '"

καὶ ἐξελέξατο ὁ κύριος Σαοὺλ γενέσθαι βασιλέα τοῦ ἔθνους. ὁ δὲ
Σαοὺλ οὐχ εὑρίσκετο ἐν τῷ λαῷ τῷ συναχθέντι πρὸς Σαμουὴλ ὅτι ὁ Σαοὺλ
ἐν τοῖς σκεύεσι ἦν. καὶ προσηύξατο Σαμουὴλ γνωσόμενος ποῦ ἐλήλυθε
Σαούλ. καὶ εἶπεν ὁ κύριος, "ἰδοὺ αὐτὸς εὑρεθήσεται ἐν τοῖς σκεύεσι."
10 καὶ Σαμουὴλ ἔδραμε ἐπὶ τὰ σκεύη καὶ ἔλαβε Σαοὺλ ἐκ τῶν σκευῶν.

καὶ εἶπε Σαμουὴλ πρὸς πάντα τὸν λαόν, "βλέπετε Σαοὺλ τὸν ἄνδρα
ὃν ἐκλέλεκται ἑαυτῷ κύριος;"

καὶ ἔγνωσαν πᾶς ὁ λαός, καὶ ἐχάρησαν. καὶ εἶπε Σαμουὴλ πρὸς τὸν
λαὸν τοὺς νόμους τοῦ βασιλέως. καὶ ἀπέστειλε Σαμουὴλ πάντα τὸν λαόν,
15 καὶ ἀπῆλθεν ἕκαστος εἰς τὸν ἑαυτοῦ τόπον.

300. VOCABULARY.

ἐκλέγομαι, --- , ἐξελεξάμην, ἐκλέλεγμαι, --- : I choose

εὑρίσκω, εὑρήσω, εὗρον, εὕρηκα, --- , εὑρέθην: I find, discover
(followed by participial indirect discourse)

θλῖψις, -εως, ἡ: affliction, distress

Σαούλ (indecl.), ὁ: Saul

σκεῦος, -ους, τό: vessel, utensil, implement; (plural) baggage,
gear, goods

301. THIRD DECLENSION NOUNS WITH STEMS ENDING IN -ει AND -ι.

	(ἡ)	θλῖψις	θλίψεις
		θλίψεως	θλίψεων
		θλίψει	θλίψεσι
		θλῖψιν	θλίψεις

This pattern will be found in several other nouns to be presented later, so it is worth knowing. It may be simpler to learn the forms than
to try to explain them all. At any rate, the stem endings -ει and -ι
may be regarded as two grades of a vowel system. θλιψι- appears in
the singular first and fourth inflectional forms: θλῖψις and θλῖψιν.
θλίψει- is supposed to have lost its final -ι- before the vowels of
the inflectional endings -ος, -ι, -ες, -ων. The forms θλίψεις (fourth
plural) and θλίψεσι are assumed to have followed the analogy of θλίψεις
(first plural from θλίψε-ες). This leaves still unexplained the accents of θλίψεως and θλίψεων. At an earlier period in the history of
the language θλίψεως is thought to have been θλίψηος. With such a

spelling the accent would be normal. When a transfer of quantity resulted in θλίψεως, the accent did not shift from the antepenult to the penult. θλίψεων is considered analogous in formation to θλίψεως.

302. EXERCISES.

a. Translate #299.

b. Review indirect discourse by translating the following sentences.

1) ἐχθὲς ὁ λαὸς ἤκουσαν τοῦ ἐσχάτου προφήτου εἰπόντος, "ἰδοὺ ἐξελεξάμην βασιλέα ὑμῖν."

2) εἰρήκει ὁ θεὸς ὅτι αὐτός ἐστιν ὁ ἔσχατος βασιλεὺς τούτου τοῦ
ἔθνους.

3) γινώσκομεν τὸ ἔθνος νῦν ἔχειν βασιλέα.

4) ἠκούσαμεν τὸν Σαοὺλ ἐν τοῖς σκεύεσιν εὑρεθέντα.

c. Translate the underlined words (1) with adjectival participles and
(2) with relative clauses.

1) I see the king who has been found.
2) We found a prophet who was choosing.
3) God has given a leader to the nation that had chosen a king.
4) The father of the child who is coming into our house died last
night.

d. Review of genitive absolutes. Translate the genitive absolutes
(1) literally and (2) more freely and in better English.

1) τῶν τέκνων εὑρηκότων ἀλλήλους ἐν τοῖς σκεύεσι οἱ ἄνδρες
ἐχάρησαν.

2) τοῦ ἀνδρὸς τούτου ἀναστρεφομένου ὧδε, χαρησόμεθα.

3) φευξομένων τῶν τριακοσίων, εἶπον οἱ ἐχθροί, "ὧδε ἐστιν ὁ
βασιλεὺς ἡμῶν.

4) τῶν καλῶν ἱερέων μεινάντων ἐν τῷ σπηλαίῳ ἐκείνῳ, ὁ ἱερεὺς
ὠργίσθη.

e. Review of relative pronouns. Translate the English words in
parentheses so as to fit their contexts.

1) δεῖ καθεύδειν ἐν τοῖς σκεύεσι τὸν (priest who fled).

2) εὑρίσκονται οἱ (judges to whom he gave) τὴν γῆν.

3) ἐβλέψαμεν τὸν (priest whose son) ἐν τῷ πολέμῳ ἀπεκτάνθη.

4) ἀκούσετε τῆς (voice which saved) τριακόσια τέκνα.

f. Review of participle usage. In the following paragraph tell
which participles are adjectival and which are adverbial in emphasis, and translate appropriately.

ἐλθόντες οἱ ἄνδρες τοῦ Μαδιὰμ εἰς τὴν γῆν Ἰσραήλ, ἔλαβον πάντα
τὸν σῖτον. προσευξαμένων τῷ θεῷ τῶν υἱῶν Ἰσραήλ, Γεδεὼν ἀπεστάλη
γενησόμενος ὁ κριτὴς τοῦ λαοῦ. ἔδωκεν δὲ ὁ θεὸς τούτῳ τριακοσίους
ἄνδρας τοὺς σαλπίζοντας. σαλπισάντων τῶν τριακοσίων νυκτός, οἱ
ἐχθροὶ σχόντες φόβον καὶ ἐγκαταλιπόντες τὴν παρεμβολὴν ἔφυγον.

135

303. WHEN THE VOICE OF THE PEOPLE WAS NOT THE VOICE OF GOD.

ὢν καλὸς ἐν ταῖς πρώταις ἡμέραις τῆς βασιλείᾱς, Σαοὺλ οὐκ ἐπείθετο τῷ θεῷ πάντοτε. εἰρήκει γὰρ κύριος τῷ βασιλεῖ καταλῦσαι τὴν βασιλείᾱν τοῦ Ἀμαλὴκ, πάντας τοὺς ἄνδρας τοῦ Ἀμαλὴκ, πάσᾱς τὰς γυναῖκας καὶ πάντα τὰ τέκνα καὶ πάντα τοῦ Ἀμαλὴκ.

5   ἀλλ' οὐκ ἐπείσατο πᾶσιν ἃ εἰρήκει ὁ θεός, ἔπεισε γὰρ ὁ λαὸς τὸν βασιλέα σῶσαι τὸν ἡγεμόνα τοῦ Ἀμαλὴκ καὶ πρόβατά τινα καλά. εἶπον γὰρ, "ἀποκτείνωμεν τοῦτον τὸν ἡγεμόνα καὶ ταῦτα τὰ καλὰ πρόβατα; οὐχί. σώσωμεν τὰ πρόβατα ταῦτα γενησόμενα θυσίᾱς κυρίῳ τῷ θεῷ ἡμῶν."

Σαοὺλ οὖν ἐπείσατο τῷ ῥήματι τοῦ λαοῦ. διὰ τοῦτο ὠργίσθη ὁ θεὸς
10   τῷ βασιλεῖ τοῦ Ἰσραὴλ καὶ εἶπε τῷ Σαμουήλ, "εἰπὲ τῷ Σαούλ, 'οὐχ ἕξει ὁ υἱός σου ταύτην τὴν βασιλείᾱν μετὰ σε. ἀλλ' ἡ βασιλείᾱ σου δοθήσεται ἄλλῳ ὄντι κρείσσονι σοῦ.'"

ἤθελε γὰρ κύριος διδάξαι Σαοὺλ ὅτι ἡ ὑπακοὴ κρείσσων ἐστι θυσίᾱς οὔσης λίαν καλῆς. ἐπείσθη οὖν Σαμουὴλ κυρίῳ καὶ εἶπε ταῦτα τὰ ῥήματα
15   τῷ βασιλεῖ. μετὰ ταῦτα ἀπέκτεινε ὁ προφήτης αὐτὸς τὸν ἡγεμόνα τῆς βασιλείᾱς τοῦ Ἀμαλὴκ, καὶ ἀπῆλθε πρὸς τὸν ἑαυτοῦ οἶκον.

304. VOCABULARY.

Ἀμαλὴκ (indecl.), ὁ: Amalek

βασιλείᾱ, -ᾱς, ἡ: kingdom, royal power, dominion, rule, reign

γυνή, γυναικός, ἡ: woman, wife

δοθήσεται (fut. indic. pass. 3rd. sing. δίδωμι: I give): it shall be
given

ἡγεμών, -όνος, ὁ: leader, governor, chief

θυσίᾱ, -ᾱς, ἡ: sacrifice

καταλύω, καταλύσω, κατέλυσα, --- , --- , κατελύθην: I destroy, overthrow

κρείσσων, κρεῖσσον: better

ὑπακοή, -ῆς, ἡ: obedience

305. PRESENT PARTICIPLE OF εἰμί (cf. #249).

ὤν (=being)	οὖσα	ὄν
ὄντος	οὔσης	ὄντος
ὄντι	οὔσῃ	ὄντι
ὄντα	οὖσαν	ὄν
ὄντες	οὖσαι	ὄντα
ὄντων	οὐσῶν	ὄντων
οὖσι	οὔσαις	οὖσι
ὄντας	οὔσᾱς	ὄντα

306. PARADIGM OF ἡ γυνή.

γυνή   γυναῖκες
γυναικός   γυναικῶν
γυναικί   γυναιξί
γυναῖκα   γυναῖκας
γύναι

You will notice that this noun like several others of the third declension is formed on two stems.

307. PARADIGM OF κρείσσων.

Masculine and Feminine   Neuter

κρείσσων   κρεῖσσον
κρείσσονος   κρείσσονος
κρείσσονι   κρείσσονι
κρείσσονα   κρεῖσσον
    or
κρείσσω   (κρείσσοσα)

κρείσσονες   κρείσσονα
    or   or
κρείσσους (κρείσσοσες)   κρείσσω   (κρείσσοσα)
κρείσσων   κρείσσων
κρείσσοσι   κρείσσοσι
κρείσσονας   κρείσσονα
    or   or
κρείσσους (κρείσσοσες)   κρείσσω   (κρείσσοσα)

The forms in parentheses are not used. They are intended merely to explain the origin of the forms after which they are placed.

308. ABLATIVE WITH A COMPARATIVE. A comparison may be expressed by a comparative adjective followed by an ablative noun or pronoun.

ἡ ὑπακοή ἐστι κρείσσων θυσίας.
Obedience is better than <u>sacrifice</u>.

309. SUBJUNCTIVE MOOD. Two verbs in this lesson, ἀποκτείνωμεν and σώσωμεν, neither make statements or ask questions as do indicative forms. These two new forms belong to the subjunctive mood, which carries with it an idea of uncertainty or of some emotional coloring.

310. DELIBERATIVE QUESTION. When the people ask Saul, "Shall we kill this leader?" they are represented as saying ἀποκτείνωμεν τοῦτον τὸν ἡγεμόνα; This question is on the surface an appeal for counsel as to what is to be done. But the rest of the story shows that the people already had their minds made up that they should not kill the leader of the Amalekites. This question then is rhetorical, asked to produce an effect, not to gain information. The future is used in English.

The subjunctive can be used also in questions of sincere appeal for information.

ποῦ ἔλθωμεν;   ποῦ ἔλθωσι;
Where shall we go?   Where will they go?

The implication is that the questioner is not sure whether there is an answer or not. But suppose we ask a similar question of a guide who knows the way and in whom we have complete confidence. In such a situation an indicative form will be used.

ποῦ ἐλευσόμεθα;   ποῦ ἐλεύσονται;
Where shall we go?   Where will they go?

The indicative reveals our assumption that an answer is to be had.

311. HORTATORY SUBJUNCTIVE. The people try to influence Saul by saying

σώσωμεν τὰ πρόβατα ταῦτα γενησόμενα θυσίας.
Let us save these sheep in order to be sacrifices.

The first person plural is used, and the translation begins
"Let us . . ."

312. PARADIGMS OF THE SUBJUNCTIVE: πιστεύω, ἔρχομαι, γίνομαι, ἀποστέλλω.
In the forms to be given two points should be observed: (1) no augment is used in the aorist subjunctive; and (2) the forms are made up
of the tense stem plus the variable vowel -ω/η- plus the personal endings. The tenses chiefly used are the present and the aorist. No
future subjunctive exists. NO ONE translation fits all constructions.

Present Active of πιστεύω

		Present Middle and Passive of πιστεύω	
πιστεύω	πιστεύωμεν	πιστεύωμαι	πιστευώμεθα
πιστεύῃς	πιστεύητε	πιστεύῃ	πιστεύησθε
πιστεύῃ	πιστεύωσι	πιστεύηται	πιστεύωνται

First Aorist Active of πιστεύω

		Second Aorist Active of ἔρχομαι	
πιστεύσω	πιστεύσωμεν	ἔλθω	ἔλθωμεν
πιστεύσῃς	πιστεύσητε	ἔλθῃς	ἔλθητε
πιστεύσῃ	πιστεύσωσι	ἔλθῃ	ἔλθωσι

First Aorist Middle of πιστεύω

		Second Aorist Middle of γίνομαι	
πιστεύσωμαι	πιστευσώμεθα	γένωμαι	γενώμεθα
πιστεύσῃ	πιστεύσησθε	γένῃ	γένησθε
πιστεύσηται	πιστεύσωνται	γένηται	γένωνται

Aorist First Passive of πιστεύω

		Aorist Second Passive of ἀποστέλλω	
πιστευθῶ	πιστευθῶμεν	ἀποσταλῶ	ἀποσταλῶμεν
πιστευθῇς	πιστευθῆτε	ἀποσταλῇς	ἀποσταλῆτε
πιστευθῇ	πιστευθῶσι	ἀποσταλῇ	ἀποσταλῶσι

Note the peculiar accent in the aorist passive.

Liquid and nasal aorists use the same endings as the second aorist,
e. g., ἀποστείλω and μείνω.

The distinction between the present and the aorist subjunctive is in
kind of action, not in time of action. The present represents progressive or repeated action while the aorist represents action as an
occurrence.

313. EXERCISES.

a. Translate #303.

b. In translating the following, distinguish carefully between indicative and subjunctive forms.

1) πιστεύσωμεν ταύτῃ τῇ γυναικί;

2) πιστεύσομεν ταύτῃ τῇ γυναικί;

3) πιστεύσωμεν ταύτῃ τῇ γυναικί.

4) πιστεύωμεν ἐκείνῳ τῷ ἡγεμόνι τοῦ Ἀμαλήκ.

5) πιστεύωμεν ἐκείνῳ τῷ ἡγεμόνι τοῦ Ἀμαλήκ;

6) πιστεύομεν ἐκείνῳ τῷ ἡγεμόνι τοῦ Ἀμαλήκ;

c. Say in Greek.

1) Let us be healing the child (pres. subj.).
2) Let the child be healed (an occurrence not a process: aorist imperative).
3) What shall I destroy? (uncertainty implied: aor. subj.).
4) What shall I destroy? (a definite answer assumed as available: fut. indic.).
5) Let us save the sacrifice.
6) Is obedience better than sacrifice?
7) Sacrifice will not be better than obedience.
8) God remembered the prophet's obedience.

d. Locate.

1) καταλύητε   6) ἀγάγωμεν

2) λαμβάνωσι   7) φεύγῃ

3) καταλυθῇς   8) μείνῃς

4) δεχώμεθα   9) φάγητε

5) σώσηται   10) πεμφθῇ

LESSON 42

314. VOCABULARY. Review thoroughly the vocabulary introduced since Lesson 36.

NOUNS

		ADJECTIVES
Ἀμαλήκ	Σαούλ	κρείσσων
ἀνήρ	σκεῦος	τριακόσιοι
βασιλεία	ὑπακοή	
Γεδεών	φωνή	
γυνή		PRONOUNS
ἡγεμών		
Ἡλί	VERBS	ἀλλήλων
θλῖψις		ὅς, ἥ, ὅ
θυσία	ἀναστρέφω	
ἱερεύς	γινώσκω	
κερατίνη	δεῖ	ADVERBS
λαμπάς	ἐκλέγομαι	
Μαδιάμ	εὑρίσκω	ἰδού
οὖς	καλέω	οὔπω
παρεμβολή	καθεύδω	
πόλεμος	καταλύω	
προφήτης	σαλπίζω	PREPOSITION
ῥῆμα	τρέχω	
Σαμουήλ	φεύγω	ὑπέρ

139

315. GENITIVE ABSOLUTE. Translate the underlined portions of the following sentences by genitive absolutes.

a. While the priest was returning, the king sounded the trumpet.
b. After the chief had destroyed the torch, the woman ran into the house.
c. Although his ear had been destroyed, the prophet was hoping to hear.
d. If the women flee, we shall be able to sleep.
e. Because voices were heard in the baggage, the king was found there.

316. INDIRECT DISCOURSE. Put the following sentences into forms using indirect discourse as explained in #288.

a. ὁ ἀνὴρ ὁ ἔχων ὦτα ἤκουσε, "σαλπίζουσι οἱ τριακόσιοι."

b. ἀπεκρίθημεν, "ἡμεῖς φευξόμεθα."

c. βλέψετε (ταύτην τὴν ἀλήθειαν) "πάντες οἱ ἄνθρωποι ἀποθανοῦνται."

d. ἔγνωμεν, "ἡ ὑπακοὴ κρείσσων τοῦ ἀργυρίου ἐστίν."

e. ἐρῶ, "ἡ βασιλείᾱ αὕτη καταλυθήσεται."

317. PRONOUNS: MOSTLY RELATIVE. Translate the English carefully.

a. εὑρήσουσι τὸν ἄνδρα (whose son) σαλπίζει ἐν τοῖς ὠσὶν τοῦ ἱερέως;

b. ποῦ καθεύδει ἡ γυνὴ (to whom) τὰ σκεύη ἐπέμψαμεν;

c. ἀνήρ τις ἦν (than whom) κρείσσων ἦς;

d. (on behalf of whom) ἐδράμομεν πρὸς τὸν ἡγεμόνα;

e. τοῦτό ἐστι τὸ τέκνον (on behalf of whom) ἐδράμομεν πρὸς τὸν ἡγεμόνα.

318. SUBJUNCTIVE. Translate carefully.

a. φεύγωσι;   g. φεύγωμεν;

b. φεύγουσι;   h. φύγωμεν;

c. φευγέτωσαν.   i. ἐφύγομεν.

d. φεύγωμεν.   j. ἐφύγομεν;

e. φευξόμεθα   k. φύγωμεν.

f. φυγέτωσαν.

319. SAUL'S SUCCESSOR CHOSEN.

    καὶ εἶπε κύριος πρὸς Σαμουήλ, "οὐκ ἔσται Σαοὺλ πάντοτε βασιλεὺς
ἐπὶ 'Ισραήλ. λάβε τὸ κέρας σου ἐλαίου, καὶ ἀποστελῶ σε πρὸς 'Ιεσσαὶ
ἐν Βηθλεέμ, ὅτι εὕρηκα ἐν τοῖς υἱοῖς αὐτοῦ ἐμοὶ βασιλέα, χριστὸν ἐμοί."

    καὶ εἶπε Σαμουήλ, "πῶς ἔλθω; ὅτι ἀκούσει Σαούλ, καὶ ἀποκτενεῖ με."

5   καὶ εἶπε κύριος, "ἐρεῖς, 'θῦσαι τῷ κυρίῳ ἥκω.' καὶ καλέσεις τὸν
'Ιεσσαὶ εἰς τὴν θυσίᾶν, καὶ γνώσῃ ἃ ἐρεῖς."

    καὶ ἐπείσατο Σαμουὴλ πᾶσιν ἃ εἰρήκει αὐτῷ κύριος. καὶ λαβὼν τὸ
κέρας ἐλαίου ἦλθεν εἰς Βηθλεέμ, καὶ οἱ πρεσβύτεροι τῆς Βηθλεὲμ εἶπον,
"τί ἥκεις;"

10   καὶ εἶπεν, "θῦσαι τῷ κυρίῳ ἥκω, ἁγιάσθητε καὶ φάγεσθε μετ' ἐμοῦ
σήμερον." καὶ ἡγίασε τὸν 'Ιεσσαὶ καὶ τοὺς υἱοὺς αὐτοῦ, καὶ ἐκάλεσεν
αὐτοὺς εἰς τὴν θυσίᾶν.

    καὶ ὅτε ἔβλεψε τὸ πρόσωπον τοῦ πρώτου υἱοῦ, εἶπεν, "ὁ χριστὸς
κυρίου ἐστὶν ὅδε."

15   ἀλλ' εἶπε κύριος πρὸς Σαμουήλ, "μὴ βλέψῃς τὸν πρόσωπον αὐτοῦ.
οὗτος γὰρ οὐ μὴ γένηται ὁ χριστός, ὅτι βλέπει τὸν πρόσωπον ἄνθρωπος,
ἀλλὰ ὁ θεὸς βλέπει τὴν καρδίᾶν."

    καὶ ἤγαγεν 'Ιεσσαὶ τοὺς ἑπτὰ υἱοὺς αὐτοῦ ἵνα βλέψῃ αὐτοὺς Σαμουήλ.
καὶ εἶπε Σαμουήλ, "οὐ μὴ χρίσω τινὰ ἐν τούτοις. ἔχεις ἄλλον υἱόν;"

20   καὶ εἶπεν 'Ιεσσαί, "ἰδοὺ ὁ μικρὸς Δαυὶδ μετὰ τῶν προβάτων ἐστί."

    καὶ εἶπε Σαμουὴλ πρὸς 'Ιεσσαί, "ἀπόστειλον καὶ λάβε Δαυὶδ ἵνα ᾖ
μεθ' ἡμῶν."

    καὶ ἀπέστειλε καὶ ἤγαγεν Δαυίδ. καὶ εἶπε κύριος πρὸς Σαμουήλ,
"χρῖσον τὸν Δαυὶδ ὅτι τοῦτον ἐξελεξάμην καὶ ἕξει τὴν βασιλείᾶν."

25   καὶ ἔλαβε Σαμουὴλ τὸ κέρας τοῦ ἐλαίου καὶ ἔχρισεν Δαυὶδ ἐν μέσῳ
τῶν ἀδελφῶν αὐτοῦ.

320. VOCABULARY.

ἁγιάζω, --- , ἡγίασα, --- , ἡγίασμαι, ἡγιάσθην: I dedicate, set apart
                                     for God, sanctify, purify

Δαυίδ (indecl.), ὁ: David

ἔλαιον, -ου, τό: olive oil

ἥκω, ἥξω, ἧξα, --- , --- , --- : I have come, am present

'Ιεσσαί (indecl.), ὁ: Jesse

ἵνα: that, in order that

κέρας, -ατος, τό: horn

οὐ μή: no, (a strong negative) by no means, not at all

πρόσωπον, -ου, τό: face

χριστός, -οῦ, ὁ: anointed, Christ

χρίω, --- , ἔχρισα, --- , --- ἐχρίσθην: I anoint

321. PRESENT SUBJUNCTIVE OF εἰμί.

ὦ   ὦμεν
ᾖς   ἦτε
ᾖ   ὦσι

322. NEGATIVES USED WITH THE SUBJUNCTIVE. The negative adverb μή is usually found alone with subjunctive forms. Less frequently οὐ μή is used.

323. SUBJUNCTIVE IN STRONG DENIALS. The aorist subjunctive with the
negative οὐ μή expresses a rather strong denial of a future possibility.

οὐ μὴ γένηται ὁ χριστὸς τοῦ 'Ισραήλ.
He <u>shall</u> <u>by</u> <u>no</u> <u>means</u> <u>become</u> the anointed of Israel.

324. SUBJUNCTIVE IN PROHIBITIONS. The aorist subjunctive with the negative
μή expresses a negative command or prohibition.

μὴ βλέψῃς τὸ πρόσωπον αὐτοῦ.
<u>Do</u> <u>not</u> <u>look</u> <u>at</u> his face.

325. SUBJUNCTIVE IN PURPOSE CLAUSES. Purpose is often expressed by the
subjunctive in clauses introduced by ἵνα.

λάβε αὐτὸν ἵνα ᾖ μεθ' ἡμῶν.
Take him <u>in</u> <u>order</u> <u>that</u> <u>he</u> <u>may</u> <u>be</u> with us.

326. EXERCISES.

a. Translate #319.

b. Complete the following sentences in the ways indicated.

   1) ἐλθὲ εἰς τὴν Βηθλεὲμ ἵνα μεθ' ἡμῶν . . . .
                        . . . you may be
                        . . . you may eat (once).
                        . . . you may eat (regularly).
                        . . . you may be purified.

   2) οὐ μὴ . . . he will choose . . . τοῦτο τὸ πρόσωπον.
                   he will anoint with olive oil
                   he will dedicate
                   he will look at

   3) μὴ . . . start to destroy yourself . . . , Σαούλ.
              start to choose
              start to dedicate yourself
              start to anoint yourself with olive oil

c. Put suitable negatives with all the verbs in the following sentences.

   1) Σαμουὴλ ____ ἥκει ἵνα ____ χρίσῃ ἐλαίῳ πάντας υἱοὺς τοῦ 'Ιεσσαι.

142

2) ____ ἥξῃ πρὸς Βηθλεὲμ πάλιν μετὰ τοῦ κέρατος τοῦ ἐλαίου.

3) ____ ἁγιάσησθε κέρατι ἐλαίου, ἀδελφοὶ Δαυίδ, ἵνα ἦτε καλοί.

4) ____ ὦμεν κακοὶ ἵνα ἥκῃ πρὸς ἡμᾶς μετὰ τοῦ κέρατος τοῦ ἐλαίου
ἵνα ἁγιάσῃ Δαυίδ.

5) τί κρεῖσσον τούτου ____ εἴπωμεν.

6) ____ ἐλευσόμεθα ὧδε πάλιν μετὰ τῶν κεράτων.

7) ____ ἔλθωμεν ὧδε πάλιν.

8) ____ ἐλευσόμεθα ὧδε πάλιν;

9) ____ ἔλθωμεν ὧδε πάλιν.

10) ____ ἁγιάζωμεν μόνον τὸ κέρας ἀλλὰ καὶ τὸ ἔλαιον.

11) ____ βλέψητε τὰ πρόσωπα τῶν ἀδελφῶν.

d. Remember by way of review that usually

1) οὐ and its compounds are used with the indicative.
2) μή and its compounds are used with other parts of a Greek verb.

e. Associate these words with your new vocabulary.

1) ceratoid: shaped like a horn.
2) Christ: God's Anointed.

LESSON 44

327. A VOLUNTEER ANSWERS A CHALLENGE.

καὶ συνάγουσιν ἀλλόφυλοι τὰς παρεμβολὰς αὐτῶν εἰς πόλεμον, καὶ
Σαοὺλ καὶ οἱ ἄνδρες Ἰσραὴλ συνάγονται. καὶ ἦλθεν ἀνὴρ δυνατὸς ἐκ τῶν
παρεμβολῶν τῶν ἀλλοφύλων, μέγας καὶ φοβερός. Γολιὰθ ἦν ὄνομα αὐτοῦ.
καὶ ἤρχετο Γολιὰθ καὶ ὠνείδιζε τὴν παρεμβολὴν τοῦ Ἰσραὴλ λέγων, "τί
5   πορεύεσθε κατὰ ἡμῶν; οὐκ ἐγώ εἰμι Γολιὰθ ὁ ἀλλόφυλος, καὶ ὑμεῖς οἱ
δοῦλοι τοῦ Σαούλ; ἐκλέξασθε ἑαυτοῖς ἕνα ἄνδρα μάχεσθαι πρός με. καὶ
ἐὰν δυνηθῇ οὗτος ὁ εἷς μόνος πατάξαι με, ἡμεῖς ἐσόμεθα ὑμῖν δοῦλοι.
ἐὰν δὲ ἐγὼ δυνηθῶ πατάξαι αὐτόν, ὑμεῖς ἔσεσθε ἡμῖν δοῦλοι καὶ δουλεύσετε ἡμῖν. ἰδοὺ ἐγὼ ὠνείδισα τὴν παρεμβολὴν Ἰσραὴλ σήμερον. πέμψον
10 μοι ἄνδρα ἕνα, καὶ μαχώμεθα μόνοι πρὸς ἀλλήλους." οὕτως ὠνείδιζε
Γολιὰθ τὸν Ἰσραήλ.

καὶ τὰ ῥήματα τοῦ Γολιὰθ τοῦ ἀλλοφύλου ἦν οὕτως φοβερὰ ὥστε ἔσχον μέγαν φόβον Σαοὺλ καὶ πᾶς ὁ Ἰσραήλ.

καὶ εἶπε Σαοὺλ πρὸς Δαυίδ, "οὐ μὴ δυνήσῃ πορευθῆναι πρὸς τὸν
15   ἀλλόφυλον ἵνα μάχῃ πρὸς αὐτόν. ὅτι τέκνον εἶ σύ, αὐτὸς δὲ ἀνὴρ μαχό-
μενος πᾶσαν τὴν ζωήν."

καὶ εἶπε Δαυὶδ πρὸς Σαούλ, "καὶ λέοντα καὶ ἄρκον ἐπάταξε ὁ δοῦλος
σου, καὶ ἀποθανεῖται ὁ ἀλλόφυλος οὗτος. οὐχὶ πορεύσομαι καὶ πατάξω
αὐτόν; τίς ἐστιν οὗτος ὃς ὠνείδισε τὴν παρεμβολὴν τοῦ θεοῦ ἡμῶν;"

20   καὶ εἶπε Σαοὺλ πρὸς Δαυίδ, "πορεύου καὶ ἔσται κύριος μετά σου."

328. VOCABULARY.

ἀλλόφυλος, -ου, ὁ: foreigner, Gentile, Philistine

ἄν: (No individual translation, used in apodosis of Type II conditions and elsewhere)

ἄρκος, -ου, ὁ or ἡ: bear

Γολιάθ (indecl.), ὁ: Goliath

δύναμαι, δυνήσομαι, --- , --- , ἠδυνήθην: I am able, have power, can

ἐάν: if

εἰ: if

εἷς, μία, ἕν: one

λέων, λέοντος, ὁ: lion

μάχομαι (present system only): I fight

μέγας, μεγάλη, μέγα: great, large, tall, big

ὀνειδίζω, --- , ὠνείδισα, --- , --- , --- : I reproach, upbraid, revile

πατάσσω, πατάξω, ἐπάταξα, --- , --- , --- : I strike, smite, kill

πορεύομαι, πορεύσομαι, --- , πεπόρευμαι, ἐπορεύθην: I go on my way,
proceed, travel

φοβερός, -ά, -όν: fearful, terrifying, causing fear

ὥστε: so that

329. CONDITIONAL SENTENCES. A conditional sentence is one whose reality or
probability depends on a supposed situation.

If it rains, the grass grows.
If it rains, we shall have no picnic.

In these sentences, "the grass grows" and "we shall have no picnic"
are not made as absolute statements. Their reality or probability
depends on the weather, that is, on the subordinate clauses "If it
rains." The subordinate clause is called the <u>protasis</u>, and the in-
dependent clause the <u>apodosis</u>.

330. TYPES OF CONDITIONAL SENTENCES. Greek of the New Testament period
used chiefly three types of conditional sentences.

a. Type I, in which the protasis is <u>assumed</u> <u>to</u> <u>be</u> <u>true</u>.

εἰ οὐ πατάξει με, ἡμεῖς οὐκ ἐσόμεθα ὑμῖν δοῦλοι.
If he does not smite me (and we assume that he will not), we
shall not be slaves to you.

The indicative is used in both clauses. The protasis is introduced by εἰ.

b. Type II, in which the protasis is <u>assumed</u> <u>to</u> <u>be</u> <u>false</u>.

εἰ μὴ ἐπάταξέ με, ἡμεῖς οὐκ ἂν ἐγενόμεθα ὑμῖν δοῦλοι.
If he had not smitten me (but he did), we would not have become
slaves to you (but we have).

εἰ μὴ ἐπάτασσέ με, ἡμεῖς οὐκ ἂν ἐγινόμεθα ὑμῖν δοῦλοι.
If he were not smiting me (but he is), we would not be becoming
slaves to you (but we are so becoming).

The aorist indicates a past contrary to fact situation; the imperfect indicates a present contrary to fact situation. In this
type of conditional sentence the Greek word ἄν has no individual
translation, but in the context (εἰ plus a secondary tense of the
indicative in the protasis, and ἄν plus a secondary tense of the
indicative in the apodosis) it is a signal of a contrary to fact
condition.

c. Type III, in which the protasis is <u>assumed</u> <u>to</u> <u>be</u> <u>neither</u> <u>true</u> <u>nor</u>
<u>false</u>, <u>but</u> <u>is</u> <u>left</u> <u>in</u> <u>doubt</u>.

ἐὰν μὴ πατάξῃ με, ἡμεῖς οὐκ ἐσόμεθα ὑμῖν δοῦλοι.
If he does not smite me (and we make no predictions about whether
he will or not), we shall not be slaves to you.

The protasis is introduced by ἐάν and uses the subjunctive. The
apodosis may use any form that expresses futurity, the time to
which Type III refers.

d. Mixed Conditions, in which a protasis of one type is used with an
apodosis of another type. The most frequently used combination is
a Type III protasis with a Type I apodosis, often called the
"present general condition."
ἐὰν μὴ πατάξῃ με, ἡμεῖς οὐκ ἐσμὲν ὑμῖν δοῦλοι.
If he does not smite me, we are not slaves to you.

331. RESULT CLAUSES WITH ὥστε. A result of some action or situation may be
expressed by ὥστε followed by either an indicative or an infinitive.

τὰ ῥήματα τοῦ ἀλλοφύλου ἦν οὕτως φοβερὰ ὥστε ἔσχον μέγαν φόβον
Σαοὺλ καὶ πᾶς ὁ Ἰσραὴλ (ὥστε σχεῖν μέγαν φόβον Σαοὺλ καὶ πάντα
τὸν Ἰσραήλ).

If an infinitive is used, one must substitute an accusative of general
reference for the nominative subject with the indicative.

332. οὐ AND μή INTRODUCING QUESTIONS.

a. A question introduced by οὐ, οὐκ, οὐχ, or οὐχί implies that the
questioner expects an affirmative answer.

οὐχ ὑμεῖς ἐμὲ πατάξετε;
You will smite me, won't you?

b. A question introduced by μή implies that the questioner expects a
a negative answer.

μὴ ὑμεῖς ἐμὲ πατάξετε;
You will not smite me, will you?

c. A question introduced by neither οὐ nor μή implies nothing about the answer expected.

ὑμεῖς ἐμὲ πατάξετε;
Will you smite me?

333. PARADIGM OF εἷς.

εἷς	μία	ἕν
ἑνός	μιᾶς	ἑνός
ἑνί	μιᾷ	ἑνί
ἕνα	μίαν	ἕν

The meaning of the word excludes a plural.

334. PARADIGM OF μέγας. With the exception of the four underlined forms in the paradigm below, μέγας is an adjective of the first and second declensions.

<u>μέγας</u>	μεγάλη	<u>μέγα</u>
μεγάλου	μεγάλης	μεγάλου
μεγάλῳ	μεγάλῃ	μεγάλῳ
<u>μέγαν</u>	μεγάλην	<u>μέγα</u>
μεγάλοι	μεγάλαι	μεγάλα
μεγάλων	μεγάλων	μεγάλων
μεγάλοις	μεγάλαις	μεγάλοις
μεγάλους	μεγάλᾱς	μεγάλα

335. EXERCISES.

a. Translate #327.

b. (1) Identify the type of each of the following conditional sentences, (2) tell the implications of each, and (3) translate.

1) εἰ συνάγουσιν οἱ αλλόφυλοι τὰς παρεμβολὰς εἰς πόλεμον, Σαοὺλ καὶ οἱ ἄνδρες αὐτοῦ συνάγονται, ἀλλὰ οὐ μάχονται.

2) εἰ συνῆγον οἱ ἀλλόφυλοι τὰς παρεμβολὰς εἰς πόλεμον, Σαοὺλ καὶ οἱ ἄνδρες αὐτοῦ ἂν συνήγοντο, ἀλλὰ οὐκ ἂν ἐμάχοντο.

3) εἰ συνήγαγον οἱ ἀλλόφυλοι τὰς παρεμβολὰς εἰς πόλεμον, Σαοὺλ καὶ οἱ ἄνδρες αὐτοῦ ἂν συνηγάγοντο.

4) ἐὰν συνάγωσιν οἱ ἀλλόφυλοι τὰς παρεμβολὰς εἰς πόλεμον, Σαοὺλ καὶ οἱ ἄνδρες αὐτοῦ συνάξονται.

c. Tell into which type of conditional sentence each of the following should be translated.

1) If you were a good teacher, you would improve with practice.
2) If you had been a good teacher, you would have improved with practice.
3) If you are made a good teacher, you will improve with practice.
4) If you are a good teacher (as I see clearly you are), you are improving with practice.

d. Translate.

1) Γολιὰθ ἦν οὕτως μέγας καὶ φοβερὸς ὥστε οὐκ εὗρεν ἕνα ἄνδρα ὃς δυνήσεται μάχεσθαι ὑπὲρ τοῦ Ἰσραήλ.

2) οὐκ εἶχε φόβον τοῦ Γολιὰθ ὁ Δαυὶδ ὥστε δυνηθῆναι ἐλθεῖν μάχεσθαι ἐπὶ τὸν μέγαν ἀλλόφυλον.

3) ὠνείδισεν οὕτως ὁ ἀλλόφυλος τὴν παρεμβολὴν τοῦ ᾽Ισραὴλ ὥστε Δαυὶδ ἠθέλησεν ἀποκτεῖναι τοῦτον τὸν φοβερὸν ἐχθρόν.

4) εἰ φόβον ἄρκου ἢ λέοντος οὐκ εἶχε ὁ Δαυίδ, οὐ δεῖ σχεῖν φόβον τοῦ Γολιάθ.

5) ἄρκοι καὶ λέοντες δύνανται γενέσθαι οὕτως φοβεροὶ ὥστε ἐπὶ αὐτοὺς οὐ μάχονται ἄνδρες.

6) εἰ ἄρκον ἢ λέοντα φοβερὸν ἀπεκτείναμεν, οὐκ ἂν ἔσχομεν φόβον τοῦ Γολιάθ.

7) ἐὰν ἡμᾶς εὕρωσιν σήμερον οἱ ἄρκοι τῆς γῆς ταύτης καὶ οἱ λέοντες, πῶς φύγωμεν;

8) εἰ χέρας εὕρομεν, τὰ πρόσωπα ἂν ἐχρίσαμεν.

e. Associate the following words with your new vocabulary.

1) <u>allophyl</u>ian: non-Indo-European or non-Semitic, i. e., <u>foreign</u>.
2) <u>arctic</u>: located under the polar constellation of the <u>Bear</u>.
3) <u>dynasty</u>: a series of rulers (<u>powerful</u> people) in the same
   family.
4) <u>Leo</u>, <u>Leon</u>, <u>Leon</u>ard, <u>Leon</u>idas: given names derived entirely or
   in part from the Greek word for
   lion.
5) <u>log</u>omachy: a <u>fight</u> about words.

LESSON 45

336. ONE LITTLE STONE.

καὶ Δαυὶδ ὁ υἱὸς τοῦ ᾽Ιεσσαὶ ἐν τῇ χειρὶ αὐτοῦ ἔλαβε τὴν ῥάβδον αὐτοῦ. καὶ ἐξελέξατο ἑαυτῷ μικροὺς λίθους τινάς. λαβὼν δὲ τὴν σφενδόνην αὐτοῦ ἐπορεύθη πρὸς τὸν ἀλλόφυλον ὃς τὸ ὄνομα τοῦ θεοῦ ἐβλασφήμει.

5   βλέψας δὲ ὁ Γολιὰθ τὸν Δαυίδ, ὠνείδισεν αὐτὸν ὅτι Δαυὶδ ἦν τέκνον καὶ τὸ πρόσωπον καλόν. καὶ ἐλάλει ὁ ἀλλόφυλος πρὸς Δαυίδ, "τί λαμβάνεις ῥάβδον καὶ λίθους τινὰς ἐρχόμενος ἐπ᾽ ἐμέ; ἔρχου πρὸς ἐμέ, καὶ δώσω σε τοῖς πετεινοῖς τοῦ οὐρανοῦ καὶ τοῖς θηρίοις τῆς γῆς."

καὶ ἐλάλησε ὁ υἱὸς τοῦ ᾽Ιεσσαὶ πρὸς τὸν ἀλλόφυλον, "σὺ ἥκεις πρὸς
10 με ἐν ῥομφαίᾳ ἀλλὰ ἐγὼ ἥκω πρὸς σε ἐν ὀνόματι κυρίου θεοῦ τῆς παρεμβολῆς ᾽Ισραήλ, τῷ ὀνόματι ὃ βλασφημεῖς σήμερον. καὶ δώσει σε κύριος

σήμερον εἰς τὴν χεῖρα μου καὶ ἀποκτενῶ σε. καὶ ἀποκόψω τὴν κεφαλήν

σου καὶ δώσω τὸ σῶμά σου καὶ τὰ σώματα τῶν ἀλλοφύλων σήμερον τοῖς

πετεινοῖς τοῦ οὐρανου καὶ τοῖς θηρίοις τῆς γῆς. λέοντα καὶ ἄρκον

15   ἀπέκτεινα καὶ ἀποκτενῶ σέ. καὶ γνῶσεται πᾶσα ἡ γῆ ὅτι ἐστὶ θεὸς ἐν

'Ισραήλ.   γνῶσεται δὲ πᾶσα ἡ παρεμβολὴ αὕτη ὅτι οὐκ ἐν ρομφαίᾳ σώζει

κύριος, ὅτι τοῦ κυρίου ἐστὶν ὁ πόλεμος, καὶ δώσει κύριος ὑμᾶς εἰς

χεῖρας ἡμῶν."

            ἐπορεύθη δὲ ὁ ἀλλόφυλος πρὸς Δαυίδ. ἔλαβεν οὖν ὁ υἱὸς τοῦ

20   'Ιεσσαι λίθον μικρὸν ἕνα καὶ ἔβαλεν αὐτὸν τῇ σφενδόνῃ καὶ ὁ μέγας

ἔπεσεν ἐπὶ πρόσωπον αὐτοῦ ἐπὶ τὴν γῆν. καὶ ἔδραμε Δαυίδ καὶ ἔλαβε

τὴν ρομφαίᾱν τοῦ ἀλλοφύλου καὶ ἐν ταύτῃ τῇ ρομφαίᾳ ἡ κεφαλὴ τοῦ ἐχθροῦ

ἀπεκόπη.

            ὅτε δὲ ἔβλεψαν οἱ ἀλλόφυλοι ὅτι ἡ κεφαλὴ τοῦ δυνατοῦ αὐτῶν ἀπε-

25   κόπη ὑπὸ τοῦ Δαυίδ, ἔφυγον.

337.   VOCABULARY.

ἀποκόπτω, ἀποκόψω, ἀπέκοψα, --- , --- , ἀπεκόπην: I cut off

βλασφημέω, --- , ἐβλασφήμησα, --- , --- , ἐβλασφημήθην: I revile,
        rail at, blaspheme, slander, speak evil of God

δώσω, -εις, -ει, etc. (fut. indic. act. of δίδωμι, which is to be
        given later): I shall give, you will give, etc.

θηρίον, -ου, τό: wild beast

κεφαλή, -ῆς, ἡ: head

λαλέω, λαλήσω, ἐλάλησα, λελάληκα, λελάλημαι, ἐλαλήθην: I utter,
                                                        speak, say

πετεινόν, -οῦ, τό: bird

πίπτω, πεσοῦμαι, ἔπεσον and ἔπεσα, πέπτωκα, --- , --- : I fall

ράβδος, -ου, ἡ: staff, rod

ρομφαίᾱ, -ᾱς, ἡ: sword

σφενδόνη, -ης, ἡ: sling

σῶμα, σώματος, τό: body, dead body, living body, person

338.   CONTRACT VERBS.

    a.   Nature of contract verbs. In this lesson the verb forms βλασφη-
         μεῖς, ἐβλασφήμει, and ἐλάλει are representatives of verbs whose
         final stem vowel joins in contraction with the thematic or variable
         vowel following it, e. g.

         βλασφημέεις becomes βλασφημεῖς, and ἐλάλεε becomes ἐλάλει.

    b.   Accent of contract verbs. The accent of contract verbs depends upon the accent in the uncontracted form.

1) If the first of the uncontracted parts is accented, the contracted syllable is circumflexed, e. g.
βλασφημέεις becomes βλασφημεῖς.

2) If the second of the two uncontracted parts is accented, the
contracted syllable receives an acute accent, e. g.
βλασφημεόμεθα becomes βλασφημούμεθα.

3) If the accent falls on neither of the uncontracted parts, the
same accent remains where it is, e. g.
ἐλάλεε becomes ἐλάλει.

339. LIST OF FORMULAS FOR CONTRACT VERBS IN -εω.

ε+ε=ει	ε+ο=ου
ε+ει=ει	ε+ου=ου
ε+η=η	ε+ω=ω
ε+ῃ=ῃ	

340. PARADIGMS OF λαλέω.

PRESENT

Active		Middle and Passive	

Indicative

λαλῶ	λαλοῦμεν	λαλοῦμαι	λαλούμεθα
λαλεῖς	λαλεῖτε	λαλῇ	λαλεῖσθε
λαλεῖ	λαλοῦσι	λαλεῖται	λαλοῦνται

Subjunctive

λαλῶ	λαλῶμεν	λαλῶμαι	λαλώμεθα
λαλῇς	λαλῆτε	λαλῇ	λαλῆσθε
λαλῇ	λαλῶσι	λαλῆται	λαλῶνται

Imperative

λάλει	λαλεῖτε	λαλοῦ	λαλεῖσθε
λαλείτω	λαλείτωσαν	λαλείσθω	λαλείσθωσαν

Infinitive

λαλεῖν	λαλεῖσθαι

Participle

λαλῶν	λαλοῦσα	λαλοῦν	λαλούμενος, -η, -ον

IMPERFECT INDICATIVE

ἐλάλουν	ἐλαλοῦμεν	ἐλαλούμην	ἐλαλούμεθα
ἐλάλεις	ἐλαλεῖτε	ἐλαλοῦ	ἐλαλεῖσθε
ἐλάλει	ἐλάλουν	ἐλαλεῖτο	ἐλαλοῦντο

341. EXERCISES.

a. Translate #336.

b. Locate by (1) tense, (2) mood, (3) voice, (4) person, (5) number,
and (6) first principal part.

1) ἐλελάλητο

2) βλασφημείσθωσαν

3) ἀποκόψῃ

4) ἐλάλει

5) ἐλαλεῖτε

6) βλασφημείτω

7) δώσεις

8) λαλεῖν

9) βλασφημοῦ

10) λαλήθητι

11) ἀποκοπῆναι

12) λαλῆται

13) λάλησον

14) λαλεῖσθε

15) λαλήσει

16) λάλει

17) λαλεῖ

18) λαλείτω

19) λαλῇ (3 places)

20) λαλῶμεν

21) πεσεῖν

22) πεσεῖσθε

23) ἐπέσομεν

24) πεσούμεθα

25) πίπτομεν

26) χρισάτω

27) χρίσον

28) ὀνείδισαι

29) ὀνειδισάσης

30) ὀνείδιζε

c. Translate.

1) ἐλελάλητο ὑπὸ τοῦ ἀλλοφύλου τὸ ῥῆμα.

2) βλασφημείσθωσαν αἱ ρομφαῖαι τοῦ ἡγεμόνος, ἀλλὰ μὴ βλασφημεί‑
τωσαν τὸ ὄνομα τοῦ βασιλέως ἡμῶν.

3) εὑρήκατε τὸν ἀλλόφυλον εἶναι μικρόν;

4) ἤθελέ τινα δυνησόμενον μάχεσθαι ρομφαίᾳ ὑπὲρ τοῦ Ἰσραήλ.

5) οὐ μὴ λαλήσητε ὅτι βληθήσονται ἡ κεφαλὴ καὶ τὸ σῶμα τοῦ βασι‑
λέως ἡμῶν τοῖς θηρίοις καὶ τοῖς πετείνοις.

6) "τῇ ἐμῇ σφενδόνῃ καὶ τῇ ἐμῇ ῥάβδῳ," ἐλάλησε Δαυίδ, "ἀποκτεῖναι
δύναμαι θηρία, λέοντας καὶ ἄρκους, καὶ βαλεῖν τὰ σώματα τοῖς
πετείνοις."

7) δεῖ ἔχειν σφενδόνην καὶ ῥάβδον ἐὰν τις ἔχῃ πρόβατα.

8) οἱ λέοντες καὶ οἱ ἄρκοι καὶ ἄλλα θηρία καὶ τὰ πετεῖνα φάγονται
πρόβατον ἀποκτανθὲν ἐν τῇ ἐρήμῳ.

9) διὰ ταῦτα Δαυίδ εἶχε πάντοτε σφενδόνην καὶ ῥάβδον.

10) ἐὰν τὴν κεφαλὴν τοῦ φοβεροῦ Γολιάθ ἀποκόψῃ ὁ Δαυίδ,
ἀποθανεῖται τὸ σῶμα τοῦ Γολιάθ.

11) οὐκ ἂν ἔσχε τὴν βασιλείαν ὁ Δαυίδ εἰ μὴ τὸν φοβερὸν Γολιάθ
ἀπέκτεινεν.

d. Associate the following words with the new vocabulary.

1) apocope: a cutting off of the last part of a word.
2) blasphemy: reviling something sacred.
3) theriomorphic: formed like an animal.
4) rhabdomantist: one who divines by rods.

342. WORDS OF ENCOURAGEMENT: John 14:21-26 in Nestle, <u>Novum Testamentum Graece</u>.

343. VOCABULARY.

ἀγαπάω, ἀγαπήσω, ἠγάπησα, ἠγάπηκα, ἠγάπημαι, ἠγαπήθην: I love

ἅγιος, -ᾱ, -ον: holy

ἐμός, -ή, -όν: my

ἐμφανίζω, ἐμφανίσω, ἐνεφάνισα, ---, --- , ἐνεφανίσθην: I manifest, exhibit

ἐντολή, -ῆς, ἡ: order, command

'Ισκαριώτης, -ου, ὁ: Iscariot

κἀγώ: καὶ ἐγώ

κόσμος, -ου, ὁ: universe, world, earth

λόγος, -ου, ὁ: word, statement, speech, teaching

μέλλω, μελλήσω, ---, ---, ---, ---: I am about to, intend to

μονή, -ῆς, ἡ: dwelling place, residence

παρά (παρ'): (with abl.) from; (with loc.) beside, with;
(with acc.) along.

παράκλητος, -ου, ὁ: advocate, helper, intercessor

πνεῦμα, -ατος, τό: spirit, wind

ποιέω, ποιήσω, ἐποίησα, πεποίηκα, πεποίημαι, ἐποιήθην: I make, do

τηρέω, τηρήσω, ἐτήρησα, τετήρηκα, τετήρημαι, ἐτηρήθην: I take care
of, guard, observe, give heed to, keep

ὑπομιμνήσκω, ὑπομνήσω, ὑπέμνησα, ---, --- , ὑπεμνήσθην: I cause to
remember, remind

344. LIST OF FORMULAS FOR CONTRACT VERBS IN -αω.

α+ε=α   α+η=ᾳ
α+ει (=ε+ε)=α   α+ο=ω
α+ει (=ε+ι)=ᾳ   α+ου=ω
α+η=α   α+ω=ω

345. PARADIGMS OF ἀγαπάω.

PRESENT

Indicative

Active		Middle and Passive	
ἀγαπῶ	ἀγαπῶμεν	ἀγαπῶμαι	ἀγαπώμεθα
ἀγαπᾷς	ἀγαπᾶτε	ἀγαπᾷ	ἀγαπᾶσθε
ἀγαπᾷ	ἀγαπῶσι	ἀγαπᾶται	ἀγαπῶνται

Subjunctive

ἀγαπῶ	ἀγαπῶμεν	ἀγαπῶμαι	ἀγαπώμεθα
ἀγαπᾷς	ἀγαπᾶτε	ἀγαπᾷ	ἀγαπᾶσθε
ἀγαπᾷ	ἀγαπῶσι	ἀγαπᾶται	ἀγαπῶνται

Imperative

ἀγάπα	ἀγαπᾶτε	ἀγαπῶ	ἀγαπᾶσθε
ἀγαπάτω	ἀγαπάτωσαν	ἀγαπάσθω	ἀγαπάσθωσαν

Infinitive

ἀγαπᾶν   ἀγαπᾶσθαι

(This represents an original
ἀγαπάεεν which became ἀγαπάεν
and later ἀγαπᾶν.)

Participle

ἀγαπῶν   ἀγαπῶσα   ἀγαπῶν   ἀγαπώμενος, -η, -ον

IMPERFECT INDICATIVE

ἠγάπων	ἠγαπῶμεν	ἠγαπώμην	ἠγαπώμεθα
ἠγάπας	ἠγαπᾶτε	ἠγαπῶ	ἠγαπᾶσθε
ἠγάπα	ἠγάπων	ἠγαπᾶτο	ἠγαπῶντο

346. **EXERCISES.**

a. Translate John 14:21-26.

b. Locate by giving (1) tense, (2) mood, (3) voice, (4) person, (5) number, and (6) first principal part.

1) ἐτετηρήκεισαν   7) ἀγαπῶ

2) ἠγαπῶ   8) ἠγάπᾱ

3) ἀγαπάτω   9) λαλοῦσι

4) τηρεῖν   10) τηροῦντος

5) λαλεῖσθε   11) πορεύθητι

6) ἀγαπᾷ

c. Translate:

1) I used to love you so that you loved me.
2) You used to love me so that I loved you.
3) We used to love each other.
4) Why don't we love each other?
5) Let's love each other again.
6) Do not love lions and bears so that they will love you.

d. Associate the following words with the new vocabulary.

1) agapanthus: a group of African flowers (love flower).
2) paraclete: one called to help, used of the Holy Spirit.
3) pneumatics: study of gases.

347. READING: I John 1:1-4

348. VOCABULARY.

ἀπαγγέλλω, ἀπαγγελῶ, ἀπήγγειλα, --- , --- , ἀπηγγέλην: I announce,
                                              report

ἀρχή, -ῆς, ἡ: beginning, rule, sovereignty

ἡμέτερος, -ᾱ, -ον: our

θεάομαι, --- , ἐθεασάμην, τεθέαμαι, ἐθεάθην: I behold, look upon,
                                                  contemplate, view

κοινωνίᾱ, -ᾱς, ἡ: fellowship, joint participation

μαρτυρέω, μαρτυρήσω, ἐμαρτύρησα, μεμαρτύρηκα, μεμαρτύρημαι, ἐμαρτυρή-
                  θην: I am witness, bear witness, testify

ὁράω, ὄψομαι, εἶδον, ἑώρακα, --- , ὤφθην: I see

ὅστις, ἥτις, ὅ τι: whoever, whatever, who, what

ὀφθαλμός, -οῦ, ὁ: eye

πληρόω, πληρώσω, ἐπλήρωσα, πεπλήρωκα, πεπλήρωμαι, ἐπληρώθην: I make
                                        full, fill, complete

φανερόω, φανερώσω, ἐφανέρωσα, πεφανέρωκα, πεφανέρωμαι, ἐφανερώθην:
                        I make visible, known, clear, manifest

χαρά, -ᾶς, ἡ: joy

ψηλαφάω, --- , ἐψηλάφησα, --- , --- , --- : I handle, touch, feel

349. FORMS OF ὅστις. In the New Testament only the following forms of
ὅστις are used. In I John 1:2 we find the form ἥτις.

                                    Singular

Nominative	ὅστις	ἥτις	ὅ τι
Genitive and Ablative	ὅτου		
Accusative			ὅ τι

                                    Plural

Nominative	οἵτινες	αἵτινες	ἅ τινα

350. LIST OF FORMULAS FOR CONTRACT VERBS IN -οω.

ο+ε=ου   ο+ῃ=οι or ῳ
ο+ει(=ε+ε)=ου   ο+ο=ου
ο+ει(=ε+ι)=οι   ο+ου=ου
ο+η=ω   ο+ω=ω

351. PARADIGMS OF πληρόω.

                                  PRESENT

     Active   Middle and Passive
                        Indicative

πληρῶ	πληροῦμεν	πληροῦμαι	πληρούμεθα
πληροῖς	πληροῦτε	πληροῖ	πληροῦσθε
πληροῖ	πληροῦσι	πληροῦται	πληροῦνται

Subjunctive

πληρῶ	πληρῶμεν	πληρῶμαι	πληρώμεθα
πληροῖς	πληρῶτε	πληροῖ	πληρῶσθε
πληροῖ	πληρῶσι	πληρῶται	πληρῶνται

Imperative

πλήρου	πληροῦτε	πληροῦ	πληροῦσθε
πληρούτω	πληρούτωσαν	πληρούσθω	πληρούσθωσαν

Infinitive

πληροῦν   πληροῦσθαι

(This represents an original
πληρόεεν which became πλη-
ροῦεν and later πληροῦν.)

Participle

πληρῶν   πληροῦσα   πληροῦν   πληρούμενος, -η, -ον

IMPERFECT INDICATIVE

ἐπλήρουν	ἐπληροῦμεν	ἐπληρούμην	ἐπληρούμεθα
ἐπλήρους	ἐπληροῦτε	ἐπληροῦ	ἐπληροῦσθε
ἐπλήρου	ἐπλήρουν	ἐπληροῦτο	ἐπληροῦντο

352. EXERCISES.

a. Translate I John 1:1-4. What does each ἵνα clause tell us?

b. Review all the contractions used in ἀγαπάω, λαλέω, and πληρόω by studying the following table.

Vowels in Suffixes

		ε	ει (=ε+ε)	ει (=ε+ι)	η	ῃ	ο	ου	ω
Final Stem Vowels	α	α	α (inf.)	ᾳ	α	ᾳ	ω	ω	ω
	ε	ει	ει (inf.)	ει	η	ῃ	ου	ου	ω
	ο	ου	ου (inf.)	οι	ω	οι/ῳ	ου	ου	ω

c. Locate by (1) tense, (2) mood, (3) voice, (4) person, (5) number, and (6) first principal part.

1) ἐθεάσω   6) φανέρου

2) ἐθεῶ   7) ἐφανέρου

3) πληροῖς   8) ἐφανεροῦ

4) πληροῦν   9) ἐμαρτυροῦντο

5) φανεροῦ

d. Associate the following words with new vocabulary.

1) <u>thea</u>ter: a place where dramas may be <u>viewed</u>.
2) <u>martyr</u>: one who <u>testifies</u> to his faith by death.

353. READING: I John 1:5-10.

354. VOCABULARY.

ἀγγελία, -ᾱς, ἡ: message

ἀδικία, -ᾱς, ἡ: unrighteousness, iniquity, injustice

ἁμαρτάνω, ἁμαρτήσω, ἡμάρτησα (ἥμαρτον), ἡμάρτηκα, --- , --- : I sin

ἁμαρτία, -ᾱς, ἡ: sin

ἀναγγέλλω, ἀναγγελῶ, ἀνήγγειλα, --- , --- , ἀνηγγέλην: I report,
           announce, declare

ἀφίημι, ἀφήσω, ἀφῆκα, --- , ἀφεῖμαι, ἀφέθην: I send away, let go, for-
           give, allow, remit

δείκνυμι (δεικνύω), δείξω, ἔδειξα, δέδειχα, --- , ἐδείχθην: I show,
           exhibit

δίδωμι, δώσω, ἔδωκα, δέδωκα, δέδομαι, ἐδόθην: I give

ἵστημι, στήσω, ἔστησα & ἔστην, ἔστηκα, --- , ἐστάθην: I cause to
           stand (transitive in pres., imperf., fut., 1st aor. act.);
           I stand, stand by (intransitive in -μι aor., perf., plup. act.
           and fut. mid. and fut. and aor. passive)

καθαρίζω, καθαριῶ, ἐκαθάρισα, --- , κεκαθάρισμαι, ἐκαθαρίσθην: I make
           clean, cleanse

ὁμολογέω, ὁμολογήσω, ὡμολόγησα, --- , --- , --- : I agree, confess,
           acknowledge

οὐδείς, οὐδεμία, οὐδέν: nobody, nothing, no, none

περιπατέω, περιπατήσω, περιεπάτησα, περιπεπάτηκα, --- , --- : I walk,
           live, conduct my life

πιστός, -ή, -όν: trusty, faithful, reliable

πλανάω, πλανήσω, ἐπλάνησα, --- , πεπλάνημαι, ἐπλανήθην: I lead astray,
           deceive

σκότος, -ους, τό: darkness

τίθημι, θήσω, ἔθηκα, τέθεικα, τέθειμαι, ἐτέθην: I put, place, lay down

φῶς, φωτός, τό: light

ψεύδομαι, ψεύσομαι, ἐψευσάμην, --- , --- : I lie, deceive by lies

ψεύστης, -ου, ὁ: liar

ὡς: as

355. PARADIGM OF οὐδείς.

οὐδείς	οὐδεμία	οὐδέν
οὐδενός	οὐδεμιᾶς	οὐδενός
οὐδενί	οὐδεμιᾷ	οὐδενί
οὐδένα	οὐδεμίαν	οὐδέν

356. RESULT CLAUSE WITH ἵνα. In I John 1:9 we have a ἵνα clause that

seems to express result rather than purpose.

. . . πιστός ἐστιν καὶ δίκαιος, ἵνα ἀφῇ ἡμῖν τὰς ἁμαρτίας καὶ καθαρίσῃ
ἡμᾶς ἀπὸ πάσης ἀδικίας.
. . . He is faithful and righteous, so that he forgives us our sins
and cleanses us from all unrighteousness.

God's faithfulness and righteousness result in the forgiveness of the
sins of those who confess them to Him. He has always been faithful
to His promises and righteous in His character. He is not faithful
and righteous just in order to forgive us.

357. MI VERBS. Some verbs, called -μι verbs from the ending of the first
principal part, are formed without the variable or thematic vowel except in the subjunctive. Consequently, the personal endings are
added directly to the stem of the tense. These verbs have peculiar
inflections only in the present, the imperfect, and the second aorist.
The stems of these verbs end in α (ἵστημι), ε (τίθημι), ο (δίδωμι).
For the paradigms of these verbs see #417 and #418 in the appendix.

358. EXERCISES.

a. Translate I John 1:5-10.

b. Answer the following questions.

1) What are the personal endings of -μι verbs in the present
indicative active? Middle and passive?

2) How does the final stem vowel of -μι verbs change from the
singular to the plural in the present and imperfect indicative
active?

3) What should be noticed about the second singular in the present
and imperfect indicative middle and passive?

4) What distinguishes the present from the aorist subjunctive in
-μι verbs?

5) What are the endings of -μι verbs in the imperfect indicative
active? Middle and passive?

c. Associate the following words with the new vocabulary.

1) cathartic: related to what cleanses.
2) deictic: pertaining to that which shows or points out.
3) homologous: agreeing or parallel in structure.
4) Peripatetics: a group of ancient philosophers who met in a
covered walking place called a peripatos.
5) photophobia: an aversion to light.
6) pseudonym: a false name.
7) scotophobia: an abnormal fear of darkness.
8) static: related to what is at rest or standing still.
9) Utopia: Sir Thomas More's description of a perfect
community which existed in no place.

359. PASSAGE TO TRANSLATE AND STUDY: I John 2:1-11.

360. VOCABULARY.

ἀγάπη, -ης, ἡ: love

ἀγαπητός, -ή, -όν: beloved

ἀληθής, -ές: true (to fact; actual as opposed to apparent), truthful

ἀληθῶς: truly, surely, certainly

ἄρτι: now, just now, just at this moment

ἕως: (prep. with gen.) until, as far as;   (conj.) until

ἤδη: now, already, now at length

ἱλασμός, -οῦ, ὁ: means of appeasing, propitiation

καθώς: as, just as

καινός, -ή, -όν: new, fresh, unused

μισέω, μισήσω, ἐμίσησα, μεμίσηκα, μεμίσημαι, --- : I hate

ὁ ἀπ'ἀρχῆς: he who has been from the beginning

οἶδα, εἰδήσω: I know

ὅλος, -η, -ον: whole, complete, entire

ὀφείλω, --- , --- , --- , --- , --- : I owe, ought

παλαιός, -ά, -όν: old, ancient

παράγω, --- , --- , --- , --- , --- : I pass away, disappear, go by
(The middle or passive form in I John 2:8 has the same meaning
as the active.)

σκάνδαλον, -ου, τό: stumbling block, cause of sin, snare

τεκνίον, -ου, τό: little child

τελειόω, --- , ἐτελείωσα, τετελείωκα, τετελείωμαι, ἐτελειώθην:
I finish, complete, accomplish

τυφλόω, --- , ἐτύφλωσα, τετύφλωκα, --- , --- : I make blind, blind

ὑπάγω, --- , --- , --- , --- , --- : I go away, depart

φαίνω, φανοῦμαι, ἔφανα, --- , --- , ἐφάνην: I give light, shine;
(pass.) come to light, appear

361. PARADIGMS OF οἶδα.

SECOND PERFECT ACTIVE

Indicative

οἶδα	οἴδαμεν
οἶδας	οἴδατε
οἶδε	οἴδασι & ἴσασι

Subjunctive

εἰδῶ	εἰδῶμεν
εἰδῇς	εἰδῆτε
εἰδῇ	εἰδῶσι

Imperative

ἴσθι	ἴστε
ἴστω	ἴστωσαν

Infinitive

εἰδέναι

Participle

εἰδώς	εἰδυῖα	εἰδός

SECOND PLUPERFECT INDICATIVE ACTIVE

ἤδειν	ἤδειμεν
ἤδεις	ἤδειτε
ἤδει	ἤδεισαν

FUTURE INDICATIVE ACTIVE

εἰδήσω	εἰδήσομεν
εἰδήσεις	εἰδήσετε
εἰδήσει	εἰδήσουσι

362. **INDEFINITE RELATIVE CLAUSES.** In I John 2:5 we find the clause ὅς δ' ἂν τηρῇ αὐτοῦ τὸν λόγον. . ., but whoever keeps his word. . . The antecedent of ὅς is not expressed. This indefiniteness is accentuated by the use of ἄν and the subjunctive. Indefinite relative clauses of this kind are parallel in construction and idea to the protasis of third type conditional sentences.

ἐὰν δέ τις τηρῇ αὐτοῦ τὸν λόγον	ὅς δ' ἂν τηρῇ αὐτοῦ τὸν λόγον
but if anyone keeps his word	but whoever keeps his word

363. **EXERCISES.** Exegesis is drawing the correct meaning from the text. This process includes a careful consideration of (1) the meaning of the roots of the words, (2) the meaning of the forms of the words, and (3) the meaning of the context. Since beginning the study of Greek, you have learned numerous items of vocabulary and scores of inflectional endings. Now we have started reading the Greek New Testament together, and our keen desire is to see more in the Greek than we have seen in even the best English translations that we have read. The way to do this is to put together in our thinking the meanings of (1) roots, (2) forms, and (3) context. Naturally skill in exegesis develops with practice. To begin to accomplish this purpose we shall work on fairly simple problems.

a. Try to answer the following questions.

    1) Does John teach the possibility of sinless perfection for a Christian here on earth in I John 2:1?

        a) Check the vocabulary meaning of ἁμαρτάνω.

        b) Identify the tense of ἁμάρτητε and ἁμάρτῃ.

        c) Read the context, especially I John 1:8, for limitations on John's meaning.

d) Now write out in one or two clear sentences what you think John means by his first statement in I John 2:1.

2) How secure is the basis of the assurance John offers in I John 2:3?

a) What is the assurance?

b) On what is the continuation of the assurance dependent?

c) What does John assume in ἐὰν . . . τηρῶμεν?

d) State John's idea clearly in your own words.

b. Associate the following words with the new vocabulary.

1) holocaust: a whole burnt offering.
2) misogynist: one who hates women.
3) phenomenon: an event that can be observed from what appears.
4) teleost: a fish belonging to a group that has complete or true bones.
5) typhlology: the systematic study of blindness.

LESSON 50

364. PASSAGE TO TRANSLATE AND STUDY: I John 2:12-21.

365. VOCABULARY.

αἰών, αἰῶνος, ὁ: eternity, universe, present age

ἀλαζονεία, -ᾱς, ἡ: boastfulness, vain display

ἀντίχριστος, -ου, ὁ: Antichrist, one who tries to take the place of the Messiah and who withstands Him

ἀφέωνται (perf. indic. pass. 3rd pl. ἀφίημι: I forgive): they have been (and therefore now are) forgiven

βίος, -ου, ὁ: life, period of life, means of living, course of life

εἰς τὸν αἰῶνα: forever

ἐξέρχομαι, ἐξελεύσομαι, ἐξῆλθον, ἐξελήλυθα, --- , --- : I come out, go out

θέλημα, -ατος, τό: will, choice, the action purposed, the act of willing

ἰσχυρός, -ά, -όν: powerful, mighty, strong

νεανίσκος, -ου, ὁ: young man, youth, lad

νικάω, νικήσω, ἐνίκησα, νενίκηκα, --- , ἐνικήθην: I conquer, win the victory over

ὅθεν: whence, wherefore

παιδίον, -ου, τό: young child, little one

πολύς, πολλή, πολύ: much, (pl.) many

πονηρός, -ά, -όν: bad, evil, wicked

σάρξ, σαρκός, ἡ: flesh

χρῖσμα, -ατος, τό: anointing

ψεῦδος, -ους, τό: lie, falsehood

ὥρᾱ, -ᾱς, ἡ: hour, season

366. NOTES ON I JOHN 2:18-21.

a. ἀλλ᾽ ἵνα (v.19). This is an ellipsis, an omission of what must be supplied to complete the meaning. From the beginning of the verse supply ἐξῆλθαν between ἀλλ᾽ and ἵνα.

b. πᾶν . . . οὐκ (v.21). No. When these two words occur in the same clause, be alert to two possible translations, (1) not all or not every, and (2) no.

367. PROBLEMS TO STUDY.

a. What type of conditional sentence is used in this passage? See v.19.

b. What does the implication of each type of condition contribute to our understanding of the passage?

c. What should we supply between ἀλλ᾽ and ὅτι in v.21?

d. List and classify, as far as you can, all the subordinate clauses in this passage under one of the following heads.

1) causal
2) comparative
3) conditional
4) purpose
5) relative
6) substantival

LESSON 51

368. PASSAGE TO TRANSLATE AND STUDY: I John 2:22-3:8.

369. VOCABULARY.

ἁγνίζω, --- , ἥγνισα, ἥγνικα, ἥγνισμαι, ἡγνίσθην: I purify

ἁγνός, -ή, -όν: pure, clean

αἴρω, ἀρῶ, ἦρα, ἦρκα, ἦρμαι, ἤρθην: I take up, lift up, raise, carry, take away, remove

αἰσχύνομαι, --- , --- , --- , ᾐσχύνθην: I am ashamed, am put to shame

ἀνομίᾱ, -ᾱς, ἡ: lawlessness, transgression, iniquity

ἀρνέομαι, ἀρνήσομαι, ἠρνησάμην, ἤρνημαι, --- : I deny, say "No," refuse to acknowledge, disown

160

γεννάω, γεννήσω, ἐγέννησα, γεγέννηκα, γεγέννημαι, ἐγεννήθην: I beget,
become a father of, bear

διάβολος, -ου, ὁ: devil, accuser

δικαιοσύνη, -ης, ἡ: righteousness

ἐλπίς, ἐλπίδος, ἡ: hope

ἐπαγγέλλομαι, --- , ἐπηγγειλάμην, ἐπήγγελμαι, --- : I promise

λύω, --- , ἔλυσα, --- , λέλυμαι, ἐλύθην: I loose, destroy

μηδείς, μηδεμία, μηδέν: no one, no, nothing

ὅμοιος, -ᾱ, -ον: like, resembling, similar, of the same kind as

παρουσίᾱ, -ᾱς, ἡ: presence, coming, arrival

ποταπός, -ή, -όν: what? of what sort? what kind of?

370. SUBSTANTIVE CLAUSES WITH ἵνα. In I John 2:27 we have a ἵνα clause
which is used as a substantive (i. e., a noun).

. . . καὶ οὐ χρείᾱν ἔχετε ἵνα τις διδάσκῃ ὑμᾶς. . .
. . . and you have no need that any one teach you. . .

The ἵνα clause stands as an appositive to χρείᾱν.

371. PRESENT PROGRESSIVE. In I John 3:8, . . . ὅτι ἀπ' ἀρχῆς ὁ διάβολος
ἁμαρτάνει the verb indicates an action begun in the past and still
going on in the present. The clause can be translated: . . . because
the devil has been sinning from the beginning.

372. POINTS TO STUDY.

a. Was John uncertain about the Lord's return? See ἐάν in I John 2:28.

b. What plausible reason can you give to explain why John used σχῶμεν
and αἰσχυνθῶμεν in 2:28 instead of ἔχωμεν and αἰσχυνώμεθα?

c. In 3:4 which noun is the subject in ἡ ἁμαρτίᾱ ἐστὶν ἡ ἀνομίᾱ?

d. Explain in 3:6 ἁμαρτάνει and ἁμαρτάνων. Is there a man, woman,
or a child who does not sin (Rom. 3:23)? What difference may we
understand between οὐχ ἁμαρτάνει and "does not sin"?

373. PASSAGE TO TRANSLATE AND STUDY: I John 3:9-24.

374. VOCABULARY.

αἰτέω, αἰτήσω, ἤτησα, ἤτηκα, ---, ---: I ask

ἀνθρωποκτόνος, -ου, ὁ: murderer

ἀρεστός, -ή, -όν: pleasing, agreeable

ἔμπροσθεν: (with gen.) in front of, before

ἐνώπιον: (with gen.) before, in the presence of, in the sight of

θάνατος, -ου, ὁ: death

θαυμάζω, θαυμάσομαι, ἐθαύμασα, --- , --- , ἐθαυμάσθην: I wonder,
wonder at

θεωρέω, θεωρήσω, ἐθεώρησα, --- , --- , --- : I look at, behold,
gaze at, see

Κάϊν (indecl.), ὁ: Cain

καταγινώσκω, --- , --- , --- , κατέγνωσμαι, --- : I blame, condemn

κλείω, κλείσω, ἔκλεισα, --- , κέκλεισμαι, ἐκλείσθην: I shut

μείζων, μεῖζον (comparative of μέγας): greater

μεταβαίνω, μεταβήσομαι, μετέβην, μεταβέβηκα, --- , --- : I pass over
(from one place to another), depart

σπέρμα, -ατος, τό: seed, offspring, posterity, children

σπλάγχνον, -ου, τό: heart, affections

σφάζω, σφάξω, ἔσφαξα, --- , ἔσφαγμαι, ἐσφάγην: I slay, slaughter

φανερός, -ά, -όν: visible, manifest

χάριν: (prep. with gen.) for, on account of, for the sake of

ψυχή, -ῆς, ἡ: soul, life

375. PROBLEMS AND QUESTIONS.

a. v. 9   Comment on the tense of ποιεῖ and ἁμαρτάνειν.

b. v. 13 What does the tense of θαυμάζετε imply?

c. v. 13 What legitimate deduction may we draw from the condition
εἰ μισεῖ?

d. v. 14 Comment on whether μεταβεβήκαμεν indicates a probable return ἐκ τῆς ζωῆς εἰς τὸν θάνατον.

e. v. 16 What is the duration of the obligation stated in ὀφείλομεν?

f. v. 23 What is the significance of the case of ὀνόματι?

376.   PASSAGE TO TRANSLATE AND STUDY: I John 4:1-21.

377.   VOCABULARY.

δοκιμάζω, δοκιμάσω, ἐδοκίμασα, --- , δεδοκίμασμαι, --- : I test, prove, approve

ἔξω: outside

ζῶ /ζάω/, ζήσω, ἔζησα, --- , --- , --- : I live, am alive

κόλασις, -εως, ἡ: correction, punishment, penalty

κρίσις, -εως, ἡ: decision, judgment, right, justice

μονογενής, -ές: only of its kind, unique

πλάνη, -ης, ἡ: going astray, error

πώποτε: ever yet

τέλειος, -ᾱ, -ον: mature, complete, perfect

ψευδοπροφήτης, -ου, ὁ: false prophet

378.   PROBLEMS: Comment on each of the following words in its context.

a. v. 1   πιστεύετε

b. v. 1   δοκιμάζετε

c. v. 2   ἐληλυθότα

d. v. 4   νενικήκατε

e. v. 12   τετελειωμένη . . . ἐστιν

f. v. 16   ἐγνώκαμεν

g. v. 16   πεπιστεύκαμεν

379. PASSAGE TO TRANSLATE AND STUDY: I John 5:1-21.

380. VOCABULARY.

αἴτημα, -ατος, τό: request, what is asked for

ἅπτω, ---, ἦψα, ---, ---, ---: I fasten to, set on fire, (mid.)
                              I fasten myself to, lay hold, assail

βαρύς, -εῖα, -ύ: heavy, burdensome

διάνοια, -ᾱς, ἡ: understanding, mind

εἴδωλον, -ου, τό: idol, image of a false god, false god

ἐρωτάω, ἐρωτήσω, ἠρώτησα, ---, ---, ---: I ask a question, make a
                              request

κεῖμαι, ---, ---, ---, --- : I lie, am located

μαρτυρίᾱ, -ᾱς, ἡ: witness, testimony, evidence

μόνον (adv.): only

νίκη, -ης, ἡ: victory

ὅταν: when, whenever

πίστις, -εως, ἡ: faith

τρεῖς, τρία: three

φυλάσσω, φυλάξω, ἐφύλαξα, πεφύλαχα, ---, ἐφυλάχθην: I guard, keep,
                                       watch, protect

381. PARADIGM OF βαρύς

βαρύς	βαρεῖα	βαρύ
βαρέος	βαρείᾱς	βαρέος
βαρεῖ	βαρείᾳ	βαρεῖ
βαρύν	βαρεῖαν	βαρύ
βαρεῖς	βαρεῖαι	βαρέα
βαρέων	βαρειῶν	βαρέων
βαρέσι	βαρείαις	βαρέσι
βαρεῖς	βαρείᾱς	βαρέα

382. PROBLEMS.

a. Classify and explain the meaning of every subordinate clause in vss. 15 and 16.

b. Clauses introduced by ἵνα may be classified as follows:

    1) Purpose clauses, giving the aim or goal which one has in performing some other action.
    2) Substantive clauses, clauses serving as a noun.
    3) Subfinal clauses, clauses expressing both purpose and content, a combination of purpose and substantive.
    4) Result clauses, giving the result of some other action.

Classify each of the ἵνα clauses in I John 5 in one of these four groups.

A P P E N D I X

NOUNS

383. FIRST OR <u>A</u> DECLENSION NOUNS.

    a. Stems ending in ε, ι, or ρ.

καρδία	καρδίαι	ἀλήθεια	ἀλήθειαι
καρδίας	καρδιῶν	ἀληθείας	ἀληθειῶν
καρδίᾳ	καρδίαις	ἀληθείᾳ	ἀληθείαις
καρδίαν	καρδίας	ἀλήθειαν	ἀληθείας

    b. Stems not ending in ε, ι, or ρ.

κώμη	κῶμαι	θάλασσα	θάλασσαι	προφήτης	προφῆται	γῆ	No
κώμης	κωμῶν	θαλάσσης	θαλασσῶν	προφήτου	προφητῶν	γῆς	
κώμῃ	κώμαις	θαλάσσῃ	θαλάσσαις	προφήτῃ	προφήταις	γῇ	Plural
κώμην	κώμας	θάλασσαν	θαλάσσας	προφήτην	προφήτας	γῆν	
				προφήτα			

384. SECOND OR <u>O</u> DECLENSION NOUNS.

ἄνθρωπος	ἄνθρωποι	ποτήριον	ποτήρια
ἀνθρώπου	ἀνθρώπων	ποτηρίου	ποτηρίων
ἀνθρώπῳ	ἀνθρώποις	ποτηρίῳ	ποτηρίοις
ἄνθρωπον	ἀνθρώπους	ποτήριον	ποτήρια
ἄνθρωπε			

385. THIRD OR CONSONANT DECLENSION NOUNS.

    a. Stems ending in a palatal mute (κ, γ, χ).

ἡ σάρξ	σάρκες	ἡ γυνή	γυναῖκες
σαρκός	σαρκῶν	γυναικός	γυναικῶν
σαρκί	σαρξί	γυναικί	γυναιξί
σάρκα	σάρκας	γυναῖκα	γυναῖκας
		γύναι	

    b. Stems ending in a linguo-dental (τ, δ, θ).

ὁ λέων	λέοντες	τὸ ὄνομα	ὀνόματα	τὸ ὕδωρ	ὕδατα		
λέοντος	λεόντων	ὀνόματος	ὀνομάτων	ὕδατος	ὑδάτων		
λέοντι	λέουσι	ὀνόματι	ὀνόμασι	ὕδατι	ὕδασι		
λέοντα	λέοντας	ὄνομα	ὀνόματα	ὕδωρ	ὕδατα		

ἡ ἐλπίς	ἐλπίδες	ἡ λαμπάς	λαμπάδες	ἡ νύξ	νύκτες
ἐλπίδος	ἐλπίδων	λαμπάδος	λαμπάδων	νυκτός	νυκτῶν
ἐλπίδι	ἐλπίσι	λαμπάδι	λαμπάσι	νυκτί	νυξί
ἐλπίδα	ἐλπίδας	λαμπάδα	λαμπάδας	νύκτα	νύκτας

    c. Stems ending in a liquid (λ, ρ).

ὁ πατήρ	πατέρες	ἡ μήτηρ	μητέρες	ὁ ἀνήρ	ἄνδρες	ὁ σωτήρ	σωτῆρες
πατρός	πατέρων	μητρός	μητέρων	ἀνδρός	ἀνδρῶν	σωτῆρος	σωτήρων
πατρί	πατράσι	μητρί	μητράσι	ἀνδρί	ἀνδράσι	σωτῆρι	σωτῆρσι
πατέρα	πατέρας	μητέρα	μητέρας	ἄνδρα	ἄνδρας	σωτῆρα	σωτῆρας
πάτερ				ἄνερ			

    d. Stems ending in a nasal (μ, ν).

ὁ αἰών	αἰῶνες	ὁ ἡγεμών	ἡγεμόνες
αἰῶνος	αἰώνων	ἡγεμόνος	ἡγεμόνων
αἰῶνι	αἰῶσι	ἡγεμόνι	ἡγεμόσι
αἰῶνα	αἰῶνας	ἡγεμόνα	ἡγεμόνας

    e. Stems ending in -ος/-ες.

τὸ ἔθνος	ἔθνη
ἔθνους	ἐθνῶν
ἔθνει	ἔθνεσι
ἔθνος	ἔθνη

    f. Stems ending in -ει/-ι.

ἡ θλῖψις	θλίψεις	ὁ ἱερεύς	ἱερεῖς
θλίψεως	θλίψεων	ἱερέως	ἱερέων
θλίψει	θλίψεσι	ἱερεῖ	ἱερεῦσι
θλῖψιν	θλίψεις	ἱερέα	ἱερεῖς
		ἱερεῦ	

386. PERSONAL PRONOUNS.

ἐγώ	σύ	αὐτός	αὐτή	αὐτό
ἐμοῦ, μου	σοῦ, σου	αὐτοῦ	αὐτῆς	αὐτοῦ
ἐμοί, μοι	σοί, σοι	αὐτῷ	αὐτῇ	αὐτῷ
ἐμέ, με	σέ, σε	αὐτόν	αὐτήν	αὐτό
ἡμεῖς	ὑμεῖς	αὐτοί	αὐταί	αὐτά
ἡμῶν	ὑμῶν	αὐτῶν	αὐτῶν	αὐτῶν
ἡμῖν	ὑμῖν	αὐτοῖς	αὐταῖς	αὐτοῖς
ἡμᾶς	ὑμᾶς	αὐτούς	αὐτάς	αὐτά

387. REFLEXIVE PRONOUNS.

ἐμαυτοῦ	ἐμαυτῆς	σεαυτοῦ	σεαυτῆς	ἑαυτοῦ	ἑαυτῆς	ἑαυτοῦ
ἐμαυτῷ	ἐμαυτῇ	σεαυτῷ	σεαυτῇ	ἑαυτῷ	ἑαυτῇ	ἑαυτῷ
ἐμαυτόν	ἐμαυτήν	σεαυτόν	σεαυτήν	ἑαυτόν	ἑαυτήν	ἑαυτό
ἑαυτῶν	ἑαυτῶν	ἑαυτῶν	ἑαυτῶν	ἑαυτῶν	ἑαυτῶν	ἑαυτῶν
ἑαυτοῖς	ἑαυταῖς	ἑαυτοῖς	ἑαυταῖς	ἑαυτοῖς	ἑαυταῖς	ἑαυτοῖς
ἑαυτούς	ἑαυτάς	ἑαυτούς	ἑαυτάς	ἑαυτούς	ἑαυτάς	ἑαυτά

388. INTENSIVE PRONOUN.

αὐτός	αὐτή	αὐτό	αὐτοί	αὐταί	αὐτά
αὐτοῦ	αὐτῆς	αὐτοῦ	αὐτῶν	αὐτῶν	αὐτῶν
αὐτῷ	αὐτῇ	αὐτῷ	αὐτοῖς	αὐταῖς	αὐτοῖς
αὐτόν	αὐτήν	αὐτό	αὐτούς	αὐτάς	αὐτά

389. RECIPROCAL PRONOUN. (In the N. T. only masculine forms are used.)

ἀλλήλων	ἀλλήλων	ἀλλήλων
ἀλλήλοις	ἀλλήλαις	ἀλλήλοις
ἀλλήλους	ἀλλήλᾱς	ἄλληλα

390. DEMONSTRATIVE PRONOUNS.

οὗτος	αὕτη	τοῦτο	ἐκεῖνος	ἐκείνη	ἐκεῖνο
τούτου	ταύτης	τούτου	ἐκείνου	ἐκείνης	ἐκείνου
τούτῳ	ταύτῃ	τούτῳ	ἐκείνῳ	ἐκείνῃ	ἐκείνῳ
τοῦτον	ταύτη	τοῦτο	ἐκεῖνον	ἐκείνην	ἐκεῖνο
οὗτοι	αὗται	ταῦτα	ἐκεῖνοι	ἐκεῖναι	ἐκεῖνα
τούτων	τούτων	τούτων	ἐκείνων	ἐκείνων	ἐκείνων
τούτοις	ταύταις	τούτοις	ἐκείνοις	ἐκείναις	ἐκείνοις
τούτους	ταύτᾱς	ταῦτα	ἐκείνους	ἐκείνᾱς	ἐκεῖνα

391. RELATIVE PRONOUN.

ὅς	ἥ	ὅ	οἵ	αἵ	ἅ
οὗ	ἧς	οὗ	ὧν	ὧν	ὧν
ᾧ	ᾗ	ᾧ	οἷς	αἷς	οἷς
ὅν	ἥν	ὅ	οὕς	ἅς	ἅ

392. GENERAL OR INDEFINITE RELATIVE PRONOUN.

ὅστις	ἥτις	ὅ τι	οἵτινες	αἵτινες	ἅτινα
ὅτου	---	---	---	---	---
---	---	ὅτῳ	---	---	---

393. INTERROGATIVE PRONOUN. (AND ADJECTIVE) 394. INDEFINITE PRONOUN. (AND ADJ.)

τίς	τί		τὶς	τὶ
τίνος	τίνος		τινός	τινός
τίνι	τίνι		τινί	τινί
τίνα	τί		τινά	τὶ
τίνες	τίνα		τινές	τινά
τίνων	τίνων		τινῶν	τινῶν
τίσι	τίσι		τισί	τισί
τίνας	τίνα		τινάς	τινά

395. NEGATIVE PRONOUNS.

μηδείς	μηδεμία	μηδέν	οὐδείς	οὐδεμία	οὐδέν
μηδενός	μηδεμιᾶς	μηδενός	οὐδενός	οὐδεμιᾶς	οὐδενός
μηδενί	μηδεμιᾷ	μηδενί	οὐδενί	οὐδεμιᾷ	οὐδενί
μηδένα	μηδεμίαν	μηδέν	οὐδένα	οὐδεμίαν	οὐδέν

396. DEFINITE ARTICLE.

ὁ	ἡ	τό		οἱ	αἱ	τά
τοῦ	τῆς	τοῦ		τῶν	τῶν	τῶν
τῷ	τῇ	τῷ		τοῖς	ταῖς	τοῖς
τόν	τήν	τό		τούς	τάς	τά

397. FIRST AND SECOND DECLENSION.

a. Two terminations.

αἰώνιος	αἰώνιον		αἰώνιοι	αἰώνια
αἰωνίου	αἰωνίου		αἰωνίων	αἰωνίων
αἰωνίῳ	αἰωνίῳ		αἰωνίοις	αἰωνίοις
αἰώνιον	αἰώνιον		αἰωνίους	αἰώνια

b. Three Terminations. (including middle participles, πιστευόμενος, -η, -ον)

καλός	καλή	καλόν		δίκαιος	δικαία	δίκαιον
καλοῦ	καλῆς	καλοῦ		δικαίου	δικαίας	δικαίου
καλῷ	καλῇ	καλῷ		δικαίῳ	δικαίᾳ	δικαίῳ
καλόν	καλήν	καλόν		δίκαιον	δικαίαν	δίκαιον
καλέ				δίκαιε		

καλοί	καλαί	καλά		δίκαιοι	δίκαιαι	δίκαια
καλῶν	καλῶν	καλῶν		δικαίων	δικαίων	δικαίων
καλοῖς	καλαῖς	καλοῖς		δικαίοις	δικαίαις	δικαίοις
καλούς	καλάς	καλά		δικαίους	δικαίας	δίκαια

398. THIRD DECLENSION.

ἀληθής	ἀληθές		κρείσσων	κρεῖσσον
ἀληθοῦς	ἀληθοῦς		κρείσσονος	κρείσσονος
ἀληθεῖ	ἀληθεῖ		κρείσσονι	κρείσσονι
ἀληθῆ	ἀληθές		κρείσσονα (κρείσσω)	κρεῖσσον
ἀληθές				

ἀληθεῖς	ἀληθῆ		κρείσσονες (κρείσσους)	κρείσσονα (κρείσσω)
ἀληθῶν	ἀληθῶν		κρεισσων	κρείσσων
ἀληθέσι	ἀληθέσι		κρείσσοσι	κρείσσοσι
ἀληθεῖς	ἀληθῆ		κρείσσονας (κρείσσους)	κρείσσονα (κρείσσω)

399. FIRST AND THIRD DECLENSION.

βαρύς	βαρεῖα	βαρύ		πᾶς	πᾶσα	πᾶν
βαρέος	βαρείας	βαρέος		παντός	πάσης	παντός
βαρεῖ	βαρείᾳ	βαρεῖ		παντί	πάσῃ	παντί
βαρύν	βαρεῖαν	βαρύ		πάντα	πᾶσαν	πᾶν

βαρεῖς	βαρεῖαι	βαρέα		πάντες	πᾶσαι	πάντα
βαρέων	βαρειῶν	βαρέων		πάντων	πασῶν	πάντων
βαρέσι	βαρείαις	βαρέσι		πᾶσι	πάσαις	πᾶσι
βαρεῖς	βαρείας	βαρέα		πάντας	πάσας	πάντα

400. IRREGULAR ADJECTIVE.

μέγας	μεγάλη	μέγα		μεγάλοι	μεγάλαι	μεγάλα
μεγάλου	μεγάλης	μεγάλου		μεγάλων	μεγάλων	μεγάλων
μεγάλῳ	μεγάλῃ	μεγάλῳ		μεγάλοις	μεγάλαις	μεγάλοις
μέγαν	μεγάλην	μέγα		μεγάλους	μεγάλας	μεγάλα

401. DECLENSION OF THE FIRST FOUR CARDINAL NUMBERS.

εἷς	μία	ἕν		δύο	τρεῖς	τρία		τέσσαρες	τέσσαρα
ἑνός	μιᾶς	ἑνός		δύο	τριῶν	τριῶν		τεσσάρων	τεσσάρων
ἑνί	μιᾷ	ἑνί		δυσί	τρισί	τρισί		τέσσαρσι	τέσσαρσι
ἕνα	μίαν	ἕν		δύο	τρεῖς	τρία		τέσσαρας	τέσσαρα

402. NUMERALS.

Cardinals	Ordinals
1. εἷς, μία, ἕν	πρῶτος
2. δύο	δεύτερος
3. τρεῖς, τρία	τρίτος
4. τέσσαρες, τέσσαρα	τέταρτος
5. πέντε	πέμπτος
6. ἕξ	ἕκτος

7. ἑπτά	ἕβδομος
8. ὀκτώ	ὄγδοος
9. ἐννέα	ἔνατος
10. δέκα	δέκατος
11. ἕνδεκα	ἑνδέκατος
12. δώδεκα (δεκαδύο)	δωδέκατος
13. δεκατρεῖς	τριτοσκαιδέκατος
14. δεκατέσσαρες	τεσσαρεσκαιδέκατος
15. δεκαπέντε	πεντεκαιδέκατος
16. δεκαέξ	ἕκτος καὶ δέκατος
17. δεκαεπτά	ἕβδομος καὶ δέκατος
18. δεκαοκτώ	ὄγδοος καὶ δέκατος
19. δεκαεννέα	ἔνατος καὶ δέκατος
20. εἴκοσι	εἰκοστός
21. εἷς καὶ εἴκοσι (εἴκοσι καὶ εἷς)	πρῶτος καὶ εἰκοστός
25. εἴκοσι πέντε	
30. τριάκοντα	
40. τεσσαράκοντα (τεσσεράκοντα)	
50. πεντήκοντα	
60. ἑξήκοντα	
90. ἐνενήκοντα	
100. ἑκατόν	
200. διακόσιοι, -αι, -α	
300. τριακόσιοι, -αι, -α	
1000. χίλιοι, -αι, -α	
10000. μύριοι (δέκα χιλιάδες)	

403. PRESENT PARTICIPLE OF εἰμί. (The second aorist active participle of βάλλω: βαλών, βαλοῦσα, βαλόν, is like this paradigm.)

ὤν	οὖσα	ὄν	ὄντες	οὖσαι	ὄντα
ὄντος	οὔσης	ὄντος	ὄντων	οὐσῶν	ὄντων
ὄντι	οὔσῃ	ὄντι	οὖσι	οὔσαις	οὖσι
ὄντα	οὖσαν	ὄν	ὄντας	οὔσας	ὄντα

404. PRESENT ACTIVE PARTICIPLE OF πιστεύω.

πιστεύων	πιστεύουσα	πιστεῦον	πιστεύοντες	πιστεύουσαι	πιστεύοντα
πιστεύοντος	πιστευούσης	πιστεύοντος	πιστευόντων	πιστευουσῶν	πιστευόντων
πιστεύοντι	πιστευούσῃ	πιστεύοντι	πιστεύουσι	πιστευούσαις	πιστεύουσι
πιστεύοντα	πιστεύουσαν	πιστεῦον	πιστεύοντας	πιστευούσας	πιστεύοντα

405. AORIST ACTIVE PARTICIPLE OF πιστεύω.

πιστεύσας	πιστεύσασα	πιστεῦσαν	πιστεύσαντες	πιστεύσασαι	πιστεύσαντα
πιστεύσαντος	πιστευσάσης	πιστεύσαντος	πιστευσάντων	πιστευσασῶν	πιστευσάντων
πιστεύσαντι	πιστευσάσῃ	πιστεύσαντι	πιστεύσασι	πιστευσάσαις	πιστεύσασι
πιστεύσαντα	πιστευσάσαν	πιστεῦσαν	πιστεύσαντας	πιστευσάσας	πιστεύσαντα

406. PERFECT ACTIVE PARTICIPLE OF πιστεύω.

πεπιστευκώς	πεπιστευκυῖα	πεπιστευκός	πεπιστευκότες	πεπιστευκυῖαι	πεπιστευκότα
πεπιστευκότος	πεπιστευκυίας	πεπιστευκότος	πεπιστευκότων	πεπιστευκυιῶν	πεπιστευκότων
πεπιστευκότι	πεπιστευκυίᾳ	πεπιστευκότι	πεπιστευκόσι	πεπιστευκυίαις	πεπιστευκόσι
πεπιστευκότα	πεπιστευκυῖαν	πεπιστευκός	πεπιστευκότας	πεπιστευκυίας	πεπιστευκότα

407. AORIST PASSIVE PARTICIPLE OF πιστεύω.

πιστευθείς	πιστευθεῖσα	πιστευθέν	πιστευθέντες	πιστευθεῖσαι	πιστευθέντα
πιστευθέντος	πιστευθείσης	πιστευθέντος	πιστευθέντων	πιστευθεισῶν	πιστευθέντων
πιστευθέντι	πιστευθείσῃ	πιστευθέντι	πιστευθεῖσι	πιστευθείσαις	πιστευθεῖσι
πιστευθέντα	πιστευθεῖσαν	πιστευθέν	πιστευθέντος	πιστευθείσας	πιστευθέντα

408. PRESENT ACTIVE PARTICIPLE OF δίδωμι.

διδούς	διδοῦσα	διδόν	διδόντες	διδοῦσαι	διδόντα
διδόντος	διδούσης	διδόντος	διδόντων	διδουσῶν	διδόντων
διδόντι	διδούσῃ	διδόντι	διδοῦσι	διδούσαις	διδοῦσι
διδόντα	διδοῦσαν	διδόν	διδόντας	διδούσας	διδόντα

409. PRESENT ACTIVE PARTICIPLE OF ποιέω.

ποιῶν	ποιοῦσα	ποιοῦν	ποιοῦντες	ποιοῦσαι	ποιοῦντα
ποιοῦντος	ποιούσης	ποιοῦντος	ποιούντων	ποιουσῶν	ποιούντων
ποιοῦντι	ποιούσῃ	ποιοῦντι	ποιοῦσι	ποιούσαις	ποιοῦσι
ποιοῦντα	ποιοῦσαν	ποιοῦν	ποιοῦντας	ποιούσας	ποιοῦντα

410. PRESENT ACTIVE PARTICIPLE OF ἀγαπάω.

ἀγαπῶν	ἀγαπῶσα	ἀγαπῶν	ἀγαπῶντες	ἀγαπῶσαι	ἀγαπῶντα
ἀγαπῶντος	ἀγαπώσης	ἀγαπῶντος	ἀγαπώντων	ἀγαπωσῶν	ἀγαπώντων
ἀγαπῶντι	ἀγαπώσῃ	ἀγαπῶντι	ἀγαπῶσι	ἀγαπώσαις	ἀγαπῶσι
ἀγαπῶντα	ἀγαπῶσαν	ἀγαπῶν	ἀγαπῶντας	ἀγαπώσᾱς	ἀγαπῶντα

VERBS

411. PERSONAL ENDINGS OF VERBS AND VERB ANALYSIS OF THE INDICATIVE.

	Active	Middle and Passive
Primary	Ω Verbs Present & Future with variable vowel -ω -εις -ει -ομεν -ετε -ουσι Perfect without variable vowel --- -ς --- -μεν -τε -ᾱσι (-νσι) MI Verbs -μι -ς -σι -μεν -τε -ᾱσι (-νσι)	Present, Future, and Perfect Indicative, and Present and Aorist Subjunctive -μαι -σαι ←(often contracted) -ται -μεθα -σθε -νται
Secondary	Imperfect, Aorist, Pluperfect, and Aorist Passive -ν -ς --- -μεν -τε -ν & -σαν	Imperfect, Aorist, and Pluperfect except Aorist Passive -μην -σο ←(often contracted) -το -μεθα -σθε -ντο
Imperative	---, -ς, & -θι -τω -τε -τωσαν	-σο -σθω -σθε -σθωσαν

VERB ANALYSIS OF THE INDICATIVE: Read down each column.

	ACTIVE						MIDDLE						PASSIVE	
	Pres.	Fut.	Impf.	Aor.	Perf.	Plup.	Pres.	Fut.	Impf.	Aor.	Perf.	Plup.	Fut.	Aor.
Aug.			*	*		*			*	*		*		*
Redup.			+	+	*	+ *			+	+	*	+ *		+
Vb.Stem	*	*	*	*	+ *	+ *	*	*	*	*	+ *	+ *	*	*
Ten. Suf. and/or Var. Vow.	+ o/ε	+ σο/ε	+ o/ε	+ σα/ε	+ κα/ε	+ κει	+ o/ε	+ σο/ε	+ o/ε	+ σα	+	+	+ θη/η+ σο/ε	+ θη/η
Pers. Endings	+ *	+ *	+ *	+ *	+ *	+ *	+ *	+ *	+ *	+ *	*	*	+ *	+ *

412. PARADIGMS OF πιστεύω.

PRESENT

	Active		Middle & Passive	
Ind.	πιστεύω	πιστεύομεν	πιστεύομαι	πιστευόμεθα
	πιστεύεις	πιστεύετε	πιστεύῃ	πιστεύεσθε
	πιστεύει	πιστεύουσι	πιστεύεται	πιστεύονται
Sub.	πιστεύω	πιστεύωμεν	πιστεύωμαι	πιστευώμεθα
	πιστεύῃς	πιστεύητε	πιστεύῃ	πιστεύησθε
	πιστεύῃ	πιστεύωσι	πιστεύηται	πιστεύωνται
Opt.	πιστεύοιμι	πιστεύοιμεν	πιστευοίμην	πιστευοίμεθα
	πιστεύοις	πιστεύοιτε	πιστεύοιο	πιστεύοισθε
	πιστεύοι	πιστεύοιεν	πιστεύοιτο	πιστεύοιντο
Impv.	πίστευε	πιστεύετε	πιστεύου	πιστεύεσθε
	πιστευέτω	πιστευέτωσαν	πιστευέσθω	πιστευέσθωσαν
Inf.	πιστεύειν		πιστεύεσθαι	
Part.	πιστεύων, -ουσα, -ον		πιστευόμενος, -η, -ον	

IMPERFECT

	Active		Middle & Passive	
Ind.	ἐπίστευον	ἐπιστεύομεν	ἐπιστευόμην	ἐπιστευόμεθα
	ἐπίστευες	ἐπιστεύετε	ἐπιστεύου	ἐπιστεύεσθε
	ἐπίστευε	ἐπίστευον	ἐπιστεύετο	ἐπιστεύοντο

FUTURE

	Active	Middle	Passive
Ind.	πιστεύσω	πιστεύσομαι	πιστευθήσομαι
	πιστεύσεις	πιστεύσῃ	πιστευθήσῃ
	πιστεύσει	πιστεύσεται	πιστευθήσεται
	πιστεύσομεν	πιστευσόμεθα	πιστευθησόμεθα
	πιστεύσετε	πιστεύσεσθε	πιστευθήσεσθε
	πιστεύσουσι	πιστεύσονται	πιστευθήσονται
Opt.	πιστεύσοιμι	πιστευσοίμην	πιστευθησοίμην
	πιστεύσοις	πιστεύσοιο	πιστευθήσοιο
	πιστεύσοι	πιστεύσοιτο	πιστευθήσοιτο
	πιστεύσοιμεν	πιστευσοίμεθα	πιστευθησοίμεθα
	πιστεύσοιτε	πιστεύσοισθε	πιστευθήσοισθε
	πιστεύσοιεν	πιστεύσοιντο	πιστευθήσοιντο
Inf.	πιστεύσειν	πιστεύσεσθαι	πιστευθήσεσθαι
Part. M.	πιστεύσων	πιστευσόμενος	πιστευθησόμενος
F.	πιστεύσουσα	πιστευσομένη	πιστευθησομένη
N.	πιστεύσον	πιστευσόμενον	πιστευθησόμενον

AORIST

	Active	Middle	Passive
Ind.	ἐπίστευσα	ἐπιστευσάμην	ἐπιστεύθην
	ἐπίστευσας	ἐπιστεύσω	ἐπιστεύθης
	ἐπίστευσε	ἐπιστεύσατο	ἐπιστεύθη
	ἐπιστεύσαμεν	ἐπιστευσάμεθα	ἐπιστεύθημεν
	ἐπιστεύσατε	ἐπιστεύσασθε	ἐπιστεύθητε
	ἐπίστευσαν	ἐπιστεύσαντο	ἐπιστεύθησαν
Subj.	πιστεύσω	πιστεύσωμαι	πιστευθῶ
	πιστεύσῃς	πιστεύσῃ	πιστευθῇς
	πιστεύσῃ	πιστεύσηται	πιστευθῇ
	πιστεύσωμεν	πιστευσώμεθα	πιστευθῶμεν
	πιστεύσητε	πιστεύσησθε	πιστευθῆτε
	πιστεύσωσι	πιστεύσωνται	πιστευθῶσι

Opt.	πιστεύσαιμι	πιστευσαίμην	πιστευθείην
	πιστεύσαις	πιστεύσαιο	πιστευθείης
	πιστεύσαι	πιστεύσαιτο	πιστευθείη
	πιστεύσαιμεν	πιστευσαίμεθα	πιστευθείημεν
	πιστεύσαιτε	πιστεύσαισθε	πιστευθείητε
	πιστεύσαιεν &	πιστεύσαιντο	πιστευθείησαν
	πιστεύσειαν		

Impv.	πίστευσον	πίστευσαι	πιστεύθητι
	πιστευσάτω	πιστευσάσθω	πιστευθήτω
	πιστεύσατε	πιστεύσασθε	πιστεύθητε
	πιστευσάτωσαν	πιστευσάσθωσαν	πιστευθήτωσαν

Inf.	πιστεῦσαι	πιστεύσασθαι	πιστευθῆναι

Part.	πιστεύσᾱς, -ᾱσα, -αν	πιστευσάμενος, -η, -ον	πιστευθείς, -εῖσα, -ἐν

PERFECT

Ind.	πεπίστευκα	πεπιστεύκαμεν	πεπίστευμαι	πεπιστεύμεθα
	πεπίστευκας	πεπιστεύκατε	πεπίστευσαι	πεπίστευσθε
	πεπίστευκε	πεπιστεύκᾱσι	πεπίστευται	πεπίστευνται

Subj.	πεπιστευκὼς ὦ	πεπιστευκότες ὦμεν	πεπιστευμένος ὦ	πεπιστευμένοι ὦμεν
	" ᾖς	" ἦτε	" ᾖς	" ἦτε
	" ᾖ	" ὦσι	" ᾖ	" ὦσι

Impv.	NONE		πεπίστευσο	πεπίστευσθε
			πεπιστεύσθω	πεπιστεύσθωσαν

Inf.	πεπιστευκέναι		πεπιστεῦσθαι

Part.	πεπιστευκώς, -υῖα, -ός	πεπιστευμένος, -η, -ον

PLUPERFECT

Ind.	(ἐ)πεπιστεύκειν	(ἐ)πεπιστεύκειμεν	(ἐ)πεπιστεύμην	(ἐ)πεπιστεύμεθα
	(ἐ)πεπιστεύκεις	(ἐ)πεπιστεύκειτε	(ἐ)πεπίστευσο	(ἐ)πεπίστευσθε
	(ἐ)πεπιστεύκει	(ἐ)πεπιστεύκεισαν	(ἐ)πεπίστευτο	(ἐ)πεπίστευντο

413. SECOND AORIST OF βάλλω.

	Active		Middle	
Ind.	ἔβαλον	ἐβάλομεν	ἐβαλόμην	ἐβαλόμεθα
	ἔβαλες	ἐβάλετε	ἐβάλου	ἐβάλεσθε
	ἔβαλε	ἔβαλον	ἐβάλετο	ἐβάλοντο
Subj.	βάλω	βάλωμεν	βάλωμαι	βαλώμεθα
	βάλῃς	βάλητε	βάλῃ	βάλησθε
	βάλῃ	βάλωσι	βάληται	βάλωνται
Opt.	βάλοιμι	βάλοιμεν	βαλοίμην	βαλοίμεθα
	βάλοις	βάλοιτε	βάλοιο	βάλοισθε
	βάλοι	βάλοιεν	βάλοιτο	βάλοιντο
Impv.	βάλε	βάλετε	βάλου	βάλεσθε
	βαλέτω	βαλέτωσαν	βαλέσθω	βαλέσθωσαν
Inf.	βαλεῖν		βαλέσθαι	
Part.	βαλών, -οῦσα, -όν		βαλόμενος, -η, -ον	

414. FUTURE AND AORIST OF LIQUID AND NASAL VERBS.

FUTURE OF ἀποστέλλω

	Active		Middle	
Ind.	ἀποστελῶ	ἀποστελοῦμεν	ἀποστελοῦμαι	ἀποστελούμεθα
	ἀποστελεῖς	ἀποστελεῖτε	ἀποστελῇ	ἀποστελεῖσθε
	ἀποστελεῖ	ἀποστελοῦσι	ἀποστελεῖται	ἀποστελοῦνται
Inf.	ἀποστελεῖν		ἀποστελεῖσθαι	
Part.	ἀποστελῶν, -οῦσα, -οῦν		ἀποστελούμενος, -η, -ον	

AORIST OF ἀποστέλλω

Active		Middle	
Ind. ἀπέστειλα	ἀπεστείλαμεν	ἀπεστειλάμην	ἀπεστειλάμεθα
ἀπέστειλας	ἀπεστείλατε	ἀπεστείλω	ἀπεστείλασθε
ἀπέστειλε	ἀπέστειλαν	ἀπεστείλατο	ἀπεστείλαντο
Subj. ἀποστείλω	ἀποστείλωμεν	ἀποστείλωμαι	ἀποστειλώμεθα
ἀποστείλῃς	ἀποστείλητε	ἀποστείλῃ	ἀποστείλησθε
ἀποστείλῃ	ἀποστείλωσι	ἀποστείληται	ἀποστείλωνται
Imper. ἀπόστειλον	ἀποστείλατε	ἀπόστειλαι	ἀποστείλασθε
ἀποστειλάτω	ἀποστειλάτωσαν	ἀποστειλάσθω	ἀποστειλάσθωσαν
Inf. ἀποστεῖλαι		ἀποστείλασθαι	
Part. ἀποστείλᾱς, -ᾱσα, -αν		ἀποστειλάμενος, -η, -ον	

415. PERFECT AND PLUPERFECT MIDDLE AND PASSIVE OF MUTE VERBS.

PERFECT

	(γράφω)	(ἄγω)	(πείθω)	(ἀποστέλλω)
Ind.	γέγραμμαι	ἦγμαι	πέπεισμαι	ἀπέσταλμαι
	γέγραψαι	ἦξαι	πέπεισαι	ἀπέσταλσαι
	γέγραπται	ἦκται	πέπεισται	ἀπέσταλται
	γεγράμμεθα	ἤγμεθα	πεπείσμεθα	ἀπεστάλμεθα
	γέγραφθε	ἦχθε	πέπεισθε	ἀπέσταλθε
	γεγραμμένοι εἰσί	ἠγμένοι εἰσί	πεπεισμένοι εἰσί	ἀπεσταλμένοι εἰσί
Subj.	γεγραμμένος ᾦ	ἠγμένος ᾦ	πεπεισμένος ᾦ	ἀπεσταλμένος ᾦ
	” ᾖς	” ᾖς	” ᾖς	” ᾖς
	” ᾖ	” ᾖ	” ᾖ	” ᾖ
	γεγραμμένοι ᾦμεν	ἠγμένοι ᾦμεν	πεπεισμένοι ᾦμεν	ἀπεσταλμένοι ᾦμεν
	” ᾖτε	” ᾖτε	” ᾖτε	” ᾖτε
	” ᾦσι	” ᾦσι	” ᾦσι	” ᾦσι

No optative or imperative are in use in the New Testament.

| **Inf.** | γεγράφθαι | ἦχθαι | πεπεῖσθαι | ἀπεστάλθαι |
| **Part.** | γεγραμμένος, -η, -ον | ἠγμένος, -η, -ον | πεπεισμένος, -η, -ον | ἀπεσταλμένος, -η, -ον |

PLUPERFECT

Ind.	(ἐ)γεγράμμην	ἤγμην	(ἐ)πεπείσμην	ἀπεστάλμην
	(ἐ)γέγραψο	ἦξο	(ἐ)πέπεισο	ἀπέσταλσο
	(ἐ)γέγραπτο	ἦκτο	(ἐ)πέπειστο	ἀπέσταλτο
	(ἐ)γεγράμμεθα	ἤγμεθα	(ἐ)πεπείσμεθα	ἀπεστάλμεθα
	(ἐ)γέγραφθε	ἦχθε	(ἐ)πέπεισθε	ἀπέσταλθε
	γεγραμμένοι ἦσαν	ἠγμένοι ἦσαν	πεπεισμένοι ἦσαν	ἀπεσταλμένοι ἦσαν

416. CONTRACT VERBS.

PRESENT ACTIVE

Ind.	ἀγαπῶ	ἀγαπῶμεν	λαλῶ	λαλοῦμεν	πληρῶ	πληροῦμεν
	ἀγαπᾷς	ἀγαπᾶτε	λαλεῖς	λαλεῖτε	πληροῖς	πληροῦτε
	ἀγαπᾷ	ἀγαπῶσι	λαλεῖ	λαλοῦσι	πληροῖ	πληροῦσι
Subj.	ἀγαπῶ	ἀγαπῶμεν	λαλῶ	λαλῶμεν	πληρῶ	πληρῶμεν
	ἀγαπᾷς	ἀγαπᾶτε	λαλῇς	λαλῆτε	πληροῖς	πληρῶτε
	ἀγαπᾷ	ἀγαπῶσι	λαλῇ	λαλῶσι	πληροῖ	πληρῶσι

No optative of contract verbs is used in the New Testament.

Impv.	ἀγάπα	ἀγαπᾶτε	λάλει	λαλεῖτε	πλήρου	πληροῦτε
	ἀγαπάτω	ἀγαπάτωσαν	λαλείτω	λαλείτωσαν	πληρούτω	πληρούτωσαν
Inf.	ἀγαπᾶν		λαλεῖν		πληροῦν	
Part.	ἀγαπῶν, -ῶσα, -ῶν		λαλῶν, -οῦσα, -οῦν		πληρῶν, -οῦσα, -οῦν	

IMPERFECT ACTIVE

Ind.	ἠγάπων	ἠγαπῶμεν	ἐλάλουν	ἐλαλοῦμεν	ἐπλήρουν	ἐπληροῦμεν
	ἠγάπας	ἠγαπᾶτε	ἐλάλεις	ἐλαλεῖτε	ἐπλήρους	ἐπληροῦτε
	ἠγάπα	ἠγάπων	ἐλάλει	ἐλάλουν	ἐπλήρου	ἐπλήρουν

PRESENT MIDDLE

Ind.	ἀγαπῶμαι	ἀγαπώμεθα	λαλοῦμαι	λαλούμεθα	πληροῦμαι	πληρούμεθα
	ἀγαπᾷ	ἀγαπᾶσθε	λαλῇ	λαλεῖσθε	πληροῖ	πληροῦσθε
	ἀγαπᾶται	ἀγαπῶνται	λαλεῖται	λαλοῦνται	πληροῦται	πληροῦνται

Subj.	ἀγαπῶμαι	ἀγαπώμεθα	λαλῶμαι	λαλώμεθα	πληρῶμαι	πληρώμεθα
	ἀγαπᾷ	ἀγαπᾶσθε	λαλῇ	λαλῆσθε	πληροῖ	πληρῶσθε
	ἀγαπᾶται	ἀγαπῶνται	λαλῆται	λαλῶνται	πληρῶται	πληρῶνται

No optative of contract verbs is used in the New Testament.

Impv.	ἀγαπῶ	ἀγαπᾶσθε	λαλοῦ	λαλεῖσθε	πληροῦ	πληροῦσθε
	ἀγαπάσθω	ἀγαπάσθωσαν	λαλείσθω	λαλείσθωσαν	πληρούσθω	πληρούσθωσαν

Inf.	ἀγαπᾶσθαι		λαλεῖσθαι		πληροῦσθαι	

Part.	ἀγαπώμενος, -η, -ον		λαλούμενος, -η, -ον		πληρούμενος, -η, -ον	

IMPERFECT MIDDLE

Ind.	ἠγαπώμην	ἠγαπώμεθα	ἐλαλούμην	ἐλαλούμεθα	ἐπληρούμην	ἐπληρούμεθα
	ἠγαπῶ	ἠγαπᾶσθε	ἐλαλοῦ	ἐλαλεῖσθε	ἐπληροῦ	ἐπληροῦσθε
	ἠγαπᾶτο	ἠγαπῶντο	ἐλαλεῖτο	ἐλαλοῦντο	ἐπληροῦτο	ἐπληροῦντο

417. COMPARATIVE PARADIGMS OF FOUR MI VERBS.

PRESENT ACTIVE

Ind.	ἵστημι	τίθημι	δίδωμι	δείκνυμι
	ἵστης	τίθης	δίδως	δείκνυς
	ἵστησι	τίθησι	δίδωσι	δείκνυσι
	ἵσταμεν	τίθεμεν	δίδομεν	δείκνυμεν
	ἵστατε	τίθετε	δίδοτε	δείκνυτε
	ἱστᾶσι	τιθέασι	διδόασι	δεικνύασι

Subj.	ἱστῶ	τιθῶ	διδῶ	δεικνύω
	ἱστῇς	τιθῇς	διδῷς (διδοῖς)	δεικνύῃς
	ἱστῇ	τιθῇ	διδῷ (διδοῖ)	δεικνύῃ
	ἱστῶμεν	τιθῶμεν	διδῶμεν	δεικνύωμεν
	ἱστῆτε	τιθῆτε	διδῶτε	δεικνύητε
	ἱστῶσι	τιθῶσι	διδῶσι	δεικνύωσι

Opt.	None in N. T.	None in N. T.	None in N. T.	None in N. T.

Impv.	ἵστη	τίθει	δίδου	δείκνυ
	ἱστάτω	τιθέτω	διδότω	δεικνύτω
	ἵστατε	τίθετε	δίδοτε	δείκνυτε
	ἱστάτωσαν	τιθέτωσαν	διδότωσαν	δεικνύτωσαν

Inf.	ἱστάναι	τιθέναι	διδόναι	δεικνόναι

Part.	ἱστάς, -ᾶσα, -άν	τιθείς, -εῖσα, -έν	διδούς, -οῦσα, -όν	δεικνύς, -ῦσα, -όν

IMPERFECT ACTIVE

Ind.	ἵστην	ἐτίθην	ἐδίδουν	ἐδείκνυν
	ἵστης	ἐτίθεις	ἐδίδους	ἐδείκνυς
	ἵστη	ἐτίθει	ἐδίδου	ἐδείκνυ
	ἵσταμεν	ἐτίθεμεν	ἐδίδομεν	ἐδείκνυμεν
	ἵστατε	ἐτίθετε	ἐδίδοτε	ἐδείκνυτε
	ἵστασαν	ἐτίθεσαν	ἐδίδοσαν	ἐδείκνυσαν

PRESENT MIDDLE

Ind.	ἵσταμαι	τίθεμαι	δίδομαι	δείκνυμαι
	ἵστασαι	τίθεσαι	δίδοσαι	δείκνυσαι
	ἵσταται	τίθεται	δίδοται	δείκνυται
	ἱστάμεθα	τιθέμεθα	διδόμεθα	δεικνύμεθα
	ἵστασθε	τίθεσθε	δίδοσθε	δείκνυσθε
	ἵστανται	τίθενται	δίδονται	δείκνυνται

Subj.	ἱστῶμαι	τιθῶμαι	διδῶμαι	δεικνύωμαι
	ἱστῇ	τιθῇ	διδῷ	δεικνύῃ
	ἱστῆται	τιθῆται	διδῶται	δεικνύηται
	ἱστώμεθα	τιθώμεθα	διδώμεθα	δεικνυώμεθα
	ἱστῆσθε	τιθῆσθε	διδῶσθε	δεικνύησθε
	ἱστῶνται	τιθῶνται	διδῶνται	δεικνύωνται

Opt.	None in N. T.	None in N. T.	None in N. T.	None in N. T.

Impv.	ἵστασο	τίθεσο	δίδοσο	δείκνυσο
	ἱστάσθω	τιθέσθω	διδόσθω	δεικνύσθω
	ἵστασθε	τίθεσθε	δίδοσθε	δείκνυσθε
	ἱστάσθωσαν	τιθέσθωσαν	διδόσθωσαν	δεικνύσθωσαν

Inf.	ἵστασθαι	τίθεσθαι	δίδοσθαι	δείκνυσθαι

Part.	ἱστάμενος, -η, -ον	τιθέμενος, -η, -ον	διδόμενος, -η, -ον	δεικνύμενος, -η, -ον

IMPERFECT MIDDLE

Ind.	ἱστάμην	ἐτιθέμην	ἐδιδόμην	ἐδεικνύμην
	ἵστασο	ἐτίθεσο	ἐδίδοσο	ἐδείκνυσο
	ἵστατο	ἐτίθετο	ἐδίδοτο	ἐδείκνυτο
	ἱστάμεθα	ἐτιθέμεθα	ἐδιδόμεθα	ἐδεικνύμεθα
	ἵστασθε	ἐτίθεσθε	ἐδίδοσθε	ἐδείκνυσθε
	ἵσταντο	ἐτίθεντο	ἐδίδοντο	ἐδείκνυντο

AORIST ACTIVE

	-μι Aor.	"κ" Aor.	"κ" Aor.	1st Aor.
Ind.	ἔστην	ἔθηκα	ἔδωκα	ἔδειξα
	ἔστης	ἔθηκας	ἔδωκας	ἔδειξας
	ἔστη	ἔθηκε	ἔδωκε	ἔδειξε
	ἔστημεν	ἐθήκαμεν	ἐδώκαμεν	ἐδείξαμεν
	ἔστητε	ἐθήκατε	ἐδώκατε	ἐδείξατε
	ἔστησαν	ἔθηκαν	ἔδωκαν	ἔδειξαν
Subj.	στῶ	θῶ	δῶ	δείξω
	στῇς	θῇς	δῷς(δοῖς)	δείξῃς
	στῇ	θῇ	δῷ (δοῖ, δώῃ)	δείξῃ
	στῶμεν	θῶμεν	δῶμεν	δείξωμεν
	στῆτε	θῆτε	δῶτε	δείξητε
	στῶσι	θῶσι	δῶσι	δείξωσι
Opt.	None in N. T.	None in N. T.	Only 3rd S. in — N. T. δῴη — —	δείξαιμι δείξαις δείξαι δείξαιμεν δείξαιτε δείξαιεν(δείξειαν)
Impv.	στῆθι	θές	δός	δεῖξον
	στήτω	θέτω	δότω	δειξάτω
	στῆτε	θέτε	δότε	δείξατε
	στήτωσαν	θέτωσαν	δότωσαν	δειξάτωσαν
Inf.	στῆναι	θεῖναι	δοῦναι	δεῖξαι
Part.	στάς, -ᾶσα, -άν	θείς, -εῖσα, -έν	δούς, -οῦσα, -όν	δείξας, -ᾶσα, -αν

MI AORIST MIDDLE

Ind.	NONE	ἐθέμην	ἐδόμην	NONE
		ἔθου	ἔδου	
		ἔθετο	ἔδοτο	
		ἐθέμεθα	ἐδόμεθα	
		ἔθεσθε	ἔδοσθε	
		ἔθεντο	ἔδοντο	
Subj.		θῶμαι	δῶμαι	
		θῇ	δῷ	
		θῆται	δῶται	
		θώμεθα	δώμεθα	
		θῆσθε	δῶσθε	
		θῶνται	δῶνται	

Impv.	θοῦ	δοῦ
	θέσθω	δόσθω
	θέσθε	δόσθε
	θέσθωσαν	δόσθωσαν

Inf.	θέσθαι	δόσθαι

Part.	θέμενος, -η, -ον	δόμενος, -η, -ον

418. PARADIGMS OF ἀφίημι.

PRESENT

	Active		Middle	
Ind.	ἀφίημι	ἀφίεμεν(ἀφίομεν)	ἀφίεμαι	ἀφιέμεθα
	ἀφεῖς	ἀφίετε	ἀφίεσαι	ἀφίεσθε
	ἀφίησι	ἀφίουσι	ἀφίεται	ἀφίενται(ἀφίονται)
Subj.	ἀφιῶ	ἀφιῶμεν	ἀφιῶμαι	ἀφιώμεθα
	ἀφιῇς	ἀφιῆτε	ἀφιῇ	ἀφιῆσθε
	ἀφιῇ	ἀφιῶσι	ἀφιῆται	ἀφιῶνται
Impv.	ἀφίει	ἀφίετε	ἀφίεσο(ἀφίου)	ἀφίεσθε
	ἀφιέτω	ἀφιέτωσαν	ἀφιέσθω	ἀφιέσθωσαν(ἀφιέσθων)
Inf.	ἀφιέναι		ἀφίεσθαι	
Part.	ἀφιείς, -εῖσα, -έν		ἀφιέμενος, -η, -ον	

IMPERFECT

Ind.	ἤφιον	ἠφίομεν	ἀφιέμην	ἀφιέμεθα
	ἤφιες	ἠφίετε	ἀφίεσο	ἀφίεσθε
	ἤφιε	ἤφιον	ἀφίετο	ἀφίεντο

AORIST

Ind.	ἀφῆκα	ἀφήκαμεν	ἀφείμην	ἀφείμεθα
	ἀφῆκας	ἀφήκατε	ἀφεῖσο	ἀφεῖσθε
	ἀφῆκε	ἀφῆκαν	ἀφεῖτο	ἀφεῖντο
Subj.	ἀφῶ	ἀφῶμεν	ἀφῶμαι	ἀφώμεθα
	ἀφῇς	ἀφῆτε	ἀφῇ	ἀφῆσθε
	ἀφῇ	ἀφῶσι	ἀφῆται	ἀφῶνται
Opt.	ἀφείην	ἀφείημεν	NONE	
	ἀφείης	ἀφείητε		
	ἀφείη	ἀφείησαν		
Impv.	ἄφες	ἄφετε	ἀφοῦ	ἄφεσθε
	ἀφέτω	ἀφέτωσαν	ἀφέσθω	ἀφέσθωσαν
Inf.	ἀφεῖναι		ἀφέσθαι	
Part.	ἀφείς, -εῖσα, -έν		ἀφέμενος, -η, -ον	

419. PARADIGMS OF οἶδα

	2ND PERFECT		2ND PLUPERFECT	
Ind.	οἶδα	οἴδαμεν	ᾔδειν	ᾔδειμεν
	οἶδας	οἴδατε	ᾔδεις	ᾔδειτε
	οἶδε	οἴδᾱσι (ἴσᾱσι)	ᾔδει	ᾔδεισαν
Subj.	εἰδῶ	εἰδῶμεν		
	εἰδῇς	εἰδῆτε		
	εἰδῇ	εἰδῶσι		
Impv.	ἴσθι	ἴστε		
	ἴστω	ἴστωσαν		
Inf.	εἰδέναι			
Part.	εἰδώς, -υῖα, -ός			

420. PARADIGMS OF εἰμί.

	PRESENT			IMPERFECT	
Ind.	εἰμί	ἐσμέν		ἤμην	ἤμεν and ἤμεθα
	εἶ	ἐστέ		ἦς and ἦσθα	ἦτε
	ἐστί(ν)	εἰσί(ν)		ἦν	ἦσαν

Subj.   ᾦ   ὦμεν
        ᾖς   ἦτε·
        ᾖ   ὦσι

FUTURE

ἔσομαι   ἐσόμεθα
ἔσῃ   ἔσεσθε
ἔσται   ἔσονται

Opt.   Only 3rd S. in N. T.
        ———
        εἴη   ———

Impv.   ἴσθι   ἔστε
        ἔστω and ἤτω ἔστωσαν

Inf.   εἶναι

Part.   ὤν, οὖσα, ὄν

421. INFREQUENT USE OF THE OPTATIVE IN THE NEW TESTAMENT.

Because the optative mood is not frequently used in the New Testament it has not been introduced in these lessons. But for reference some forms have been made available in the paradigms just given since verb forms in this mood appear in the writings of Luke and Paul.

422. OPTATIVE OF WISH.

The optative may be used to express a wish. The negative is μή.

μή γένοιτο, may it not happen. (Rom.3:4, 6 and elsewhere)

μηκέτι εἰς τὸν αἰῶνα ἐκ σοῦ μηδεὶς καρπὸν φάγοι.
May no one eat fruit of you any more forever. (Mk.11:14)

οὗτος διδάσκοι τὴν ἀλήθειαν πάντοτε.
May he always teach the truth.

423. POTENTIAL OPTATIVE.

A mild or unemphatic future statement may be made by use of the optative with ἄν. The negative is οὐ.

ἔλθοιεν ἂν τῇ τρίτῃ ἡμέρᾳ.
They may (might) go on the third day.

αὕτη οὐκ ἂν δέχοιτο τὸν προφήτην.
This woman would not welcome the prophet.

424. TYPE FOUR CONDITION (Less Vivid Future Condition).

The subordinate clause of the type three (more vivid future) condition expresses a contingency, the realization of which is somewhat doubtful. In type four the realization of the conditional clause is presented as even more doubtful than in type three. The protasis uses εἰ and the optative, the apodosis ἄν and the optative.

εἰ ὁ ἄγγελος φαίνοιτο, αὐτὸν ἂν δεξαίμεθα.
If the messenger should appear, we would receive him.

εἰ μὴ εὕροιτε τὴν οἰκίαν ἑτοίμην, οὐκ ἂν εἰσέλθοιτε.
If you should not find the house ready, you would not enter.

Although no complete type four conditional sentence occurs in the New Testament, the protasis is used in mixed conditions. The apodosis occurring alone is equal to the potential optative.

425. GENERAL OBSERVATIONS ABOUT ACCENT.

a. Final -αι and -οι are considered short in determining accent.
b. An acute accent on the ultima becomes a grave when another word, not an enclitic, follows without intervening punctuation.

426. EXAMPLES OF RECESSIVE ACCENT.

a. In finite verbs of three or more syllables.

1) Having a short ultima: acute on antepenult. ἀπολύσομεν, ἤγαγον
2) Having a long ultima: acute on penult. ἀπολύει, ἀποθνῄσκω

b. In finite verbs of two syllables.

    1) Having a short ultima and a long penult: <u>circumflex</u> <u>on penult</u>. εἶχε
    2) Having a short ultima and a short penult: <u>acute on penult</u>. ἔχε
    3) Having a long ultima and a long penult: <u>acute</u> <u>on penult</u>. χαίρω
    4) Having a long ultima and a short penult: <u>acute</u> <u>on penult</u>. λέγει

c. In finite verbs of one syllable.

    1) Long: <u>circumflex</u>. ἦν
    2) Short: <u>acute</u> or <u>grave</u>. σχές, σχὲς τόπον.

427. EXAMPLES OF PERSISTENT ACCENT.

a. In adjectives.

    1) Accented on the ultima in masculine nominative singular. (See #107)

        a) Acute on the first and fourth (plus vocative) inflectional forms
            both singular and plural.
        b) Circumflex on second and third inflectional forms both singular
            and plural.

    2) Accented on the antepenult in masculine nominative singular. (See #75)

        a) Acute used throughout the paradigm.
        b) Antepenult accented when ultima is short.
        c) Penult accented when ultima is long.

b. In nouns.

    1) Accented on the antepenult in nominative singular.

        a) In the second declension.

            (1) Nouns in -ος like masculine column of δίκαιος. (See #75)
            (2) Neuter like neuter column of δίκαιος. (See #75)

        b) In the first declension. (See #105)

            (1) On the antepenult when ultima is short: <u>acute</u>.
            (2) On the penult when ultima is long: <u>acute</u> (EXCEPT in second
                 inflectional form plural where ultima is circumflexed).

    2) Accented on the penult in nominative singular.

        a) In the second declension. (See #49)

            (1) With the acute on the penult in nominative singular:
                 <u>acute</u> <u>on</u> <u>the</u> <u>penult</u> <u>throughout</u> <u>the</u> <u>paradigm</u>.
            (2) With the <u>circumflex</u> on the penult in nominative singular:
                 <u>circumflex</u> <u>made</u> <u>acute</u> <u>when</u> <u>ultima</u> <u>becomes</u> <u>long</u>.

        b) In the first declension: acute on penult in nominative singular.
            (See #73, 105)

            (1) Acute retained when ultima is long except for (3) below.
            (2) Circumflex used on penult in nominative plural when the
                 penult is long.
            (3) Circumflex used on ultima in second inflectional form of
                 plural.

    3) Accented on the ultima in nominative singular.

        a) Nouns in -ος like masculine column of χαλός.
        b) Neuter nouns like neuter column of χαλός.
        c) Feminine nouns like feminine column of χαλός.

428. ACCENTS IN PARTS OF SPEECH OTHER THAN FINITE VERBS, ADJECTIVES, and NOUNS:
      to be learned by observation.

able, to be able: δυνατὸς εἶναι, δύνασθαι,
      ἰσχύειν
Abram: Ἀβράμ
about, concerning: περί
again: πάλιν
all, once for all: an implication of the
         aorist tense
am: εἰμί
am glad: χαίρω
am made: γίνομαι
and: καί, δέ
anoint: χρίω
another: ἄλλος
around: περί
at: ἐπί
attendant: ὑπηρέτης
away from: ἀπό

B

be, to be: γίνεσθαι, εἶναι
beautiful: καλός
because of: διά
become: γίνομαι
believe: πιστεύω
Benjamin: Βενιαμίν
better: κρείσσων, κρεῖσσον
bread: ἄρτος
bring, carry: ἄγω, φέρω
brother: ἀδελφός
but: ἀλλά, δέ

C

camel: κάμηλος
can, to be able: δυνατὸς εἶναι, δύνασθαι,
      ἰσχύειν
carry: ἄγω, φέρω
certain or someone: τὶς
child: τέκνον
choose: ἐκλέγομαι
come: ἔρχομαι
command: vb. ἐντέλλομαι n. ἐντολή
concerning: περί
continually: an implication of the present
        and imperfect tenses
cup: ποτήριον
cure, heal: θεραπεύω

D

dedicate: ἁγιάζω
destroy: καταλύω, λύω
die: ἀποθνῄσκω
dinner: δεῖπνον
door: θύρᾱ
drink: πίνω

E

each other: ἀλλήλων
eat: ἐσθίω
Egypt: Αἴγυπτος
Egyptian: Αἰγύπτιος
enemy: ἐχθρός
excellent: καλός

F

far distant: μακρός
farmer: γεωργός
father: πατήρ
fear: φόβος
fever: πυρετός
festival, feast: ἑορτή
find: εὑρίσκω
fish: ὀψάριον
flee: φεύγω

for the sake of: ὑπέρ
for the same reason: διὰ τὸ αὐτό
free: ἐλεύθερος
from, away from: ἀπό
from, out of: ἐκ
fruit: καρπός

G

garden: κῆπος
gift: δωρεά
give: δίδωμι
go: ἔρχομαι, ἄγω
go away: ἀπέρχομαι
God: θεός
good: καλός
greetings: χαῖρε

H

happy: μακάριος
harden: σκληρύνω
have: ἔχω
he: αὐτός, ἐκεῖνος, οὗτος
heal: θεραπεύω
hear: ἀκούω
heart: καρδίᾱ
her: αὕτη, ἐκείνη
here: ὧδε
himself: ἑαυτοῦ, αὐτός
his: the genitive of a masculine per-
      sonal pronoun
hope: ἐλπίζω
house: οἶκος
how: πῶς

I

I: ἐγώ
in, within: ἐν
into: εἰς
is: ἐστίν
itself: αὐτό, ἑαυτοῦ

J

Jordan: Ἰορδάνης
Joshua: Ἰησοῦς
Judah: Ἰούδας
judge: κριτής
just, righteous: δίκαιος

K

kill: ἀποκτείνω, φονεύω
king: βασιλεύς

L

lamb: ἀρνίον
land: γῆ
last: ἔσχατος
Lazarus: Λάζαρος
leader: ἡγεμών
learn: μανθάνω
leave: ἀπέρχομαι
let go: ἀπολύω
life: ζωή
long ago: πάλαι
lord: κύριος
love: vb. ἀγαπάω n. ἀγάπη

M

man: ἀνήρ, ἄνθρωπος
Mark: Μᾶρκος
Mary: Μαρίᾱ
messenger: ἄγγελος
mother: μήτηρ

my: ἐμός, ἐμοῦ
myself: ἐμαυτοῦ, αὐτός

N

nation: ἔθνος
need: χρείᾱ
Nicodemus: Νικόδημος
night: νύξ
no: οὐ, μή, οὐχί
noble: καλός
not: οὐ, οὐκ, οὐχ, μή

O

obedience: ὑπακοή
of: genitive case
on behalf of: ὑπέρ
once, once for all: an implication of the
                     aorist tense
or: ἤ
ourselves: ἑαυτῶν, αὐτοί
out of: ἐκ
over: ὑπέρ
own: ἴδιος

P

paschal lamb, passover: πάσχα
perhaps: τάχα
persuade: πείθω
Peter: Πέτρος
Philip: Φίλιππος
place: τόπος
priest: ἱερεύς
promise: ἐπαγγελίᾱ
prophet: προφήτης
purify: ἁγιάζω, καθαρίζω

R

Rachel: 'Ραχήλ
ready: ἕκαστος
receive: λαμβάνω, δέχομαι
recognize: ἐπιγινώσκω
release: ἀπολύω
remain: μένω
remember: μνημονεύω

S

sacrifice: θυσίᾱ
same: αὐτός
Sarai: Σαρα
save: σώζω
say: λαλέω, λέγω
school: σχόλη
see: βλέπω, ὁράω
send: πέμπω
send forth: ἀποστέλλω
servant: ὑπηρέτης
serve: δουλεύω, λατρεύω
she: αὐτή, αὕτη, ἐκείνη

sheep: πρόβατον
sister: ἀδελφή
slave: δοῦλος
small: μικρός
son: υἱός
speak: λέγω, λαλέω
stay: μένω
strong: δυνατός

T

take: λαμβάνω
teach: διδάσκω
that: ἐκεῖνος, ὅτι, ἵνα
the: ὁ, ἡ, τό
themselves: ἑαυτῶν, αὐτοί
there: ἐκεῖ
these: οὗτοι
they: ἐκεῖνοι, -αι, -α; οὗτοι, αὗται, ταῦτα
thing: implication of the neuter, ῥῆμα
this: οὗτος
those: ἐκεῖνοι
throw: βάλλω
to: πρός
today: σήμερον
tomorrow: αὔριον
truth: ἀλήθεια

U

upon: ἐπί

village: κώμη
voice: φωνή

W

want: θέλω
war: πόλεμος
was: ἦν
we: ἡμεῖς
welcome: δέχομαι
what: τίς
where: ποῦ
which: ὅς, ἥ, ὅ
who: ὅς, ἥ, ὅ (relative pronoun)
     τίς (interrogative)
why: τί
wicked: κακός
wine: οἶνος
with: σύν, μετά
woman: γυνή
word: λόγος, ῥῆμα
write: γράφω

Y

yes: ναί
yesterday: ἐχθές
you: σύ, ὑμεῖς
yourself: σεαυτοῦ, ἑαυτῶν

Ἀβραμ (indecl.), ὁ: Abram (125)
ἀγαπάω, ἀγαπήσω, ἠγάπησα, ἠγάπηκα, ἠγάπημαι,
  ἠγαπήθην: I love (343)
ἀγάπη, -ης, ἡ: love (360)
ἀγαπητός, -ή, -όν: beloved (360)
ἀγγελία, -ᾶς, ἡ: message (354)
ἄγγελος, -ου, ὁ: angel, messenger (83)
ἁγιάζω, ---, ἡγίασα, ---, ἡγίασμαι, ἡγιάσθην: I dedicate, set apart for God,
  sanctify, purify (320)
ἅγιος, -α, -ον: holy (343)
ἁγνίζω, ---, ἥγνισα, ἥγνικα, ἥγνισμαι,
  ἡγνίσθην: I purify (369)
ἁγνός, -ή, -όν: pure, clean (369)
ἄγω, ἄξω, ἤγαγον, --- , --- , ἤχθην: I
  lead, bring, go (113)
ἀδελφή, -ῆς, ἡ: sister (131)
ἀδελφός, -ου, ὁ: brother (10)
ἀδικία, -ᾶς, ἡ: unrighteousness, iniquity,
Αἰγύπτιος, -α, -ον: Egyptian (131) [injustice,
Αἴγυπτος, -ου, ἡ: Egypt (131) (354)
αἷμα, -ατος, τό: blood (224)
αἴρω, ἀρῶ, ἦρα, ἦρκα, ἦρμαι, ἤρθην: I take
  up, lift up, raise, carry, take away,
  remove (369)
αἰσχύνομαι, --- , --- , --- , ᾐσχύνθην: I
  am ashamed, am put to shame (369)
αἰτέω, αἰτήσω, ᾔτησα, ᾔτηκα, --- , --- :
  I ask (374)
αἴτημα, -ατος, τό: request, what is asked
  for (380)
αἰών, αἰῶνος, ὁ: eternity, universe, present age (365)
αἰώνιος, -α (but distinct feminine endings
  are rarely used, -ος, -ου, etc. being
  usually found in forms agreeing with
  feminine nouns), -ον: eternal, everlasting (247)
ἀκούω, ἀκούσω, ἤκουσα, ἀκήκοα, --- ,
  ἠκούσθην: I hear, listen (followed
  by acc. or gen. direct object) (93)
ἀλαζονεία, -ᾶς, ἡ: boastfulness, vain display (365)
ἀλήθεια, -ᾶς, ἡ: truth, truthfulness (104)
ἀληθής, -ές: true (to fact; actual as opposed to apparent), truthful (360,398)
ἀληθινός, -ή, -όν: true, genuine (as opposed to spurious), real (247)
ἀληθῶς: truly, surely, certainly (360)
ἀλλά (ἀλλ'): but (stronger than δέ) (72,180)
ἀλλήλων: of one another, of each other (292)
ἄλλος, -η, -ο: other, another; οἱ ἄλλοι:
  the rest, the others (148)
ἀλλόφυλος, -ου, ὁ: foreigner, Gentile, Philistine (328)
Ἀμαλήκ (indecl.), ὁ: Amalek [not in N. T.]
  (304)
ἁμαρτάνω, ἁμαρτήσω, ἡμάρτησα (ἥμαρτον),
  ἡμάρτηκα, --- , --- : I sin (354)
ἁμαρτία, -ᾶς, ἡ: sin (354)
ἄν: (not translated by an individual English word, but forming part of a signal system for certain constructions)
  (328)
ἀναγγέλλω, ἀναγγελῶ, ἀνήγγειλα, --- , --- ,
  ἀνηγγέλην: I report, announce, declare (354)
ἀναστρέφω, --- , ἀνέστρεψα, --- , --- ,
  ἀνεστράφην: I overturn, return, (pass.)
  sojourn, dwell (286)
ἀνήρ, ἀνδρός, ὁ: man, husband (279)
ἀνθρωποκτόνος, -ου, ὁ: murderer (374)
ἄνθρωπος, -ου, ὁ: man, human being (10)
ἀνομία, -ᾶς, ἡ: lawlessness, transgression,
  iniquity (369)
ἀντί: (with gen.) instead of, in place of,
  in exchange for, in return for,
  against (200)

ἀντίχριστος, -ου, ὁ: Antichrist, one who
  tries to take the place of the Messiah and who withstands Him (365)
ἀπαγγέλλω, ἀπαγγελῶ, ἀπήγγειλα, --- , --- ,
  ἀπηγγέλην: I announce, report (348)
ἀπέρχομαι, ἀπελεύσομαι, ἀπῆλθον, ἀπελήλυθα, --- , --- : I go away, depart
  from (186)
ἀπό: (with abl.) from, away from (41)
ἀποθνήσκω, ἀποθανοῦμαι, ἀπέθανον, --- ,
  --- , --- : I die (113, 173)
ἀποκόπτω, ἀποκόψω, ἀπέκοψα, --- , --- ,
  ἀπεκόπην: I cut off (337)
ἀποκρίνομαι, --- , ἀπεκρινάμην (rare),
  --- , ἀπεκρίθην (frequent):
  I answer (247)
ἀποκτείνω, ἀποκτενῶ, ἀπέκτεινα, --- , --- ,
  ἀπεκτάνθην: I kill (142)
ἀπολύω, ἀπολύσω, ἀπέλυσα, --- , ἀπολέλυμαι, ἀπελύθην: I release, set free,
  let go (53)
ἀποστέλλω, ἀποστελῶ, ἀπέστειλα, ἀπέσταλκα,
  ἀπέσταλμαι, ἀπεστάλην: I send away,
  send forth (142)
ἅπτω, --- , ἧψα, --- , --- , --- : I fasten to, set on fire, (mid.) I fasten
  myself to, cling to, lay hold of,
  assail (380)
ἀργύριον, -ου, τό: silver, money (195)
ἀρεστός, -ή, -όν: pleasing, agreeable
  (374)
ἄρκος, -ου, ὁ or ἡ: bear (328)
ἀρνέομαι, ἀρνήσομαι, ἠρνησάμην, ἤρνημαι,
  --- : I deny, say "No," refuse to
  acknowledge, disown (369)
ἀρνίον, -ου, τό: lamb, little lamb (41)
ἄρτι: now, just now, just at this moment (360)
ἄρτος, -ου, ὁ: bread, loaf (27)
ἀρχή, -ῆς, ἡ: beginning, rule, sovereignty (348)
αὔριον: tomorrow, on the next day (180)
αὐτός, -ή, -ό: self, same, even,
  very, he, she, it (135)
ἀφίημι, ἀφήσω, ἀφῆκα, --- , ἀφεῖμαι, ἀφέθην: I send away, let go, forgive,
  allow, remit (354)

B

βάλλω, βαλῶ, ἔβαλον, βέβληκα, βέβλημαι,
  ἐβλήθην: I throw, cast, put (195)
βαρύς, -εῖα, -ύ: heavy, burdensome (380)
βασιλεία, -ᾶς, ἡ: kingdom, royal power,
  dominion, rule, reign (304)
βασιλεύς, -έως, ὁ: king (148)
Βενιαμίν (indecl.), ὁ: Benjamin (186)
Βηθλεέμ (indecl.), ἡ: Bethlehem (205)
βίος, -ου, ὁ: period of life, means of
  living, course of life (365)
βλασφημέω, --- , ἐβλασφήμησα, --- , --- ,
  ἐβλασφημήθην: I revile, rail at,
  blaspheme, slander, speak evil of
  God (337)
βλέπω, βλέψω, ἔβλεψα, --- , --- , --- :
  I see, look at (10)

Γ

γάρ: for, assuredly; indeed, yea, then,
  why (41)
Γεδεών (indecl.), ὁ: Gideon (279)
γενεά, -ᾶς, ἡ: generation (269)
γεννάω, γεννήσω, ἐγέννησα, γεγέννηκα,
  γεγέννημαι, ἐγεννήθην: I beget, become a father of, bear (369)
γεωργός, -οῦ, ὁ: farmer (93)

γῆ, γῆς, ἡ: earth, land. country, ground (125)

γίνομαι, γενήσομαι, ἐγενόμην, γέγονα, γεγένημαι, ἐγενήθην: I come into being, am born, am made, am ordained, become, come to pass, happen (173)

γινώσκω, γνώσομαι, ἔγνων, ἔγνωκα, ἔγνωσμαι, ἐγνώσθην: I come to know, perceive, understand (286)

γλῶσσα, -ης, ἡ: tongue, language (105,180)

Γολιάθ (indecl.), ὁ: Goliath /not in N.T./ (328)

γράφω, --- , ἔγραψα, γέγραφα, γέγραμμαι, ἐγράφην: I write (210)

γυνή, γυναῖκος, ἡ: woman, wife (131, 304)

Δ

Δαυίδ (indecl.), ὁ: David (320)

δέ: but, and, now (not in temporal sense) (142)

δεῖ (pres. indic. act. 3rd sing. δέω): it is necessary (followed by an infinitive with an acc. of general reference), one must, one ought (292)

δείκνυμι (δεικνύω), δείξω, ἔδειξα, δέδειχα, --- , ἐδείχθην: I show, exhibit (354)

δεῖπνον, -ου, τό: dinner, supper (41)

δέχομαι, --- , ἐδεξάμην, δέδεγμαι, ἐδέχθην: I receive, accept, welcome (205)

διά: (with gen.) through, by; (with acc.) because of, on account of (180)

διάβολος, -ου, ὁ: devil, accuser (369)

διάνοια, -ας, ἡ: understanding, mind (380)

διδάσκαλος, -ου, ὁ: teacher (180)

διδάσκω, διδάξω, ἐδίδαξα, --- , --- , ἐδιδάχθην: I teach (frequently used with a double accusative) (180)

δίδωμι, δώσω, ἔδωκα, δέδωκα, δέδομαι, ἐδόθην: I give (354)

δίκαιος, -ᾱ, -ον: righteous, just (72)

δικαιοσύνη, -ης, ἡ: righteousness (369)

διώκω, διώξω, ἐδίωξα, --- , δεδίωγμαι, ἐδιώχθην: I pursue, run after, put to flight, persecute (148)

δοκιμάζω, δοκιμάσω, ἐδοκίμασα, --- , δεδοκίμασμαι, --- : I test, prove, approve (377)

δουλεύω, δουλεύσω, ἐδούλευσα, δεδούλευκα, --- , --- : I serve as a slave, am a slave to, am subject to (with dat. dir. obj.) (53)

δοῦλος, -ου, ὁ: slave, bondslave (41)

δύναμαι, δυνήσομαι, --- , --- , ἠδυνήθην: I am able, have power, can (328)

δυνατός, -ή, -όν: able, capable, strong, powerful, possible (180)

δύο (nom., abl., gen., acc.), δυσί (loc., instr., dat.): two (253)

δωρεά, -ας, ἡ: gift (72)

E

ἐάν: if (328)

ἑαυτοῦ, -ῆς, -οῦ: of himself, herself, itself (200)

ἐγκαταλείπω, ἐγκαταλείψω, ἐγκατέλιπον, --- , --- , ἐγκατελείφθην: I abandon, forsake, desert, leave behind (269)

ἐγώ, ἐμοῦ: I (125)

ἔθνος, -ους, τό: nation, people; (pl.) nations, Gentiles (261)

εἰ: if (328)

εἴδωλον, -ου, τό: idol, image of a false god, false god (380)

εἰμί, ἔσομαι, --- , --- , --- , --- : I am (83, 86)

εἰς: (with acc.) into, in, towards, for, among (41)

εἰς τὸν αἰῶνα: forever (365)

εἷς, μία, ἕν: one (328)

ἐκ (ἐξ): (with abl.) from, out of, from within, of (i.e. belonging to)(41)

ἕκαστος, -η, -ον: each, every (195)

ἐκεῖ: there (180)

ἐκεῖνος, -η, -ο: that, he, she, it (135)

ἐκλέγομαι, --- , ἐξελεξάμην, ἐκλέλεγμαι, --- : I choose (300)

ἔλαιον, -ου, τό: olive oil (320)

ἐλεύθερος, -ᾱ, -ον: free (72)

Ἑλληνικός, -ή, -όν: Greek (180)

ἐλπίζω, ἐλπιῶ, ἤλπισα, ἤλπικα, --- , --- : I hope (83, 142)

ἐλπίς, -ίδος, ἡ: hope (369)

ἐμαυτοῦ, -ῆς: of myself (200)

ἐμός, -ή, -όν: my (343)

ἔμπροσθεν: (with gen.) in front of, before (374)

ἐμφανίζω, ἐμφανίσω, ἐνεφάνισα, --- , --- , ἐνεφανίσθην: I manifest, exhibit (343)

ἐν: (with loc.) in, within, among, by means of. during (41)

ἐντέλλομαι, ἐντελοῦμαι, ἐνετειλάμην, ἐντέταλμαι, --- : I order, command (195)

ἐντολή, -ῆς, ἡ: order, command (343)

ἐνώπιον: (with gen.) before, in the presence of, in the sight of (374)

ἐξέρχομαι, ἐξελεύσομαι, ἐξῆλθον, ἐξελήλυθα, --- , --- : I come out, go out (365)

ἔξω: outside (377)

ἑορτή, -ῆς, ἡ: festival, feast (224)

ἐπαγγελία, -ας, ἡ: promise (135)

ἐπαγγέλλομαι, --- , ἐπηγγειλάμην, ἐπήγγελμαι, --- : I promise (369)

ἐπεί: after, when, since, because (131)

ἐπί: (with gen.) on, over, upon; (with loc.) on, at, upon, concerning; (with acc.) on, over, to, against (224)

ἐπιγινώσκω, ἐπιγνώσομαι, ἐπέγνων, ἐπέγνωκα --- , ἐπεγνώσθην: I observe, perceive, recognize, know (173)

ἐπιθυμία, -ας, ἡ: longing, desire (72)

ἑπτά (indecl.): seven (173)

ἔργον, -ου, τό: work, task, deed, action (269)

ἔρημος, -ου, ἡ: desert, wilderness (253)

ἔρχομαι, ἐλεύσομαι, ἦλθον, ἐλήλυθα, --- , --- : I come, go (113, 173)

ἐρωτάω, ἐρωτήσω, ἠρώτησα, --- , --- , --- : I ask a question, make a request (380)

ἐσθίω, φάγομαι, ἔφαγον, --- , --- , --- : I eat (27, 113)

ἔσχατος, -η, -ον: last (224)

ἕτοιμος, -η, -ον: prepared, ready (113)

ἔτος, -ους, τό: year (173, 263)

εὑρίσκω, εὑρήσω, εὗρον, εὕρηκα, --- , εὑρέθην: I find, discover (300)

ἐχθές: yesterday (180)

ἐχθρός, -οῦ, ὁ: enemy (142)

ἔχω, ἕξω, ἔσχον, ἔσχηκα, --- , --- : I have, hold (10, 104)

ἕως: (prep. with gen.) until, as far as; (conj.) until (360)

Z

(ζάω) ζῶ, ζήσω, ἔζησα, --- , --- , --- : I live, am alive (377)

ζωή, -ῆς, ἡ: life (247)

H

ἤ: or, than (135)

ἡγεμών, -όνος, ὁ: leader, governor, chief (304)

ἤδη: now, already, now at length (360)

ἥκω, ἥξω, ἧξα, --- , --- , --- : I have come, am present (320)

Ἠλί (indecl.), ὁ: Eli (286)

ἡμεῖς, ἡμῶν: we (125)

ἡμέρα, -ας, ἡ: day (239)

ἡμέτερος, -ᾱ, -ον: our (348)

Θ

θάλασσα, -ης, ἡ: sea (239)
θάνατος, -ου, ὁ: death (374)
θαυμάζω, θαυμάσομαι, ἐθαύμασα, --- , ---
    ἐθαυμάσθην: I wonder, wonder at (374)
θεάομαι, --- , ἐθεασάμην, τεθέαμαι, ἐθεά-
    θην: I behold, look upon, contem-
    plate, view (348)
θέλημα, -ατος, τό: will, choice, the ac-
    tion, the act of willing (365)
θέλω, θελήσω, ἠθέλησα, --- , --- , --- : I
    will, am willing, wish, desire (180)
θεός, -οῦ, ὁ: God, god, deity (160)
θεραπεύω, θεραπεύσω, ἐθεράπευσα, --- , τε-
    θεράπευμαι, ἐθεραπεύθην: I treat,
    cure, heal (53)
θεωρέω, θεωρήσω, ἐθεώρησα, --- , --- ,
    --- : I look at, behold, gaze at,
    see (374)
θηρίον, -ου, τό: wild beast (337)
θλῖψις, -εως, ἡ: affliction, distress (300)
θύρα, -ᾱς, ἡ: door (224)
θυσίᾱ, -ᾱς, ἡ: sacrifice (304)
θύω, --- , ἔθυσα, --- , τέθυμαι, ἐτύθην:
    I sacrifice, kill, slay, offer (224)

I

Ἰακώβ (indecl.), ὁ: Jacob (186)
Ἰάκωβος, -ου, ὁ: James (104)
ἴδιος, -ᾱ, -ον: one's (my, our, your, his,
    her, its, their) own, belonging to
    one's self (72)
ἰδού: behold, see, look (286)
ἱερεύς, ἕως, ὁ: priest (286)
Ἱεροσόλυμα, -ων, τά: Jerusalem (a place
    name with plural form but singular
    meaning) (205)
Ἰεσσαί (indecl.), ὁ: Jesse (320)
Ἰησοῦς, -οῦ, -οῦ, -οῦν, -οῦ, ὁ: Jesus,
    Joshua (224)
ἱλασμός, -οῦ, ὁ: means of appeasing, pro-
    pitiation (360)
ἵνα: that, in order that (320)
Ἰορδάνης, -ου, ὁ: Jordan (135)
Ἰούδας, -α, -ᾳ, -αν, -α, ὁ: Judah,
    Judas (186)
Ἰσκαριώτης, -ου, ὁ: Iscariot (343)
Ἰσραήλ (indecl.), ὁ: Israel (210)
ἵστημι, στήσω, ἔστησα & ἔστην, ἕστηκα, --- ,
    ἐστάθην: I cause to stand (transi-
    tive in pres., imperf., fut., 1st aor.
    act.); I stand, stand by (intransi-
    tive in -μι aor., perf., plup. act.,
    fut. mid. and fut. aor. passive) (354)
ἰσχυρός, -ᾱ, -όν: powerful, mighty,
    strong (365)
ἰσχύω, ἰσχύσω, ἴσχυσα, --- , --- , --- :
    I am able, strong, powerful; I pre-
    vail (53)
Ἰωσήφ (indecl.), ὁ: Joseph (173)

Κ

κἀγώ: καὶ ἐγώ (343)
καθαρίζω, καθαριῶ, ἐκαθάρισα, --- , κεκα-
    θάρισμαι, ἐκαθαρίσθην: I make clean,
    cleanse (354)
καθεύδω (only pres. and imperf. tenses in
    N. T.): I sleep (286)
καθώς: as, just as (360)
καί: and, and so, and yet, and indeed;
    also, too, even, still (10)
Κάϊν (indecl.), ὁ: Cain (374)
καινός, -ή, -όν: new, fresh, unused (360)
κακός, -ή, -όν: bad, evil, wicked (53,
    104)
καλέω, καλέσω, ἐκάλεσα, κέκληκα, κέκλημαι,
    ἐκλήθην: I call, invite (286)
καλός, -ή, -όν: beautiful, good, excellent,
    fair, noble (41, 104)
κάμηλος, -ου, ὁ or ἡ: camel (135)
καρδίᾱ, -ᾱς, ἡ: heart (72)
καρπός, -οῦ, ὁ: fruit (27)

κατά: (with gen.) down upon, against;
    with abl.) down from; (with acc.)
    down along, through, by, according to
    (239)
καταβαίνω, καταβήσομαι, κατέβην, κατα-
    βέβηκα, --- , --- : I go down, come
    down, descend (247)
καταγινώσκω, --- , --- , --- , κατέγνωσ-
    μαι, --- : I blame, condemn (374)
καταλύω, καταλύσω, κατέλυσα, --- , --- ,
    κατελύθην: I destroy, overthrow (304)
Καφαρναούμ (indecl.), ἡ: Capernaum (247)
κεῖμαι, --- , --- , --- : I lie, am lo-
    cated (380)
κέρας, -ατος, τό: horn (320)
κερατίνη, -ης, ἡ: trumpet, horn (279)
κεφαλή, -ῆς, ἡ: head (337)
κῆπος, -ου, ὁ: garden (41)
κλείω, κλείσω, ἔκλεισα, --- , κέκλεισμαι,
    ἐκλείσθην: I shut (374)
κοινωνίᾱ, -ᾱς, ἡ: fellowship, joint par-
    ticipation (348)
κόλασις, -εως, ἡ: correction, punishment,
    penalty (377)
κόσμος, -ου, ὁ: universe, world, earth (343)
κρείσσων, κρεῖσσον: better (304)
κρίσις, -εως, ἡ: decision, judgment (377)
κριτής, -οῦ, ὁ: judge (269)
κύριος, -ου, ὁ: master, Lord (125)
κώμη, -ης, ἡ: village, town (104)

Λ

Λάζαρος, -ου, ὁ: Lazarus (53)
λαλέω, λαλήσω, ἐλάλησα, λελάληκα, λελάλη-
    μαι, ἐλαλήθην: I utter, speak, say
    (337)
λαμβάνω, λήμψομαι, ἔλαβον, εἴληφα, εἴλημ-
    μαι, --- : I take, receive, seize
    (113, 173)
λαμπάς, -άδος, ἡ: torch (279)
λαός, -οῦ, ὁ: people (210)
λατρεύω, λατρεύσω, ἐλάτρευσα, --- , --- ,
    --- : I serve, worship (261)
λέγω, ἐρῶ, εἶπον, εἴρηκα, εἴρημαι, ἐρρέθην:
    I say, speak, declare, tell (10)
λέων, -οντος, ὁ: lion (328, 385)
λίαν: exceedingly, very, very much (180)
λίθος, -ου, ὁ: stone (253)
λόγος, -ου, ὁ: word, statement, speech,
    teaching (343)
λύω, --- , ἔλυσα, --- , λέλυμαι, ἐλύθην:
    I loose, destroy (369)
Λώτ (indecl.), ὁ: Lot (125)

Μ

Μαδιάμ (indecl.), ὁ: Midian (279)
μαθητής, -οῦ, ὁ: disciple, student, pupil
    (180)
μακάριος, -ᾱ, -ον: happy, blessed (72)
μακρός, -ᾱ, -όν: long, far distant (142)
μανθάνω, --- , ἔμαθον, μεμάθηκα, --- ,
    --- : I learn (180)
Μαρίᾱ, -ᾱς, ἡ: Mary (72)
Μᾶρκος, -ου, ὁ: Mark (10)
μαρτυρέω, μαρτυρήσω, ἐμαρτύρησα, μεμαρτύ-
    ρηκα, μεμαρτύρημαι, ἐμαρτυρήθην: I am
    a witness, bear witness, testify (348)
μαρτυρίᾱ, -ᾱς, ἡ: witness, testimony,
    evidence (380)
μάχομαι (pres. system only): I fight (328)
μέγας, μεγάλη, μέγα: great, large, tall,
    big (328)
μείζων, μεῖζον (comparative of μέγας):
    greater (374)
μέλλω, μελλήσω, --- , --- , --- , --- :
    I am about to, intend to (343)
μένω, μενῶ, ἔμεινα, μεμένηκα, --- , --- :
    I stay, remain, wait for (142)
Μεσοποταμίᾱ, -ᾱς, ἡ: Mesopotamia (125)
μέσος, -η, -ον: middle, in the middle of
    (239)
μετά (μεθ' before a vowel with a rough
    breathing): (with gen.) with; (with
    acc.) after (93)

182

μεταβαίνω, μεταβήσομαι, μετέβην, μεταβέβηκα, ---, --- : I pass over (from one
   place to another), depart (374)
μή: not (used with impv., inf., part., subj.)
μηδείς, μηδεμία, μηδέν: no one, no, |(93)|
   nothing (369)
μήτηρ, μητρός, ἡ: mother (205, 385)
μικρός, -ᾱ, -όν: small, little (83)
μισέω, μισήσω, ἐμίσησα, μεμίσηκα, μεμίσημαι, --- : I hate (360)
μνημονεύω, ---, ἐμνημόνευσα, ---, ---,
   --- : I remember, call to mind (83)
μονή, -ῆς, ἡ: dwelling place, residence
   (343)
μονογενής, -ές: only of its kind, unique
   (377)
μόνον (adv.): only (380)
μόνος, -η, -ον: alone, only (247)
Μωϋσῆς, -έως, -εῖ, -ῆν, ὁ: Moses (210)

N

ναί: yes (72)
νεανίσκος, -ου, ὁ: young man, youth, lad (365)
νεφέλη, -ης, ἡ: cloud (239)
νεώτερος, -ᾱ, -ον: newer, younger, (or in
   harmony with Hellenistic usage) youngest (186)
νικάω, νικήσω, ἐνίκησα, νενίκηκα, ---,
   ἐνικήθην: I conquer, win the victory
   over (365)
νίκη, -ης, ἡ: victory (380)
Νικόδημος, -ου, ὁ: Nicodemus (10)
νόμος, -ου, ὁ: law (253)
νῦν: now (72)
νύξ, νυκτός, ἡ: night (239)

Ξ

ξηρός, -ᾱ, -όν: dry (239)

O

ὁ, ἡ, τό: the (10, 77)
ὅθεν: whence, wherefore (365)
οἶδα, εἰδήσω: I know (360, 419)
οἶκος, -ου, ὁ: house, family (41)
οἶνος, -ου, ὁ: wine (41)
ὅλος, -η, -ον: whole, complete, entire
   (360)
ὅμοιος, -α, -ον: like, resembling, similar,
   of the same kind as (369)
ὁμολογέω, ὁμολογήσω, ὡμολόγησα, ---, ---,
   --- : I agree, confess, acknowledge
   (354)
ὁμοῦ: together (83)
ὀνειδίζω, ---, ὠνείδισα, ---, ---, --- :
   I reproach, upbraid, revile (328)
ὄνομα, -ατος, τό: name (253)
ὁράω, ὄψομαι, εἶδον, ἑώρακα, ---, ὤφθην:
   I see (348)
ὀργίζομαι, ---, ---, ---, ---, ὠργίσθην: I am
   provoked to anger, am angry (269)
ὅς, ἥ, ὅ: who, which, that, what (292)
ὅστις, ἥτις, ὅ τι: whoever, whatever, who,
   what (348)
ὅταν: when, whenever (380)
ὅτε: when (83)
ὅτι: that, because (53)
οὐδείς, οὐδεμία, οὐδέν: nobody, nothing,
   no, none (354)
οὐ, οὐκ, οὐχ: not (27, 41, 125)
οὐκέτι: no longer, no more (72)
οὐ μή (plus aor. subj.): no (a strong
   negative), by no means, not at all (320)
οὖν: consequently, therefore, then (125)
οὔπω: not yet (286)
οὐρανός, -οῦ, ὁ: heaven (247)
οὖς, ὠτός, τό: ear (292)
οὗτος, αὕτη, τοῦτο: this (131)
οὕτως: thus, so (200)
οὐχί (emph. form of οὐ): not at all, no,
   no indeed (125)

ὀφείλω: I owe, ought (360)
ὀφθαλμός, -οῦ, ὁ: eye (348)
ὄχλος, -ου, ὁ: crowd, multitude, throng
   (247)
ὀψάριον, -ου, τό: fish (41)

Π

παιδίον, -ου, τό: young child (365)
πάλαι: long ago, of old, in past time (186)
παλαιός, -ᾱ, -όν: old, ancient (360)
πάλιν: again, back (83)
πάντοτε: always, at any time (72)
παρά (παρ'): (with abl.) from; (with loc.)
   beside, with; (with acc.) along (343)
παράγω: I pass away, disappear, go by (360)
παράκλητος, -ου, ὁ: advocate, helper, intercessor (343)
παρεμβολή, -ῆς, ἡ: camp, army (279)
παρουσία, -ᾱς, ἡ: presence, coming, arrival (369)
παρρησία, -ᾱς, ἡ: freedom (of speech),
   confidence, boldness, openness (72)
παρρησίᾳ (instrumental of παρρησία used as
   an adverb): freely, frankly, plainly
πᾶς, πᾶσα, πᾶν: all, every (239) |(72)|
πάσχα (indecl.), τό: Passover, paschal
   lamb (224)
πατάσσω, πατάξω, ἐπάταξα, ---, ---, --- :
   I strike, smite, kill (328)
πατήρ, πατρός, ὁ: father (200, 263)
πείθω, πείσω, ἔπεισα, πέποιθα, πέπεισμαι,
   ἐπείσθην: I persuade; (mid.) I believe, obey (with dat. dir. obj. in mid.)
πέμπω, πέμψω, ἔπεμψα, πέπομφα, --- |(210)|
   ἐπέμφθην: I send (41)
πεντακισχίλιοι, -αι, -α: five thousand
   (247)
πέραν: (with abl. or gen.) beyond, across,
   on the other side of (247)
περί: (with gen. in figurative sense)
   around, about, concerning; (with acc.
   in local sense) around, about (72,93)
περιπατέω, περιπατήσω, περιεπάτησα, περιπεπάτηκα, ---, --- : I walk, live,
   conduct my life (354)
πετεινόν, -οῦ, τό: bird (337)
Πέτρος, -ου, ὁ: Peter (10)
πίνω, πίομαι, ἔπιον, πέπωκα, ---, --- :
   I drink (41, 113)
πίπτω, πεσοῦμαι, ἔπεσον and ἔπεσα, πέπτωκα,
   ---, --- : I fall (337)
πιστεύω, πιστεύσω, ἐπίστευσα, πεπίστευκα,
   πεπίστευμαι, ἐπιστεύθην: I believe,
   trust (with dat. dir. obj.) (160)
πίστις, -εως, ἡ: faith (380)
πιστός, -ή, -όν: trusty, faithful, reliable (354)
πλανάω, πλανήσω, ἐπλάνησα, ---, πεπλάνημαι, ἐπλανήθην: I lead astray, deceive (354)
πλάνη, -ης, ἡ: going astray, error (377)
πληγή, -ῆς, ἡ: plague, calamity, blow
   (224)
πληρόω, πληρώσω, ἐπλήρωσα, πεπλήρωκα, πεπλήρωμαι, ἐπληρώθην: I make full,
   fill, complete (348)
πλοῦτος, -ου, ὁ: wealth, riches (104)
πνεῦμα, -ατος, τό: spirit, wind (343)
ποιέω, ποιήσω, ἐποίησα, πεποίηκα, πεποίημαι, ἐποιήθην: I make, do (343)
πόλεμος, -ου, ὁ: war, battle (292)
πολλάκις: often, many times (125)
πολύς, πολλή, πολύ: much, (pl.) many (365)
πονηρός, -ᾱ, -όν: bad, evil, wicked (365)
πορεύομαι, πορεύσομαι, ---, ---, πεπόρευμαι,
   ἐπορεύθην: I go on my way, proceed,
   travel (328)
ποταπός, -ή, -όν: what? of what sort?
   what kind of? (369)
ποτήριον, -ου, τό: cup (41)
ποῦ: where? (180)
πρεσβύτερος, -ᾱ, -ον: elder (200)

πρό: (with abl.) before, in front of, earlier than, preferable to, in lieu of (210)
πρόβατον, -ου, τό: sheep (135)
πρός: (with loc.) near; (with acc.) to, towards, with (142)
προσεύχομαι, προσεύξομαι, προσηυξάμην, --- , --- : I pray (247)
πρόσωπον, -ου, τό: face (320)
προφήτης, -ου, ὁ: prophet (286)
πρῶτος, -η, -ον: first, chief, principal (224)
πῦρ, πυρός, τό: fire (239)
πυρετός, -οῦ, ὁ: fever (53)
πώποτε: ever yet (377)
πῶς: how? (104)

Ρ

ῥάβδος, -ου, ἡ: staff, rod (337)
Ῥαχήλ (indecl.), ἡ: Rachel (186)
ῥῆμα, -ατος, τό: word, statement, thing, matter (286)
ῥομφαία, -ας, ἡ: sword (337)

Σ

σαλπίζω, σαλπίσω, ἐσάλπισα, --- , --- , --- : I sound a trumpet (279)
Σαμουήλ (indecl.), ὁ: Samuel (286)
Σαούλ (indecl.), ὁ: Saul (300)
Σαρα, -ας, ἡ: Sarai (125)
σάρξ, σαρκός, ἡ: flesh (365)
σεαυτοῦ, -ῆς: of yourself (200)
σήμερον: today (93)
σῖτος, -ου, ὁ: wheat, corn, grain, food (173)
σκάνδαλον, -ου, τό: stumbling block, cause of sin, snare (360)
σκεῦος, -ους, τό: vessel, utensil, implement; (pl.) baggage, gear, goods (300)
σκληρύνω, σκληρυνῶ, ἐσκλήρυνα, --- , --- , ἐσκληρύνθην: I harden, make stubborn
σκοτία, -ας, ἡ: darkness (93) (239)
σκότος, -ους, τό: darkness (354)
Σόδομα, -ων, τά: Sodom (a place name with plural form but singular meaning) (142)
σπέρμα, -ατος, τό: seed, offspring, posterity, children (374)
σπήλαιον, -ου, τό: cave (104)
σπλάγχνον, -ου, τό: heart, affections (374)
στῦλος, -ου, ὁ: pillar (239)
σύ, σοῦ: you (sing.), thou (125)
σύν: (with instrum.) with (72)
συνάγω, συνάξω, συνήγαγον, --- , συνῆγμαι, συνήχθην: I gather, bring together (173)
συναγωγή, -ῆς, ἡ: assembly, synagogue (180)
σφάζω, σφάξω, ἔσφαξα, --- , ἔσφαγμαι, ἐσφάγην: I slay, slaughter (374)
σφενδόνη, -ης, ἡ: sling (337)
σχολή, -ῆς, ἡ: school (180)
σώζω, σώσω, ἔσωσα, σέσωκα, σέσωσμαι, ἐσώθην: I save, preserve, rescue, keep safe (269)
σῶμα, -ατος, τό: body, dead body, living body, person (337)
σωτήρ, -ῆρος, ὁ: savior, deliverer, preserver (253)

Τ

τάχα: perhaps (125)
τεκνίον, -ου, τό: little child (360)
τέκνον, -ου, τό: child (41)
τέλειος, -α, -ον: mature, complete, perfect (377)
τελειόω, --- , ἐτελείωσα, τετελείωκα, τετελείωμαι, ἐτελειώθην: I finish, complete, accomplish (360)
τηρέω, τηρήσω, ἐτήρησα, τετήρηκα, τετήρημαι, ἐτηρήθην: I take care of, guard, observe, give heed to, keep (343)
τίθημι, θήσω, ἔθηκα, τέθεικα, τέθειμαι, ἐτέθην: I put, place, lay down (354)
τίς, τί: who? which? what? τί may mean "why?" (166)
τις, τι: (masc. & fem.) one, anyone, someone, a certain; (neut.) anything, something (166)
τόπος, -ου, ὁ: place, spot, locality (135)
τότε: then, at that time (83)
τρεῖς, τρία: three (380, 401)

τρέχω, --- , ἔδραμον, --- , --- , --- : I run (286)
τριακόσιοι, -αι, -α: three hundred (279)
τυφλόω, --- , ἐτύφλωσα, τετύφλωκα, --- , --- : I make blind, blind (360)

Υ

ὕδωρ, ὕδατος, τό: water (239)
υἱός, -οῦ, ὁ: son (160)
ὑμεῖς, ὑμῶν: you (pl.) (125)
ὑπάγω, --- , --- , --- , --- , --- : I go away, depart (360)
ὑπακοή, -ῆς, ἡ: obedience (304)
ὑπέρ: (with abl.) for, on behalf of, for the sake of, about; (with acc.) over, beyond (292)
ὑπηρέτης, -ου, ὁ: assistant, servant, attendant (142)
ὑπό: (with abl.) by; (with gen.) under; (with acc.) under (210)
ὑπομιμνήσκω, ὑπομνήσω, ὑπέμνησα, --- , --- ὑπεμνήσθην: I cause to remember, remind (343)
ὑψηλός, -ή, -όν: high, lofty (239)

Φ

φαίνω, φανοῦμαι, ἔφανα, --- , --- , ἐφάνην: I give light, shine; (pass.) come to light, appear (360)
φανερός, -ά, -όν: visible, manifest (374)
φανερόω, φανερώσω, ἐφανέρωσα, πεφανέρωκα, πεφανέρωμαι, ἐφανερώθην: I make visible, known, clear, manifest (348)
Φαραώ (indecl.), ὁ: Pharaoh (131)
φέρω, οἴσω, ἤνεγκα, --- , --- , ἠνέχθην: I carry, bring, endure (27, 113)
φεύγω, φεύξομαι, ἔφυγον, --- , --- , --- : I flee from, flee away, take flight
Φίλιππος, -ου, ὁ: Philip (10) (279)
φοβερός, -ά, -όν: fearful, terrifying, causing fear (328)
φόβος, -ου, ὁ: fear (160)
φονεύω, φονεύσω, ἐφόνευσα, --- , --- , ἐφονεύθην: I kill, murder (131)
φυλάσσω, φυλάξω, ἐφύλαξα, πεφύλαχα, --- , ἐφυλάχθην: I guard, keep, watch, protect (380)
φωνή, -ῆς, ἡ: voice, sound (292)
φῶς, φωτός, τό: light (354)

Χ

χαῖρε: greetings, hail, welcome, good morning, farewell, good-by (10)
χαίρω, --- , --- , --- , --- , ἐχάρην: I rejoice, am glad (224)
Χαλέβ (indecl.), ὁ: Caleb (253)
Χαναάν (indecl.), ἡ: Canaan (253)
χαρά, -ᾶς, ἡ: joy (348)
χάριν: (prep. with gen.) for, on account of, for the sake of (374)
χείρ, χειρός, ἡ: hand (239)
χρεία, -ας, ἡ: need, necessity (72)
χρῖσμα, -ατος, τό: anointing (365)
χριστός, -οῦ, ὁ: anointed, Christ (320)
χρίω, --- , ἔχρισα, --- , --- , ἐχρίσθην: I anoint (320)
χρόνος, -ου, ὁ: time (83)

Ψ

ψεύδομαι, ψεύσομαι, ἐψευσάμην, --- , --- : I lie, deceive by lies (354)
ψευδοπροφήτης, -ου, ὁ: false prophet (377)
ψεῦδος, -ους, τό: falsehood, lie (365)
ψεύστης, -ου, ὁ: liar (354)
ψηλαφάω, --- , ἐψηλάφησα, --- , --- , --- : I handle, touch, feel (348)
ψυχή, -ῆς, ἡ: soul, life (374)

Ω

ὧδε: here (180)
ὥρα, -ας, ἡ: hour, season (365)
ὡς: as (354)
ὥστε: so that (328)
(·): Greek semicolon (27)
(;): Greek question mark (27)

A or First Declension: See Declensions
Ablative Case: See Case
Accents
  combined with breathings, 6
  enclitics, 170
  kinds---acute, circumflex, grave, 7
  on 1st aor. act. infinitives, 98
  persistent, 50, 427
  proclitics, 169
  recessive, 38, 426
  résumé of, 123, 428
  rules for, 6, 123, 425-428
Accusative Case: See Case
Active Voice
  definition, 29
  paradigms: See each Tense
Acute Accent, 7: See also Accents
Adjectives
  agreement of, 59
  as substantives, 110
  declension of cardinal numbers, 333,
    401: See also Cardinals & Ordinals
  definite article as, 58
  definite article as possessive adj., 77
  definition, 58
  demonstrative, 132, 137
  first and second declension, 74, 75,
    107, 397: See also Declensions
  first and third declension, 241, 281,
    399
  indefinite, 168
  interrogative, 167
  irregular, 334, 400
  method of indicating declensional pat-
    tern, 76
  modifying genitives used as, 109
  positions of,
    ambiguous, 108d
    attributive, ascriptive, 80, 108a
    attributive, restrictive, 108b
    predicate, 108c
  second declension, 60
  third declension, 241, 307, 398
Agreement
  collective nouns with plural verbs, 257
  neuter noun in plural as subject of
    singular verb, 258
  of adjectives, 59
  of relative pronouns with antecedent,
    295
  of subject with verb, 16
Alphabet, 3
Antepenult, 36: See also Syllables
Aorist Tense
  definition, 94, 114
  distinction between present and
    aorist imperatives, 97
  first
    imperative active, 96, 412
    imperative middle, 206a, 412
    indicative active, 95, 412
    indicative middle, 196, 412
    infinitive active, 98, 412
    infinitive middle, 207a, 412
    participle active, 255, 412
    participle middle, 270a, 412
    passive imperative, 227, 412
    passive indicative, 227, 412
    passive infinitive, 227, 412
    passive participle, 281, 412
    passive subjunctive, 312, 412
    subjunctive active, 312, 412
    subjunctive middle, 312, 412
  K-Aorist, 417
  liquid and nasal
    imperative active, 145, 414
    imperative middle, 206, 414

Aorist Tense---Continued
  liquid and nasal---Continued
    indicative active, 145, 414
    indicative middle, 196, 414
    infinitive active, 145, 414
    infinitive middle, 207c, 414
    participle active, 255, 414
    participle middle, 270a, 414
    subjunctive system, 312
  MI aorist paradigms, 262, 417
  optative active, middle & passive, 412
    417, 418
  paradigms, 412, 413, 417
  passive reference list, 232
  second
    definition and analysis, 114
    imperative active, 115b, 413
    imperative middle, 206b, 413
    indicative active, 115a, 413
    indicative middle, 196, 413
    infinitive active, 115c, 413
    infinitive middle, 207b, 413
    participle active, 255, 413
    participle middle, 270a, 413
    passive imperative, 228
    passive indicative, 228
    passive infinitive, 228
    passive participle, 281
    passive subjunctive, 312
    subjunctive active, 312, 413
    subjunctive middle, 312, 413
    variations with A for O or E, 116
  translated in indirect discourse, 289
Apodosis: See Conditional Sentences
Article
  agreement with noun, 23
  definite, 23, 396
    as weak possessive, 77
    paradigm, 77, 396
    plural, 57
    with proper nouns, 128
  indefinite, 24
Attendant Circumstance, Adverbial Participle of, 266c
Attributive Position, 108
  kinds---ascriptive and restrictive, 108
  of adjectives, 80, 108
  of participles, 248, 265
Augment
  in pluperfect, 217
  kinds---syllabic, temporal, 86
  only in indicative, 96

B

Breathings, 6
  combined with accents, 6
  rough, 6
  smooth, 6

C

Cardinal Numerals
  declensions of δύο, 253; of εἷς, 333
  numerals one to four, 401
  numerals one to ten thousand, 402
Case
  ablative
    of agent, 220
    of separation or source, 44
    with a comparative, 308
  accusative
    direct object, 21
    of double direct object, 183
    of extent of time, 242
    of general reference, 288b
      with inf. in indir. disc., 288
      in result clauses, 331

Case---Continued
  dative
    of direct object, 56
    of indirect object, 55
  distinction between genitive and
    ablative, 45
  genitive
    absolute, 283
    of direct object, 84
    of material or content, 244
    of possession, 43
    of time, 243
    used as adjective, 109
  instrumental
    of association, 78
    of manner, 79
  locative
    of place, 46
    of time, 90
  nominative
    in predicate, 89
    subject, 20
  vocative of direct address, 22
Cause, Adverbial Participle of, 266b
Circumflex Accent, 7: See also Accents
Clauses
  apodosis, 329
  causal, 64
  definite relative, 295, 296
  definite temporal, 88
  indefinite relative, 362
  ὅτι clause in indirect discourse, 288c
  protasis, 329
  purpose with ἵνα, 382
  result with ἵνα, 356, 382
  result with ὥστε, 331
  subfinal with ἵνα, 382
  substantive with ἵνα, 370; with relative,
    with ἵνα, list of, 382   295
Concession, Adverbial Participle of, 266e
Conditional Sentences
  parts of, apodosis and protasis, 329
  types I-III, 330
  type IV, less vivid future, 424
Conjugation
  definition, 34
  forms, 412-420
Consonants, 4
  consonant changes in aorist and future
    passives with stems ending in
    mute, 231
  consonant changes in perfect middle and
    passive system of verbs with stems
    ending in mute or liquid, 218
Contract Verbs
  in -αω, 344, 345, 410, 416
  in -εω, 338, 339, 340, 409, 416
  in -οω, 350, 351, 416
  nature of, 338

D

Dative Case: See Case
Declensions: Also look under other headings
  definition, 49
  first
    endings, 106
    masculine nouns, 136, 383
    paradigms, 73, 105, 383
    table of endings, 156
  first and second
    paradigm of adjectives, 74, 75, 107,
      397
    table of endings, 157
  first and third, paradigm of adjectives,
    241, 381, 399
  numerals, 401
  second
    paradigms, 49, 57, 384
    table of endings, 156

Declensions---Continued
  third
    adjectives, 241, 307, 333, 398
    nouns, 240, 254, 263, 280, 287, 293
      301, 306, 385
Defective Verbs, 174a
Definite Article: See Article
Definite Temporal Clauses: See Clauses
Deliberative Subjunctive, 310
Demonstrative Adjectives and Pronouns, 132,
  137, 390
Diphthongs
  length, 5
  proper and improper, 5

E

Enclitics, 170
Endings
  adjective, table, 157
  first declension, 73, 106
  noun, table, 156
  second declension, 48
  verb,
    primary middle, 175
    secondary active, 114
    secondary middle, 197
    tables, 154, 189
    table of personal endings, 411

F

First Declension. See Declensions
Future Tense
  definition of, 61
  first passive indicative, 229, 412
  indicative active compared to present
    active, 62
  indicative active of οἶδα, 361
  indicative middle, 175c, d, 412
  infinitive active, middle, and passive,
    412
  liquid and nasal, 143, 414
  optative, 412
  participle active, 250, 412
  participle middle, 270a, 412
  passive participles, 282
  second passive, 230
  stems ending in certain consonants, 100

G

Gender
  agreement in adjectives and nouns, 59
  definition---masculine, feminine, and
    neuter, 14
  in vocabulary, 42
  neuter noun in plural as subject of a
    singular verb, 258
General Relative Pronoun,
Genitive Case: See Case
Grave Accent, 7: See also Accents

H

Hortatory Subjunctive, 311

I

Imperative Mood
  active endings, table, 154
  contract present, middle and passive,
    340, 345, 351, 416
  distinction between present and aorist,
    97
  first aorist
    active, 96, 412
    middle, 206a, 412
    passive, 227, 412

Imperative Mood---Continued
    liquid and nasal aorist
        active, 145, 414
        middle, 206c
    MI verbs
        aorist active, 262, 417, 418
        aorist middle, 417, 418
        present, active and middle, 417, 418
    present
        active, 33, 34, 68, 412
        middle and passive, 187, 412
        of εἰμί, 182, 420
    second aorist
        active, 115, 116, 413
        middle, 206b, 413
        passive, 228
    perfect middle and passive, 412
Imperfect Tense
    definition, 85
    indicative
        active, 86
        active of εἰμί, 182, 420
        middle and passive, 196, 213, 412
        middle and passive of contract, 416
        MI   verbs, 417, 418
Indefinite
    adjectives, 168
    article, 24
    pronouns, 168, 394
    relative clauses, 362
Indicative Mood
    active endings, table, 154, 189, 411
    compared with participle in the middle,
        271
    contract verbs
        imperfect active, 340, 345, 351, 416
        present active middle and passive,
            340, 345, 351, 416
    first
        aorist active, 95, 412
        aorist middle, 196, 412
        passive aorist, 227
        passive future, 229
        perfect active, 149, 412
        pluperfect active, 161, 412
    future
        active of liquid and nasal verbs,
            143, 414
        middle of liquid and nasal verbs,
            176, 414
        middle, 175, 177, 412
        of εἰμί, 182
    imperfect
        active, 86, 412
        middle and passive, 196, 412
        of εἰμί, 182, 420
    liquid and nasal aorist
        active, 145
        middle, 196
    MI aorist
        active, 262, 417, 418
        middle, 417, 418
    middle endings, table, 189
    perfect middle and passive, 214, 216,
        412, 415
    pluperfect middle and passive, 215,
        216, 412, 415
    present
        active, 33, 34, 412
        middle, 175, 412
        of εἰμί, 182, 420
    second
        aorist active, 115, 116, 413
        aorist middle, 196, 413
        passive aorist, 228
        passive future, 230
        perfect active, 150
        pluperfect active, 162
    secondary middle endings, 197, 411
Indirect Discourse, 288
    with an infinitive, 288b
    with a ὅτι clause, 288c
    with a participle, 288a

Infinitive
    active endings, table, 154
    complementary, 63
    contract, present middle and passive,
        340, 345, 351, 416
    first
        aorist active, 98, 412
        aorist middle, 207a, 412
        aorist passive, 227
        perfect active, 149, 412
    in indirect discourse, 288b
    liquid and nasal
        aorist active, 145, 414
        aorist middle, 207c, 414
        future active, 414
        future middle, 414
    MI verbs
        aorist active, 262, 417, 418
        aorist middle, 417, 418
        present active, middle and passive,
            417, 418
    perfect middle and passive, 214, 216,
        412, 415
    present
        active, 63, 68, 412
        middle, 175, 190, 412
        of εἰμί, 182, 420
    second
        aorist active, 115, 116, 413
        aorist middle, 207b, 413
        passive aorist, 228
        passive future, 230
        perfect active, 150
    with accusative of general reference, 288
Instrumental Case: See Case
Intensive Pronoun: See Pronouns
Interrogative
    adjective, 167, 393
    pronoun, 167, 393
Iota-subscript, 5b
Irregular Adjectives.
    See Adjectives.

L

Liquid and Nasal Verbs. See each Tense
    present stems in, 144
    future, 143, 414
    aorist, 145, 414
Locative Case: See Case

M

Manner
    adverbial participle of, 266f
    instrumental of, 79. See Case
Means, adverbial participle of, 266g
Middle Voice
    definition, 174
    paradigms: See each Tense
MI verbs, 357: See each Tense
    comparative paradigms of four verbs, 417
    paradigm of ἀφίημι, 418; of εἰμί, 420
    present participle, 408
Mood: See each of the following headings
    imperative, 31
    indicative, 30
    optative, 421, 422, 423
    subjunctive, 309-312
Movable N, 99
Mute Stems
    aorist and future passives, 231
    future active, 100
    perfect and pluperfect middle and pass-
        ive system, 218, 415

N

Negative
    οὐ and μή introducing questions, 332

Negative---Continued
　　pronouns--- οὐδείς, 354, 355; μηδείς, 395
　　with subjunctive, 322
　　　　in prohibitions, 324
　　　　in strong denials, 323
Nominative Case: See Case
Nouns
　　collective, 257
　　definition, 12
　　first or A declension, 73, 105, 106,
　　　　136, 383: See Declensions
　　neuter in plural as subject of a singu-
　　　　lar verb, 258
　　pattern of nouns in vocabulary, 54
　　second or O declension, 49, 57, 60, 384
　　third or consonant declension, 240, 254,
　　　　263, 280, 287, 293, 301, 306, 381,
　　　　385

Number
　　agreement: See Agreement
　　of nouns, 13
　　of verbs, 32
　　singular and plural, 13
Numerals: See Cardinals & Ordinals, 402

O

O or Second Declension. See Declensions
Objects
　　direct, 17
　　　　accusative, 21
　　　　dative, 56
　　　　genitive, 84
　　double direct, accusative, 183
　　indirect, dative, 55
Optative Mood
　　forms, 412, 413, 417, 418, 420
　　in Type IV condition, 424
　　infrequent use in the N. T., 421
　　of wish, 422
　　potential, 423
Ordinal Numerals, 402

P

Paradigm, definition, 34, 49
Participles
　　adjectival and substantival emphases, 265
　　adverbial emphasis---attendant circum-
　　　　stance, cause, concession, condition,
　　　　manner, means, purpose, time, 266
　　aorist
　　　　active, 255, 405
　　　　middle, 270a
　　　　passive, 281, 407
　　compared with the indicative in the
　　　　middle, 271
　　contract, present middle and passive,
　　　　340, 345, 351, 409, 410
　　declensions, 249, 250, 255, 264, 270,
　　　　281, 282, 403-410
　　function, 248
　　future
　　　　active, 250
　　　　middle, 270a
　　　　passive, 282
　　in indirect discourse, 288a
　　MI
　　　　aorist active, 262
　　　　present active, 408
　　perfect
　　　　active, 264, 406
　　　　middle and passive, 270b
　　present
　　　　active, 249, 404
　　　　middle and passive, 270b
　　　　of εἰμί, 305, 403
　　significance of tense in---kind of
　　　　action, relative time, 256
　　supplementary, 272

Passive Voice
　　definition, 212
　　paradigms: See each Tense
Penult, 36: See Syllables
Perfect Tense
　　definition, 149
　　first
　　　　indicative active, 149, 412
　　　　indicative and infinitive middle and
　　　　　　passive of omega verbs, 214, 412
　　imperative middle and passive, 412
　　indicative and infinitive middle and
　　　　passive of verb stems ending in
　　　　mute or liquid, 216, 415
　　participle
　　　　active, 264, 406, 412
　　　　middle and passive, 270b, 412
　　second
　　　　indicative active, 150
　　　　of οἶδα, 361, 419
　　subjunctive active, middle and passive,
　　　　412
Periphrastic, third plural in the perfect
　　and pluperfect indicative middle and
　　passive, 219
Persistent Accent. See Accents
Person: in verbs, 33
Personal Endings of Verbs, 411. See also
　　Verbs
　　primary middle, 175
　　secondary middle, 197
Personal Pronouns
　　αὐτός as, 138, 139, 386
　　demonstratives as, 132, 137
　　first person, 127, 181
　　second person, 127, 181
　　third person, 181
Pluperfect Tense
　　augment in, 217
　　definition, 161
　　first active, 161, 412
　　indicative and infinitive middle and
　　　　passive
　　　　of omega verbs, 215, 412
　　　　of verbs with stems ending in mute
　　　　　　or liquid, 216, 415
　　second
　　　　indicative active, 162
　　　　active of οἶδα, 361, 419
Possession
　　definite article as weak possessive, 77
　　genitive of, 43
Predicate position
　　of adjectives, 108c
　　of participles, 266
　　of pronouns, 132, 139a
Prepositions, 47
Present Tense
　　active
　　　　imperative, 33, 34, 68, 154, 412
　　　　indicative, 33, 34, 68, 154, 412
　　　　infinitive, 63, 68, 154, 412
　　　　of εἰμί, 182, 420
　　　　of liquid and nasal verbs, 144
　　　　participles, 249, 404, 412
　　　　participle of εἰμί, 305, 420
　　active, middle and passive subjunctive,
　　　　312, 412
　　contract verbs, active, middle and
　　　　passive, 340, 345, 351
　　definition, 28
　　middle and passive
　　　　imperative, 187, 189, 412
　　　　indicative and infinitive, 175, 189,
　　　　　　412
　　　　participle, 270, 412
　　optative, 412, 417, 418
　　progressive, 371
Principal Parts of Verbs
　　explanation, 101
　　reference list, 237
Proclitics, 169

Pronouns
    demonstrative, 132, 137, 390
    general or indefinite relative, 349, 392
    indefinite, 168, 394
    intensive, 138, 139, 388
    interrogative, 167, 393
    negative, 355, 395
    personal, 127, 139, 181, 386: See also
        Personal Pronouns
    reciprocal, 297, 389
    reflexive, 201, 202, 387
    relative, 294, 295, 391
Protasis. See Conditional Sentences.
Punctuation
    question mark, 27
    semicolon, 27, 146d
Purpose
    ἵνα clause of, 325, 382
    participle of, 266h

Q

Question
    deliberative, 310
    οὐ and μή introducing, 332

R

Recessive Accent: See Accents
Reduplication, types of, 151
Result Clauses: See also Clauses
    with ἵνα, 356, 382
    with ὥστε, 331
Rough Breathing, 6: See Breathings

S

Second Declension: See Declensions
Second Aorist: See Aorist, second
Sentence, definition, 11
Smooth Breathing, 6: See Breathings
Subject, of a sentence, 16
Subjunctive Mood
    aorist and present paradigms, 312, 412
    contract present active, middle, and
        passive, 340, 345, 351, 416
    definition, 309
    deliberative question, 310
    hortatory, 311
    in conditional sentences, 330
    in indefinite relative clauses, 362
    in prohibitions, 324
    in purpose clauses, 325
    in strong denials, 323
    present of εἰμί, 321
    with ἵνα, 325, 382

Substantive
    adjectives as, 110
    clauses, 370
    participles as, 265
Syllabic Augment: See Augment
Syllables
    length, 37
    names---ultima, penult, antepenult, 36
    number, 35

T

Temporal Augment: See Augment
Tenses: See also each of the following
        Tenses
    aorist, 94, 95, 114
    future, 61, 62
    imperfect, 85
    perfect, 149, 150
    pluperfect, 161, 162
    present, 28, 371
    significance in participles, 256
Third Declension: See Declensions
Time
    accusative of extent of, 242
    genitive of, 243
    locative of, 90
    participle of, 266a

U

Ultima, 36: See also Syllables

V

Verbs
    agreement in, 16
    analysis of indicative, 411
    contract: See Contract Verbs
    defective, 174a, 212a
    definition, 15
    liquid and nasal. See that heading and
        also each Tense
    MI, 357, 417, 418
    moods of: See Moods
    omega, 34, 214, 412, 413
    person in, 33
    personal endings, table of, 411
    tenses of: See Tenses
    voices of: See Voice
Vocative Case: See Case
Voice: See also each Tense
    active, 29
    middle, 174
    passive, 212
Vowels, 4
    length, 4
    diphthongs, 5

Page 27 — ηρθιε
10 — ᾱσθιε